105084

D1337254

Uptime

"This new edition provides a wealth of new knowledge of "what" to do for managers of physical assets and maintenance professionals."

Normand Champigny, Asset management practice
IBM Business Consulting Services
Canada

"*Uptime* is a "must read" for anyone with an interest in maximizing the productivity and value of their physical assets. *Uptime* applies to all physical assets whether they are industrial, facilities or a fleet of vehicles."

Brian Malloch, President
Plant Engineering and Maintenance Association of Canada

"Jim Reyes-Picknell brings valuable insight to the 2nd edition of *Uptime*. He offers innovative ideas, especially in the area of human resource management and team building, to a setting that can really benefit. John Campbell would be delighted."

Michael G. Currie, Director
Asset Management
Matrikon Inc.

"Over the past thirty years I have read quite a few maintenance management books and *Uptime — Strategies for Excellence in Maintenance Management* is certainly one of the best."

David A. de Castro, President
Brasman Engenharia
Brazil

"The second edition of *Uptime* is the most comprehensive overview of the art and science of maintenance management that I have found, and should be required reading for both students and seasoned professionals alike. Those companies that heed the overriding message of the book, namely that maintenance of physical assets is an investment, and not a cost, will be the pace setters of the future."

Dr. Peter F. Knights, Associate Professor
School of Engineering, The University of Queensland,
Australia

"I would recommend *Uptime* as essential reading for all managers who are interested in improving their business productivity and for all maintenance personnel involved in the journey to excellence."

Bob Thiele, Executive General Manager
Business Processes
Placer Dome

Uptime

Strategies for Excellence in Maintenance Management

2nd Edition

John D. Campbell
James V. Reyes-Picknell

New York

Most Productivity Press books are available at quantity discounts when purchased in bulk. For more information contact our Customer Service Department (888-319-5852). Address all other inquiries to:

Productivity Press
444 Park Avenue South, 7th Floor
New York, NY 10016
United States of America
Telephone 212-686-5900
Fax: 212-686-5411
E-mail: info@productivitypress.com
ProductivityPress.com

Library of Congress Cataloging-in-Publication Data
Campbell, John Dixon.
    Uptime : strategies for excellence in maintenance management / John D. Campbell, James V. Reyes-Picknell.— 2nd ed.
        p. cm.
    Includes bibliographical references and index.
    ISBN 1-56327-335-7 (alk. paper)
    1. Plant maintenance—Management.   2. Total productive maintenance—Management.   I. Reyes-Picknell, James V. II. Title.
    TS192.C36   2006
    658.2'02—dc22

                                          2006003335

10 09 08 07 06   5 4 3 2 1

Table of Contents

Foreword   vii

Acknowledgments   xi

Introduction   xiii

Part I – Leadership

Chapter 1   Building a Maintenance Strategy   3
Chapter 2   People   41

Part II – Essentials

Chapter 3   Work Management   79
Chapter 4   Basic Care   113
Chapter 5   Materials   135
Chapter 6   Performance Management   157
Chapter 7   Management and Support Systems
             for Maintenance   179

Part III – Choosing Excellence

Chapter 8   Asset-Centric Approaches 1: Being Proactive   221
Chapter 9   Asset-Centric Approaches 2: Continuous
             Improvement   251
Chapter 10   Team-Based Methods   267
Chapter 11   Process Optimization   289

Part IV – Epilogue

Chapter 12   Excellence   309

Appendix A   315
Appendix B   323
Bibliography   343
Index   347
About the Author   000

Foreword to the Second edition

It's been about eight years since the first edition of *Uptime — Strategies for Excellence in Maintenance Management* was published. A lot has happened in that time. The expected "new economy" didn't materialize as rapidly as expected, but it is cropping up in selected sectors and industries. Y2K was a wake-up call for many businesses, my own included, and was one of many things that have led to the rapid and dramatic advances in computer and software technology. While computers, the Internet, and Y2K were making the headlines, a quieter evolution was also taking place. The world of the maintenance manager was changing, and it continues to change.

In their quest for growing revenues, higher profits, and increased shareholder value, companies have grabbed all the low-hanging fruit. Production processes have been upgraded and automated; computerization supports many business decisions; purchasing has become strategic procurement; supply chains have been rationalized and streamlined; many functions like information technology, knowledge management, and payroll have been outsourced; and administrative functions are being replaced by intranet and portal technology. One of the last areas where profits can be squeezed from an existing organization is the maintenance of physical assets. The plants and equipment we use to produce our goods and the fleets we use to deliver services still break down and still require maintenance. Until very recently, we considered maintenance to be a necessary expense—perhaps even an evil.

Today, the money maintenance managers spend comes straight off earnings. If they don't spend, their companies can be more profitable. The assets they are charged with maintaining generate much of the revenue that goes to the top line. The maintenance manager of only ten years ago could be a highly skilled craftsman with people and management skills. The maintenance manager of tomorrow must be a savvy businessperson.

As we entered the new millennium, I looked at the last chapter in the first edition of *Uptime* and was pleased that much of what I suggested would happen is happening. The watchwords of the future were going to be "flexibility" and "reliability." They are.

Interpreting condition monitoring data was a growing challenge. Today, it's often left up to computers and experts. Expert systems were in their infancy but growing. They were being programmed then; today, they are "learning" by themselves. Technicians were to become more multiskilled among trades and cross-skilled with operators, but that trend has not progressed rapidly. Real "teams" are still a rarity and may require a generation to take hold. Universities were beginning to recognize and teach maintenance management as a distinct specialty, and that trend has continued. Today, for example, we are teaching maintenance management principles in the University of Toronto's Physical Asset Management Certificate program. The roles of design engineer and maintainer are slowly blurring. The need to match increasingly sophisticated and complex assets with an equal level of expertise in maintenance strategy and tactics was growing, but a greater need for this has emerged. With demands often driven by legislation and regulation in an increasingly litigious society, safety, environmental concerns, and even our license to operate in some industries depend on reliable assets. As companies look for the fixes without the need to invest, the need for sophistication has never been more challenging. Accounting terminology is increasingly commonplace in all aspects of our businesses. Indeed, the new millennium is proving to be every bit as challenging as predicted—and then some.

Around the time that *Uptime* was first published in 1995, I hired an ex-Navy engineer who had served time in several other industries in maintenance and asset management. Since graduating with a degree in Mechanical Engineering in 1977, Jim Picknell has worked as a ship's engineer, a rotating equipment specialist in petrochemicals, a maintenance and reliability engineering manager in shipbuilding and aerospace, all before he joined my relatively young practice. His focus on reliability seemed a good fit with my predicted vision of the future.

Since then, Jim and I have worked closely together, building a strong practice in Physical Asset Management. We have become, in addition to good friends, leading thinkers whose opinions are sought after. We have worked in a very diverse set of industries on remarkably challenging problems, and we have learned a great deal. Our joint experiences range from "Mickey Mouse" to rocket science: Our clients have included operators of world-class amusement parks and world-leading space launch and vehicle maintenance facilities. We've helped improve maintenance management practices in large scrap metal operations; open pit, surface, and underground mines; large hospital complexes; Ivy League universities; oil refineries; airlines; thermal and nuclear power generation plants; gas transmission pipelines and stations; electric transmission and distribution networks; fertilizer plants; automotive plants; furniture and office equipment plants; pulp and paper mills; tissue converting plants; sawmills; plywood and engineered wood products plants; asphalt and cement plants; and elsewhere.

As our practice grew, we saw and heeded the need to change our services. Some of these changes were propelled by a shift in focus from computer system installation (i.e., the old silver bullet) to complex reliability improvement efforts aimed at satisfying a variety of business and regulatory-driven requirements. Others were motivated when industry moved from simply putting solutions in place to recognizing the need to change those who use the solutions and then sustain the change for long-term payback.

Jim and I have worked to satisfy these changing needs in a dynamic, constantly evolving business environment. I'm not able to continue this pace for very much longer, but Jim is. I am passing the torch to him and have asked him to write this second edition of my original book and to share what we have learned with you. He has kindly agreed to take on this work, and this book is the result. Enjoy and learn.

John Dixon Campbell
November 2002

Note: John completed this foreword near the end of his long and courageous battle with cancer, only days before he passed away on November 11, 2002. His friends and colleagues have since created an award and scholarship in his name at the University of Toronto where he studied.

Acknowledgments

The first edition of *Uptime* was based on observations of clients and other successful companies that were high performers in maintenance management. This edition of *Uptime* began during discussions with John Dixon Campbell in 2000. The dust generated by Y2K was beginning to settle, and the consulting industry, which had done very well in the previous few years, was heading into a period of upheaval. Our maintenance management practice was doing very well and had grown substantially since *Uptime* was first published in 1995. Developments in computing technology and the explosive growth of the Internet had changed the landscape for Management Information Systems dramatically, and that part of the book was clearly out of date. Nevertheless, we had been using *Uptime* very successfully with a number of clients, and we had learned a great deal about its application in the changing business environment. During the two-year period preceding his death, John and I discussed these topics frequently and thus, the first person to be acknowledged here is John Campbell—my good friend and mentor. Without his leadership of our practice, his dedication to excellence, and his insights, the inspiration for this edition of *Uptime* would not exist.

Many friends, clients, and colleagues influenced the material contained in this second edition of *Uptime*, several of whom also helped by contributing content and/or reviewing the draft of the book and providing valuable comments. I would like to thank Adrian Baban, David A. de Castro, Gabriel Rodríguez Gustá, Roy Korompis, Dr. Peter F. Knight, Professor Andrew K. S. Jardine, Tony Rodriguez, Ark Skupien, Ben Stevens, Bob Thiele, Murray Wiseman, and especially Mike Currie, Len Middleton, Doug Stretton and Geoff Walker, for their highly detailed reviews that resulted in numerous and significant improvements to the original draft. Your insights have enhanced this work considerably.

All of the consultants and clients I have worked with have helped me learn and have had an impact on my personal and professional development. They are too numerous to be named here, but they know who they are and they are all thanked.

I am grateful to my mother, Ruth Picknell, who transcribed the original chapters of *Uptime* into electronic form, making it easier for me to edit.

I am also indebted to Bev Campbell, John's wife, for her encouragement and support, and for helping me work with the publisher of this work.

Finally, I would like to acknowledge my wife, Aileen—a "non-maintenance professional"—who read and commented on the first draft and helped me remain true to John's original intent of making the book an easy and informative read. Early in our marriage, while I was writing and struggling with words, concepts, experience, and the long and grueling task of getting my ideas across to readers, it was Aileen who made all things possible. Without her unwavering support and encouragement, this work would not have been finished.

John dedicated the first edition of *Uptime* to his wife, Bev. This second edition is dedicated to both our spouses, Bev and Aileen.

Introduction

Your operations run 24/7, generating millions in revenue every day. The markets are good, production is running flat out, and your customers are happy. You have some minor stoppages, but they are fixed quickly—total loss of production is relatively minor. Then, late in the week, there is a major equipment outage. It takes several days to get a critical part and a few more days to fix the problem. Total downtime: 5 days. By now, customers are screaming for product. You resort to buying and repackaging a competitor's product for resale to satisfy your customers. Throughout this time, a good part of your production staff was idle. Your maintenance crews, already short-staffed because you haven't been able to find qualified tradesmen, worked around the clock at premium rates. You can't make up for the lost production. You're backed up and already running flat out. This one incident has reduced annual revenues, taking more than 2 percent from your bottom line.

Only a few hours or a few miles away, your competitors were able to ramp up production to help you make up for your lost production. They were happy to help—your situation generated more revenue for them and at a premium price! They don't have a problem with outages and, although they compete for the same labor pool as you, they don't seem to be short-staffed. Their operations are similar to yours, their product is virtually identical, but they are more profitable. What's their secret?

You arrange a visit to the competitor's plant, hoping to find an answer. The plant manager is your host and gives you a tour. The plant is not new, but you are immediately impressed with how clean and orderly everything is. Much of the equipment is the same as yours, but better cared for. You see operators using checklists and helping the maintainers do repairs. There's a crew of maintenance people who do nothing but condition monitoring—today they're doing a combination of vibration checks, oil analysis, and thermal imaging. The storeroom is tidy and manned only during the day shift. At night it has a card access; bar code readers record stock transactions. Maintenance performance statistics are posted alongside production; safety statistics are posted on boards throughout the plant, and they are current. You notice that the plant's recorded accident rate is 0.5; yours is 2. It's probably a given that your competitor's insurance costs are lower than yours, too.

When you ask, the plant manager explains that maintenance is a critical business process and a key to the company's success. He views maintenance as an investment in productive capacity. You've been viewing it as a necessary evil—a cost center.

And it is precisely this scenario and these divergent views of maintenance that are the crux of the message of *Uptime: Strategies for Excellence in Maintenance Management*. What may, at first glance, be a seemingly trivial difference of opinion separates a successful operation from one beset by outages, staffing problems, and a host of related costs and other irritants.

This edition of *Uptime* is an updated and expanded affirmation of the premise promulgated in the first edition and provides current insights and practical suggestions for implementing maintenance management as a viable and valuable asset for any industry seeking to improve its operating systems.

Intended as a senior level reference for both maintenance and nonmaintenance professionals alike, this book provides an overview of Maintenance Management. It examines various elements that maintenance managers deal with and offers guidelines for maintenance success, specifically, useful information about "what" works well and "how" to achieve it. Whenever possible, I have attempted to stay away from excessive details that are likely to be more confusing than illuminating to lay readers; I have tried to balance this by providing enough information to help the dedicated maintenance professional make informed choices. Brief "Uptime Summary" sections appear at the end of each chapter. These outline key points for executives and managers who want to focus on significant points without getting bogged down in minutiae. Managers who want a quick read are encouraged to read the Introduction, the 11 Uptime Summary sections at the end of each chapter, and the Epilogue.

Uptime: Strategies for Excellence in Maintenance Management was published in 1995. Since then, John Campbell and I, along with our colleagues, have used it to help hundreds of companies move toward excellence. While applying the concepts and theories described in *Uptime*, all of us have learned a great deal more about them: where they work, where they don't, and how to apply them. Collectively, our team has gained over 500 years of experience in a wide array of circumstances, industries, and environments. We have seen tremendous growth in the use of information technology and an explosion in the number of opportunities that it provides. Company after company has reported that using the various strategies presented in *Uptime* has made it easier to take advantage of those opportunities. The feedback has been gratifyingly positive; suggestions and comments from those learning and using the strategies have been invaluable.

We have now entered the 21st Century. Although the first edition of *Uptime* is still widely read and popular, changing technologies, a rapidly changing business environment, and knowledge gained from experiences with industries using the book to enhance their performance clearly called for revisions and updates, a task John and I began with passion and conviction. Not long after we began rewriting, John was stricken with cancer. Before he passed away in late 2002, he expressed his desire that the book be completed and that I should continue alone the work that we had begun together. This edition of *Uptime* is a response to that request; hopefully, it is a work that honors the man who inspired it.

I have attempted to remain true to the original intent of providing an easily read handbook that maintenance professionals, plant managers, fleet managers and other nonmaintenance professionals can all understand and use. Several readers commented that the original edition might have been enhanced by instructions on "how to" implement the various strategies it described. While *Uptime* was not, and is still not, a "how to" book, it does describe what experience tells us works the best. For the most part, this book describes "what" to do. Because we all choose our own solutions and the methods that will work best for us, it is pointless to prescribe methods. Where appropriate, insight into what works and what does not have been included.

The original model of excellence created by John Campbell, the Pyramid of Excellence (presented later in this introduction), has stood the test of time. It has been copied and, on occasion, attacked. And while it has worked well, it also needed updating. In this work, the Pyramid of Excellence has been modified to reflect what we now know and reframe the context for various maintenance management strategies.

For those who are new to the subject of Maintenance Management or those who are interested in expanding their store of maintenance vocabulary, Appendix B contains a glossary of common terms.

Those familiar with the first edition of *Uptime*, may find the following discussion of the changes that have been made interesting. New readers may want to skip to the next section of this introduction.

CHANGES

The original introduction and all of the chapters have undergone some level of revision, in some cases minor, in others substantial. A brief summary of those changes follows:

The first edition was subdivided into four parts: Leadership, Control, Continuous Improvement, and Quantum Leaps. While this four-part structure has been retained, the individual parts have been revised and given new titles: Leadership, Essentials, Choosing Excellence, and Epilogue.

Part 1, Leadership, discusses strategy and managing change. New material includes a revised approach to strategy development and an increased emphasis on the importance of people.

Part 2, Essentials, has been transformed and augmented with the following changes:

- Planning and Scheduling is now Work Management and includes material that covers shutdowns and mobile work forces. Materials management is dealt with in an entirely new chapter.
- Tactics has been included in the chapter on Basic Care, with an emphasis on certain minimum requirements for success.
- The section on Measuring and Benchmarking has been expanded.
- Management Information Systems for Maintenance has been updated to reflect changes in technology and to include technologies that support condition-based monitoring, fault diagnostics, and decision optimization.

Part 3, Choosing Excellence, discusses three approaches to the pursuit of excellence: asset centric, team based, and process centric.

- Reliability Centered Maintenance is covered in more depth, with some consideration of its use in "Greenfield" applications. An entirely new chapter covers RCFA, PM Optimization, and Decision Optimization techniques.

- Total Productive Maintenance is discussed in depth and has been redirected to include theories on effective teamwork.

Part IV of the first edition, Quantum Leaps, is now included in the expanded discussion of Process Optimization. Part 4, Epilogue, outlines key take-away points for management.

Appendices A and C from the original *Uptime* have been retained and expanded as A and B, respectively. The original Appendix B has been omitted.

THE NEED FOR UPTIME

There is substantial evidence that physical and financial well-being are interrelated and that there is a clear link between wellness and success and, conversely, failure and physical or emotional distress. How well we take care of ourselves and our businesses has an impact on personal and professional happiness. Good health, your own or your company's, depends on wellness, and that means keeping all your systems and parts in proper working order. But just as many of us neglect our physical health, favoring short-term gratification over a long and healthy life that we can enjoy, many organizations neglect essential elements of success. It may be just human nature, but the results of this behavior are clearly negative. The human body and the corporate body suffer because we don't pay enough attention to physical health through maintenance.

Many businesses today are increasing their dependence on automation and decreasing their dependence on labor. As technology grows, it expands into new areas and enables us to do more with less so that we are more profitable, safer, and less vulnerable to labor shortages. At the same time, we become more dependent on our physical assets, which, in turn, are dependent on solid maintenance. Keeping these assets running efficiently requires efficient and cost-effective maintenance.

What we gain by maintaining our physical assets diligently is *Uptime*—the capacity to produce and provide goods and services. We also expand our ability to produce high quality goods and services quickly and satisfy our customers consistently. Finally, we –provide a safe and controlled work or service environment, with minimum risk to the health and safety of our employees, our customers, the public at large, and our environment.

Many senior executives and managers do not fully appreciate the total cost of maintenance, which is often buried as a component of "operating costs." Broken down, maintenance costs include the direct costs of repairs and any proactive work (labor, materials, and contractors), the cost of downtime (lost revenue and lost reputation), and fines or other penalties resulting from flawed products or flawed operating systems. Though they vary in direct proportion to the capital intensity of a given business, budgeted maintenance costs can be as high as half of production costs (see Figure 1).

Sector	Percentage
Mining	20–50
Primary metal	15–25
Electric utilities	15–25
Manufacturing	5–15
Processing	3–15
Fabrication and assembly	3–5

Figure 1. Ratio of Direct Maintenance Cost to Total Operating Costs

Although high enough, the numbers in Figure 1 are not "total costs"—they do not include the sales value of lost production nor the cost associated with rework, rejected product, recycled materials, fines, or other penalties. Understanding the total costs enables rational decision making and justifies increases in maintenance budgets because the result is lower total costs to the business. The more capital-intensive[1] a business becomes, the less it depends on operators and the more it depends on maintenance. The costs associated with this dependence on maintenance grow as a direct result of our increased dependence on physical assets for production. But

1. By "capital intensive" I mean that the company makes extensive use of physical assets including plant, equipment, physical systems, fleets of vehicles, fixed assets, facilities, and utility infrastructure.

if we manage our assets well, those costs will decline as will the cost per unit of output.

For managers concerned with the end result—what is produced and how to sell it—maintenance is sometimes a matter of tweaking here and tightening there. But keeping a company's inner workings working is a complex job and deserves far more attention. Moreover, this kind of detailed work does not come cheaply. Several key concerns impact the cost of asset maintenance. Some of them are difficult to quantify:

- What maintenance activities do we focus on? Can we become more predictable and less reactive?
- How do we attract and keep capable people to maintain sophisticated equipment systems?
- What is the optimum level of inventory of maintenance parts, materials, and consumables? Where can we get them?
- Do we need specialist maintenance engineering support?
- What organization arrangements are appropriate?
- How much and what do we contract out?

Today's global competitive stakes make it more important than ever to get the answers right. Business is under enormous pressure to be financially productive. Maintenance is a major production cost and if it is too expensive, plants shut down and production is outsourced or moved offshore. Everywhere, the dictum is the same: maximize the output of goods and services and minimize input of resources—financial, human, and physical. Provide the best value to both the customer and the shareholder, but at the same time be safe, and environmentally conscious.

Providing value clearly has to do with giving the best quality and service, quickly and at the lowest price. To satisfy customers, an enterprise must respond quickly to service its goods throughout their useful life cycle. In connection with this, we see "Product Life-cycle Management" emerging as a new discipline closely related to maintenance management but focused on maintaining the products sold to customers. But because we also want to expose ourselves and our customers to minimal risk (whether financial, market, operational, environmental, or safety related), its follows that:

$$Value = \frac{Quality \times Service}{Cost \times Time \times Risk}$$

The higher the quality and service we can deliver for a given cost and response time, the more value the customer perceives. It is essential that the physical resources employed—equipment, fleets, facilities or plants—be available when needed and produce at the required rate and quality, at reasonable cost. It goes almost without saying that environmental and safety risks must be consistently minimized.

World-class enterprises are paying a lot of attention to the value equation. Their quest is not only to reduce costs, but also variation, cycle time, and risks. Quality programs like Six Sigma achieve these benefits through scientific approaches aimed at eliminating problems, waste, and variation. Likewise, expectations for asset performance have increased dramatically, especially where those assets are used extensively in the delivery of products or services.

There is a cost to getting it all right. The strategies described in this book require an initial investment, and improvement is contingent on a commitment to expend the necessary effort and finances. The payback can be quite high.

New manufacturing and processing philosophies and cost-effective designs of capital equipment have spawned corresponding maintenance responses. For example, modular equipment designs are "maintained" by substitution: entire modules are replaced and electronics are designed to be increasingly fault tolerant. Some "smart" technologies are even eliminating maintenance through systems that have the ability to self-correct. But these systems are not yet widespread nor are they practical in many designs. Until they are, maintenance is likely here to stay. That is not to say that we must practice it in some hidebound, traditional manner.

Innovative companies lead the effort to improve on design through technology, often driven by substantial competitive, regulatory, or other market forces. Numerous industries and companies are working to gain a competitive edge with some of the most effective and well-established approaches in maintenance management. We can all gain from their successes and avoid their failures. Total Productive Maintenance (TPM), Reliability Centered Maintenance (RCM), Root Cause Failure Analysis (RCFA), Computerized Maintenance Management Systems (CMMS), and sophisticated performance management systems like the Balanced Score Card, whole-life cycle management processes (such as Logistics Engineering and Terotechnology), diagnostic systems, condition-monitoring systems, and outsourcing are all being utilized with varying degrees of success. Considerable research is being carried out in all these fields and organizations like the International Foundation for Research in Maintenance (IFRIM), various universities' maintenance and reliability related laboratories, and the Society of Maintenance and Reliability Professionals (SMRP) are all working to extend and refine both our knowledge and our practices.

Each of these concepts can add significant value, increasing asset effectiveness and reliability. But none is the whole solution to boost productivity and each can be overused if used in isolation. Unfortunately, many enterprises embrace a single new approach as if it alone were the answer to the complex and highly integrated business process that is maintenance management. This book puts these methods into perspective and shows how they work together to achieve optimal results.

THE UPTIME PYRAMID OF EXCELLENCE IN MAINTENANCE MANAGEMENT

Maintenance management is important to all business sectors and critical to those that are capital-intensive. As managers who are not directly involved in maintenance gain a better understanding of its importance, the ability of an enterprise to provide customer value will increase. Figure 2 is a graphic depiction of the structured framework used for applying these successful practices in your business. That framework is an overall strategy, or roadmap, that can be used to guide your choices about how you will manage maintenance in your business. Although it is not necessary to follow a prescribed approach to climb the Pyramid of Excellence, it is important to embrace all the elements in the lower two levels, Leadership and the Essentials. Achieving at least a level of competence in these two levels improves your ability to survive as a maintenance manager in today's demanding business environment. If you are striving for superior performance, then you will likely embrace at least one of the methods on the third level, Choosing Excellence, the key to transitioning from competence to excellence.

Consider three people with varying degrees of competence at swimming. One is uncomfortable in the water and cannot swim at all, one can swim well, and the third is an Olympic champion swimmer. When dropped into the water, the first will bob to the

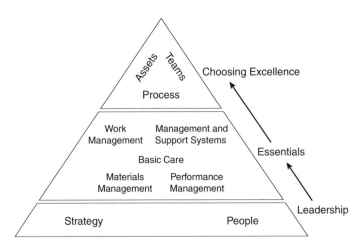

Figure 2. The Uptime Pyramid of Excellence

surface, thrash about, make a lot of noise, get nowhere, and eventually drown. The second swimmer will quickly gain his composure, determine which way he needs to go, and swim to safety. The Olympic champion will do much the same, but he will be better at it. He will make it look easy, getting to safety more quickly and maybe even helping the others along the way. Extend this to maintenance management and you will find some interesting parallels: some people don't belong in the process, some function or manage reasonably well, and some excel.

Any company that has physical assets to maintain will, by default, apply at least some of the elements from the "Essentials" level to varying degrees of competence. Even if a company does nothing more than run everything in a totally reactive mode, it will manage a workforce and materials, comply with some minimal level of regulated maintenance requirements, monitor costs, and use some sort of management systems to do so. If this is done badly, the company (like the poor swimmer) will eventually drown in high maintenance costs, fines for noncompliance with regulations, lost revenues, and poor safety records. In all likelihood, this will happen because no one has consciously applied the principles represented by the "Leadership" part of the Pyramid of Excellence and described in Part I of the book.

More successful companies will consciously apply the "Leadership" elements and may even achieve some level of excellence in executing the "Essentials." If they apply the principles consciously and consistently, they (like the reasonably good swimmer) will survive and may even do reasonably well, encountering only occasional problems along the way. High performing companies will consciously and consistently attend to "Leadership" and "Essentials," adding elements from "Choosing Excellence" to the mix. Like the Olympic swimmer, they will make the process look easy because they are so good at it. One measure of their success is that others will invariably attempt to emulate them.

How well a company executes 'management maintenance by using all or some of core elements presented in this work depends primarily on how well it motivates its people. This factor is a key determinant of how far and how quickly a company moves toward improvement and success.

As noted above, the Pyramid of Excellence is not a prescriptive "one size fits all" approach to implementing successful practices. It is intended as an underlying strategy that provides many possible routes to achieving superior results. It does not need to be followed in sequence from bottom to top, although that is a useful approach. An incentive to mastering the elements of the Pyramid of Excellence is that most of them are already being successfully utilized in high-performing organizations.

Within the pages of *Uptime*, you will find some of the most current theories that examine maintenance management from a business perspective and some of the most recent practices that dovetail with these theories. It is hoped that the book will be of great interest to the general manager who seeks to understand more about maintenance and for the maintenance and engineering professional who wants to appreciate the bigger picture in which maintenance plays an important role. Both will gain valuable insights into the various successful maintenance management techniques and methods available today.

PART I

Leadership

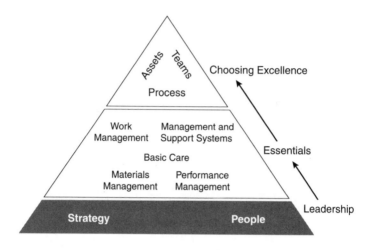

Companies that choose excellence are setting out on a journey toward high performance. They begin with a clear appreciation of where they are, where they want to go, what they will do to get there, and how long it will take. They also review these four criteria regularly to ensure the parameters set still match the needs of their business. They recognize that the key to success is people and that proactive change is sustained only by highly motivated people. Such people will execute a well thought-out strategy if they have participated in its creation, if they take ownership of it, and if the results help them achieve what they want. Success in this journey means success for your company, your people, and you—it is a W³ (Win-Win-Win) proposition. Any approach that is less than W³ will result in less than the desired results.

1

Building a Maintenance Strategy

*The measure of success is not whether you have
a tough problem to deal with, but whether it's the
same problem you had last year.*

JOHN FOSTER DULLES

If you know where you are going and you have a basic idea of how you will get there, then you have a strategy. The various twists and turns, the route you choose, the method of transportation you use, how fast you go, whom you go with, etc., are all tactical choices. Strategy describes the overall direction. It is no more complicated than that. Asset management—the management of the physical infrastructure of a business is all about execution of an asset management strategy. Tactics are the choices you make to implement the strategy and manage the people, processes, and physical asset infrastructure that make up your business.

Regardless of what you are doing and whether or not you document your strategy, you are following one. Even if you have no stated direction, you will still be following a strategy—albeit not consciously. This often results in a totally reactive approach to problem solving. Because you have not chosen your own direction, you are letting events and others choose it for you. A company that makes no proactive attempt to avoid failures of physical assets or their consequences is operating on a run-to-failure strategy in maintenance, regardless of how it defines its strategy. Ideally, your actions and your stated strategy are aligned.

If you have a sound strategy that is known to everyone in your organization, you will be solving new problems—not reliving the old ones. If you do not have a sound strategy, you will benefit immeasurably from creating one, communicating it, and then focusing on your tactical choices for how to achieve it.

It is important at this juncture to clear up a bit of confusion about the definitions of the word "strategy." One definition applies to high-level business; the other is unique to the field of physical asset management. In this chapter, "strategy" is used in the business sense. It refers to an overall direction and high-level flexible plan that leads to good choices. An example is the choice to implement methods that will move a company from a reactive approach to maintenance toward a proactive approach. Choosing excellence in this way will result in lower costs, more reliable and predictable operation, improved safety performance and environmental compliance.

Generally, physical asset management uses the word "strategy" to refer to the overall approach to managing the entire life cycle of specific physical assets. For example, a maintenance strategy for a backup centrifugal pump might be a decision to test the pump periodically and repair it only when it is found inoperable. A life-cycle asset strategy might be choosing to acquire fleet assets and dispose of them when the overall life-cycle cost of ownership is minimized. This strategy considers acquisition, depreciation, disposal, cost of capital, taxation, etc. A popular, simple, but often expensive strategy is to run assets until they have deteriorated to the point where they have no value other than their scrap disposal value.

Strategy need not be complicated—in fact, many of the most successful strategies are little more than simple guidelines or sets of rules. They do not prescribe details, but they suggest alternative routes or actions to take as circumstances shift, all the while keeping the ultimate goal or destination in sight. A good example of this elegant simplicity is Sun Tzu's *Art of War*. Written in about 500 B.C., it is nothing more than a collection of pretty simple rules that no one seriously challenges. Indeed, Sun Tzu's work has been translated and is used as a business tool even today!

To be practical, however, your strategy must go beyond simplicity. It must be supported by tactical plans for how to implement it and those plans must be executed. Without the plans you will not have a clear idea of what you are doing or how. Unless you carry them out, you will have produced little more than an interesting intellectual exercise. Tactical plans address the short, medium, and long-term activities, the human resource needs (people, skills, knowledge, change management), and the investments and budgeting required for getting it all done.

If you were to go to your corner service station and ask the owner-mechanic if he knows who his key customers are, he would probably be able to tell you right away. He deals with them directly every day. He understands their needs because he has made it his business to know them. His livelihood depends on it. He knows what he is there to do, he knows the rules, and he follows them.

In larger enterprises, like manufacturing and processing plants, most employees and specialist managers don't interface with or know their customers directly, nor do they understand their customers' real needs. This crucial information is left to sales staff or marketing departments. They, in turn, pass along what they learn to a corporate development department, and it is there that a company's strategic plan is usually fashioned. Eventually, it is sent for approval to the executive floor. In this compartmentalized approach to business management, putting together a maintenance management strategy linked to the company's overall business plan can be daunting, to say the least. Yet, with companies' increasing dependence on physical assets to deliver value, it is increasingly important to align physical asset management strategy with corporate strategy. It is also critical to ensure that the strategy is communicated and accepted throughout the organization. Without "buy-in" from everyone, it will not be implemented successfully.

Keep in mind that what works for maintenance is not much different from what works for the business. Know where you are, how well you are doing, and where you are going. A good business strategy has the following elements:

- A description of the business you are in and its current products and services, and a description of key customers and what factors keep them as key customers.
- An assessment of the regulatory, economic, and financial environment, especially as companies are increasingly global in scale.
- A description of your future business vision (say, five years from now). Sometimes this is presented as a stretch goal meant to motivate and galvanize employees into action.

- A statement of mission (what you are there to do), guiding principles (the rules you will follow), major objectives to be accomplished (milestones), and the business plan to achieve them.

Supporting the strategy are various activities and analyses that helped develop it, that justify it, and that provide a context for it. It is helpful to document these and include a background description of the strategy, something particularly useful for those who are unfamiliar with it. Examples of this background documentation include:

- An analysis of your past financial performance and overall targets.
- A review of the competitive environment and state of the marketplace.
- The strengths, weaknesses, and key competitive dimensions of the business.
- An honest appraisal of your ability to achieve this vision (can you do it?), which will help you recognize your strengths and weaknesses.

Once a company defines and communicates its business strategy, the same approach can be applied to developing a maintenance strategy. The maintenance strategy, like the business strategy, must remain flexible and respond to changing business requirements. In mining, for example, changes to maintenance strategy are prompted by factors such as mine life, growth, operation, and closure.

THE BUSINESS OF MAINTENANCE MANAGEMENT

Maintenance management supports a business by keeping its productive assets (plant, equipment, vehicle fleet, etc.) available for use. The product that maintenance delivers is "availability"— uptime. It also provides, indirectly, improved yield and process rate, quality, safety, and environmental performance.

Downtime is unproductive time, whether it is caused by lack of market demand, repairs, or scheduled maintenance. We can minimize the amount of time spent on scheduled maintenance by doing only the right maintenance. We can minimize the downtime created by unscheduled maintenance by being more reliable—that is, by consistently and conscientiously performing the right scheduled maintenance. We can also reduce downtime by utilizing spare or excess capacity to save operating and maintenance costs or by serving additional market demand. The role of maintenance must be fully integrated with production and marketing strategies so that the company can meet its production targets to meet market demand. This means optimizing our asset capacity for the business, not just for the shift. Ron Moore[1] provides an excellent discussion of this integration of key business functions in his book *Making Common Sense Common Practice*. *Uptime* focuses primarily on the maintenance aspects of that integrated manufacturing strategy.

Maintenance keeps an asset performing to the standard that is required by a business to achieve its objectives. This is a rather straightforward statement, but its full meaning relies on an understanding of the term *objectives*. One obvious objective is a healthy bottom line. From a purely financial perspective, maintainance can have significant influence on a company's bottom line. In any capital-intensive industry, production costs (i.e., the total of operations and maintenance costs) and revenues rise as the volume of sales increases. As Figure 1-1 illustrates, there are substantial fixed costs (and variable costs) that must be recovered before a company makes any profit. Note that this is a simplified representation—fixed and variable costs are rarely as linear as shown. What should be obvious, however, is that all companies want to maximize profit and increase the slice of the diagram labeled "margin."

Increasing the margin can be done in a number of ways. You can increase sales revenues by increasing either price or volume of production, or you can reduce fixed and/or variable costs. Maintenance may or may not have an impact on these business objectives.

Price is often set by market conditions, and maintenance is unlikely to have any impact on it at all. It can, however, have a profound influence on production volume. If your product or service is in demand and the market will buy more, then this is of value to your business. More uptime increases your production capacity so that you can produce and sell more, generating greater revenues at higher margins. A cautionary note that must be considered is that

---

1. Ron Moore, *Making Common Sense Common Practice: Models for Manufacturing Excellence* (Woburn, MA: Butterworth-Heinemann, 2002).

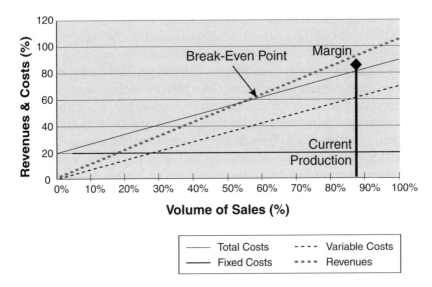

Figure 1-1. Capital-Intensive Industries

if your business is market (or externally) constrained, you will be unable to sell the additional product and increasing production volumes overall will not help. In fact, in this situation, you may already have excess production capacity and increasing uptime seems valueless. Increased uptime, however, has other advantages.

If you can increase uptime substantially, then it may be possible to meet the market demand using only a portion of your fixed asset capacity. In this case, you can shut down and idle excess capacity, reducing both fixed and variable costs. For example, an aircraft parts manufacturer was able to meet demand using two production shifts instead of three. While the company's fixed costs remained the same, its variable costs were cut by one-third. Another case demonstrates how uptime can be used to alleviate a different problem: capacity constraint that may be related to a bottlenecked production process. In this example, a large open-pit copper mine was operating a fleet of 100 haul trucks, but capacity was constrained by the shovels used to load them. By increasing truck reliability, the company was able to increase overall haul truck availability by 3 percent. This increase meant that 97 trucks could now haul the same capacity that 100 had previously been hauling. The mine was able to remove 3 trucks from service and reduce both fixed and variable costs. In a similar case, the mine sold its extra haul trucks and recovered some of its capital investment. One newspaper printing plant is selling its spare printing capacity to other newspapers.

Of course you can also do maintenance more effectively (doing the right things) and efficiently (doing them well) overall. This has the effect of reducing both fixed and variable costs. Maintenance, in fact, is often related to both fixed and variable costs. Even an idle physical plant requires a minimal amount of maintenance in order to preserve it for potential future use or resale. That is a fixed cost. If maintenance demand increases or decreases, it is evident that the cost of parts and labor will also increase or decrease in unison, but the cost of managing them will not. Management costs are more or less fixed in most businesses, regardless of the variable demand. Changing fixed maintenance costs requires a reduction in the physical plant itself or a reduction in the management effort. Reducing the physical plant will also lower the financing component of fixed costs. If this can be done at the design stage, it has a substantial positive business impact. Management effort can be reduced through increased dependency on self-managing teams as described later in this book.

Direct maintenance labor and parts costs are variable. The more maintenance we do, the more labor we expend. In most cases that also requires the use of parts and materials. As a rule of thumb, direct maintenance labor and parts costs are roughly equal in most industries in North America. If a company spends $5 million per year on maintenance labor, it will be spending close to $5 million per year on parts and materials consumed in maintenance activities. It makes little difference whether that labor cost is paid to a company's own employees or contractors.

Direct maintenance (variable) costs can be reduced. An effective maintenance effort results in higher asset reliability, increased uptime, and more productive capacity for the effort and cost expended. An efficient maintenance organization delivers its maintenance program (and hence the results it obtains) at lower cost. The objective is to combine these two seemingly diverse matters and thus improve the overall system. The results can be very impressive. One government report in the United Kingdom, for example, showed that a 10 percent improvement in maintenance performance could create a 40 percent increase in bottom-line business performance.

Quantifying both the direct and indirect costs of maintenance to your company (including costs of downtime, lost sales, penalties, etc.) provides a tool for prioritizing maintenance activities and justifying maintenance improvement expenditure. An investment in maintenance can reduce downtime and its associated costs. Your business may also benefit indirectly as a result of an effective maintenance program. Regulatory compliance, compliance with quality programs, insurance, ability to borrow, and the elimination of extended warranty costs can all be of value.

Regulatory Compliance

Extensive regulation has had a profound impact on the financial industries as well as on executives of major corporations—some of whom have recently been prosecuted and/or jailed for their roles in financial meltdowns, such as those which occurred at Enron and WorldCom. It won't be long before similar legal action is taken against executives whose management systems have failed to prevent deaths due to industrial accidents. Legislation on this has already been enacted in the United Kingdom and it can be assumed that similar legislation will eventually evolve in the United States and elsewhere.

Most companies are doing all they can to comply with pertinent regulations about safety, the environment, maintenance of lifting apparatus, and so on. Not following regulations that pertain to your industry, be it mining regulations, food and drug regulations, nuclear regulations, chemical regulations, workplace safety regulations, etc., you are liable to be caught, fined, or even face jail time. Your company can lose its license to operate and be shut down, throwing many out of work. Even if this worst case scenario does not occur, being cited for noncompliance can severely dent your company's financial forecasts and damage its reputation. Consider, for example, how Exxon's reputation suffered after the Exxon Valdez oil spill.

At a bare minimum, then, your maintenance program must comply with regulations. Inspectors from various government regulating bodies are very good at spotting areas of noncompliance; they are also diligent about warning companies to change things before accidents happen. It is wiser to view these agencies as friends than as foes and to heed their advice. But while getting a "clean bill of health" from your inspectors is certainly welcome and laudable, it indicates only that you are doing the minimum. To be truly successful, you must reach higher. One way to do this is to be scrupulously attentive to maintenance management.

Quality Programs

Today, most companies follow rigid programs of quality assurance such as ISO 9001-2000 and quality-focused improvement programs such as Six Sigma. A common feature of most quality programs is documenting business processes and then showing that everyone complies with them. Six Sigma's overall process is to measure, analyze, improve, and control. You can also use methods like Reliability Centered Maintenance (RCM) to define what it is you are analyzing and improving. No matter which quality assurance program you choose to implement, maintenance effectiveness has an impact on both the results and on your ability to document what you are doing. Having well-defined, efficient, and effective maintenance processes provides a solid foundation.

Insurance

Your company's insurance will stipulate that you comply with all the applicable regulations, and your premiums will depend on both your performance relative to your industry and on your industry's performance overall. Industrial insurers also have inspectors who can help to identify risks that could lead to future claims. These inspectors serve two masters—they help you identify risks so that you can take appropriate action and they also help their own companies minimize their exposure to excessive levels of risk. If they deem your operation to be unsafe or excessively risky, you will either pay more for your coverage or you will become uninsurable. By managing an effective maintenance program, you reduce risks to your business, making it more "insurable" and possibly even reducing your insurance premiums.

One insurance company in Canada offered its client, a global mining firm, reduced annual premiums if the company agreed to use analytical approaches like RCM to determine its maintenance requirements and could show compliance with the program developed that way. The company saved over $2 million per year, easily paying for the analysis work many times over.

Banks

Many companies borrow money to buy capital equipment or lease equipment for operations. That equipment will have a resale or disposal value at the end of its forecasted useful life and will depreciate in value over time. It will also have ongoing maintenance costs associated with its upkeep. Banks realize that a well-maintained asset will last longer, run more reliably, generate more free cash flow, and have a higher resale value down the road. Like the insurance companies, banks want to reduce all potential risks associated with loaning your company money. Banks want you to repay your loans or keep current with your lease payments. If your business risk is minimized, so is theirs. Increasing your cash flow through higher asset reliability and utilization reduces your business risk. Some banks will consider what you are doing to manage your assets and give you more favorable terms on loans and leases if you are doing things well.

Warranties

When you acquire a new asset, it usually comes with a basic warranty on materials and workmanship as well as with an option to purchase an extended warranty. Often those extended warranties cost 2 to 3 percent of the capital cost of the asset. To make good on any claims against an extended warranty, the manufacturer will need verification that you have followed maintenance and servicing instructions, which sometimes go well beyond the minimum maintenance. In addition, if you perform an RCM analysis (discussed in detail later in this book), you may discover that some of the manufacturer's recommended maintenance tasks are inappropriate for a variety of reasons. Warranties, however, are part of the cost of doing business, and if you are concerned about the validity of the warranty, you should follow the manufacturer's instructions and bear the associated cost, even though doing so seems unnecessary. Warranties often do not cover the costs or other consequences associated with unplanned downtime. If the manufacturer's maintenance program isn't quite right for your business you suffer what is often the worst of the consequences.

Warranties are a form of insurance. You pay for them up front and you pay to keep them in force. You also follow the instructions of those who do not own or operate the assets and have no material concern in your costs or business results. In some ways, you are often betting against yourself by paying a great deal to ensure that some of your costs will be recovered if the equipment or technology fails to work properly. In some respects, a manufacturer may also find warranties detrimental. If there is a problem and if you have followed maintenance instructions, the manufacturer is contractually bound to repair or replace the asset. One attractive way to avoid both situations is to bet on yourself. Instead of buying extended warranties, negotiate suppliers for a cost reduction on the purchase of their products. Spend the money that you would have spent on an extended warranty on an RCM analysis, which will provide information that helps you choose the right maintenance (at the right time) for your operating environment and circumstances.

A good maintenance management strategy considers all of these factors and their potential to help or harm your business. It also considers ways to work with the status quo in a way that allows you to set yourself up for success. Throughout this book, you will learn about various ways that companies have become successful at maintaining their assets. Doing so provides the essentials of a production system that generates revenue. Doing so cost-effectively is even more important. It makes little sense to invest heavily in maintenance if this investment does not increase sellable output, improve safety and environmental performance, or reduce fixed and variable costs. Before setting off on a massive improvement program, it makes sense to build your case in a way that shows that there will be a return on the investment. Doing that requires some knowledge of your strategy and the tactics you plan to use, their costs, and the resulting payback.

Until recently, many maintenance managers came from technical or trade backgrounds, and they seldom thought in terms of return-on-investment. Although they understood the concept, they did not live it. Today's maintenance manager cannot afford this. He or she must understand and live the concept and pay strict attention to the business aspects of their role.

Maintenance management deals with planning, organizing, directing, and using the resources necessary to keep your physical assets running well and contributing to your business. Several questions can help you determine whether this is being done cost effectively:

- Can the assets be designed for better maintainability and higher reliability? Will the added investment be worth it?
- What is the impact of financing on the capability of new assets? Does the payback cover at least the cost of capital?
- How do operating expectations, procedures, and practices affect asset performance?
- How do the efficiency and effectiveness of our maintenance efforts impact asset life-cycle costs?

Clearly, maintenance is only part of the asset life cycle, which covers everything from the time when the productive capacity needs of the asset (e.g., a vehicle, press, or pump) is set until the time of disposal. Operations, maintenance, and modifications occur together as a cycle occupying one step in a multistep life-cycle asset management process (see Figure 1-2).

On a linear time scale, the "Operate, Maintain, and Modify" cycle takes up most of the "life" of the asset. Modifications are made if the asset no longer meets the demands of the business. Today, many organizations are rethinking their approach to managing this entire asset life cycle and adopting a different approach: Physical Asset Management. This approach goes well beyond the

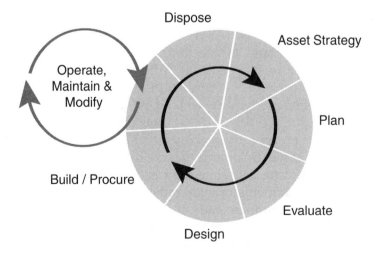

Figure 1-2. Typical Asset Life Cycle

traditional boundaries of maintenance and engineering by embracing financial considerations, market realities, and the human capital necessary to make it all happen.

Traditionally, most businesses were organized to think and act in functional silos—"I design, you operate, and someone else fixes." Many companies still operate this way. Within this framework, however, it is often easy to miss the overall business process. Those who use this approach often miss out on insights that others in the organization can contribute, and these insights can often make a tremendous difference in the way assets are perceived and maintained. The more input that is provided, the easier it is to understand the need for an asset, design it to meet customers' requirements, build and operate it so that it performs precisely and consistently, and maintain it easily and inexpensively.

Electric utilities were once publicly owned monopolies charged with providing uninterrupted service. To ensure high reliability (i.e., uninterrupted service), they built in a great deal of hardware redundancy and usually overdesigned their systems. Costs were simply passed on to users and/or the taxpayers and justified on the basis of need for high reliability. Now deregulated, these utilities are learning to compete in markets where overdesign reduces profitability. They already knew that reliability can be bought; they are now learning that it cannot be bought at any price. They are recognizing the need for more economical approaches to keep asset investment costs and operating costs down and reliability and service costs up. Their business has changed and so has their approach to managing their physical assets.

Good asset management begins by asking why the asset is required and how it relates to the business plan. Once this has been established, the purpose, function, and standards of performance must be set. Costs and benefits are evaluated and the asset is justified and ranked as an investment option by the company. After approval, detailed design and specifications are completed. The asset is constructed or procured and installed. Once it gets a thumbs-up in testing, it is operated and maintained (and often modified as requirements change and as time goes on). When the asset's economic usefulness ends, it is disposed of.

Reaping the cost-benefits of an asset rests on all nine steps. Ideally, maintenance, operations, engineering, materials, accounting, and any other relevant departments can and will be involved each step of the way. Even before the systems are built, the decisions about what to build, how to build it, how to operate it, and how to maintain it will have impact on the business for years to come. Capable engineers must design the systems. Once the systems are in place, capable maintainers must keep them running.

It is almost paradoxical that the operators who run the systems and the maintainers have very limited influence on the asset or system's total life-cycle costs. Instead, it is at the design stage that most decisions that have an impact on total life-cycle costs are made. Figure 1-3 illustrates the commitment and spending patterns during critical phases of an asset's life cycle. As the figure illustrates, maintainability and reliability considerations have the greatest impact early in the process, during the design phase. Almost as soon as the asset is built and placed in service, the maintainability and reliability considerations decline dramatically and plateau until the disposal phase, but their costs continue to rise steadily.

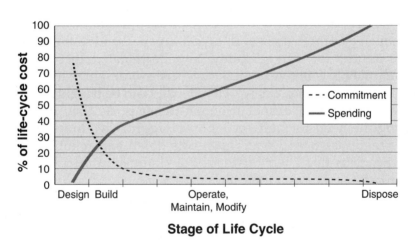

Stage of Life Cycle

Figure 1-3. Life-Cycle Costs: Commitment vs. Spending

The operations and maintenance stage of the asset life cycle is dramatically influenced by the reliability of the design. If you are running and maintaining a system that is inherently unreliable, no amount of maintenance effort will improve it. You will need costly design modifications. Using the practical knowledge of experienced maintainers and operators at the design stage can result in significant savings in operating and maintenance (O&M) costs.

These individuals can provide excellent insight into issues that are best dealt with before construction begins. In some cases, they may even help avoid excessive capital costs. For example, by including high reliability and maintainability as design considerations for a fleet of buses, it is possible to get more available service time from individual buses. This, in turn, affects desired overall fleet utilization as fewer buses will be required. Because fewer buses are required, less capital is spent up front.

In the United Kingdom, the privatization of the electricity industry led to a tremendous improvement in performance. This occurred because risk in asset management was explicitly acknowledged, and this led to the development of decision-making models that consciously traded off cost vs. risk vs. performance. The net result was a 30 to 40 percent across-the-industry reduction in cost (and labor) with a simultaneous improvement in asset performance, which was measured as a reduction in customer outage duration. Financial values were placed on customer service levels, image, environmental compliance or breach, and regulatory compliance or breach, allowing optimization of the total picture.

Most people tend to think of the steps in the asset life cycle as being sequential, but this is not always the case. The design, procure, build, and operate phases may actually overlap. Operate and maintain certainly overlap during the entire life cycle of an asset. When the need arises, both of these are overlapped by modification. Complex systems take years to design and build and are rarely built exactly as designers originally envisioned them. Compare any "as built" drawings to the engineering drawings and you will see that. Design of the maintenance program ideally overlaps with the design of the asset. Up-front definition of the right maintenance can lead to substantial benefits in life-cycle cost reduction. Design flaws are often found when this up-front analysis is performed—they can be corrected on the drawing board instead of in the field. Maintainability issues become apparent and can be rectified so that downtime is minimized once the asset enters service. Knowledge of maintenance requirements can drive the identification and purchase of spare parts. Often, spares are bought at the recommendation of manufacturers not maintainers. But ask yourself who benefits from this and you will discover that having the spares available when the asset starts can help avoid unnecessary downtime.

Today, demographics are a critical issue for all industries. As the baby boom generation approaches retirement age, a massive succession problem looms. The generations that follow are smaller in numbers. Post-boomers grew up (or are growing up) in the "information age" and learned far more about computers and high technology than about skilled trades. Few children or grandchildren of the baby boomers have shown an interest in learning a trade; their parents and grandparents have encouraged them to get college degrees and become professionals. Two strategic issues arise from this. Just who will replace the retiring boomers who are trade skilled? And how will we capture the knowledge that is leaving as older workers retire?

Dealing with these issues will be challenging, and solutions will not be quick fixes. Immigration, an old and reliable solution, will not work. Other countries are facing the same problems or do not have the ability or resources to train people in trade skills. Outsourcing is an option, but even the outsource service providers are facing similar problems. Part of the solution lies in doing more work with fewer people—in other words, becoming more efficient. Another part of the solution is doing less work—becoming more effective. Two particularly good ways to do the latter is through the Proactive Maintenance programs discussed in this work and through designing in reliability. Providing trades training and apprentice programs are also part of the solution and can be applied to newcomers from overseas who lack skills but are willing to learn them.

FRAMEWORK FOR THE STRATEGY

There are several ways to build a strategy. Stephen R. Covey tells us to begin with the end in mind.[2] If you have a good idea of your current state (where you are now), you can create an overall vision (the end result you want to achieve), then state what you will do to achieve it. If you do not have enough knowledge about your current state, it makes good sense to perform detailed analyses of this before launching into the vision and main tactical choices.

---

2. Stephen R. Covey, *The 7 Habits of Highly Effective People* (New York: Simon & Schuster, 1989).

Maintenance strategy is based on the framework model depicted in Figure 1-4. Foremost in any business plan are the needs and wants of the customers, shareholders, and other stakeholders. The key objectives for each function and element in the business strategy are drafted with them in mind. Maintenance is likely to have the following business targets:

- Maximize the production rate of a particular product through high reliability (e.g., increase availability of the bottling line from 93 to 96 percent).
- Reduce costs per unit of output by doing only the safe minimum amount of maintenance (e.g., safely reduce maintenance costs per ton of concentrate from $42 to $35).
- Add productive capability for additional plant by supplying advice to the design team (e.g., designate experienced engineer to work with the design and commissioning team for the expansion of our processing line with a goal of increasing line availability from 90 to 97 percent).
- Eliminate stores inventories through vendor partnering, increased predictive and preventive maintenance, and elimination of emergency work. (e.g., reduce the value of stores inventory by 25 percent while maintaining stores service levels of 95 percent).
- Support quality improvement initiatives through the application of precision maintenance on all production assets (e.g., introduce laser alignment techniques to improve rotating equipment reliability by eliminating all failures due to installation or repair misalignment).

A maintenance strategy is like any other tool of business. It is not meant to hammer away in only one direction. Instead, it serves as a road map that allows and includes alternatives. For this reason, it must remain flexible. If the company's situation changes, so does the maintenance strategy. If a business shuts down excess capacity, it makes little sense to continue to maintain plants that will be shut down.

The company's business strategy sets the high level direction for maintenance management. But every company has its own unique culture and values, and it is important to remember that these will come into play and may get in the way of change. If the company has always been highly responsive to market shifts, it is likely to have a reactive culture that demands rapid response to

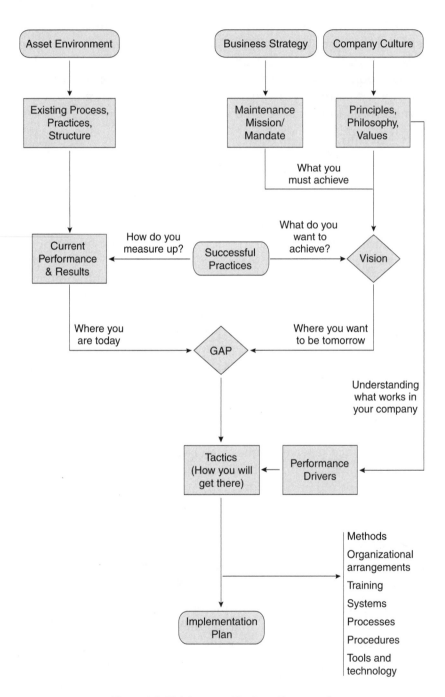

Figure 1-4. Maintenance Strategy Framework

any event. A maintenance manager in such a company will have difficulty shifting from a reactive "fix it when it breaks" mode to a proactive mode that focuses on avoiding breakdowns.

Successful maintenance practices can be learned from both outside and within the company. Many companies, for example, create their own road maps based on benchmarking results and observing what their best plants or others are doing already. Regardless of where you get your direction, the description of excellence as you desire it is your vision.

Your asset environment is usually a given. Unless you are building a new facility or buying a new fleet of vehicles, the plant, technology, and even the people are already there. Your current practices, good, bad, or somewhere in between are also a given. If they do not match your vision, they need to be changed. When the gap between your present reality and your vision is understood, it can be closed. Closing that gap will require a plan that gets you there, and your plan must include all the people, behavior, system, process, and other changes that will be involved in the changes. Understand what drives behavior in your organization and what you can do that will influence changes in that behavior. Those activities are the performance drivers for making the change happen. They will require the most work.

The more change you want to see, the more detailed your plans must be. One organization, for example, restructured so radically that every job was altered. Some jobs were eliminated entirely, but employees whose jobs were eliminated were invited to apply for the fewer jobs that remained. The transition required several well-defined plans, including plans for people. The "new" maintenance engineering manager set key three-year objectives:

1. To reengineer the entire maintenance management process, with particular emphasis on proactive and planned corrective work, increasing planned work to 85 percent and proactive effort to 60 percent of the total.
2. To specify, select, and implement a computerized maintenance and inventory management system integrated with procurement by the end of the second year.
3. To introduce a multiskilling pilot project in conjunction with the union local within 6 months for completion by the end of the second year.

4. To augment the short-, medium-, and long-range maintenance planning capabilities with 1 planner for every 25
   tradesmen and 1 maintenance engineer.
5. To reduce by 25 percent the direct maintenance cost per unit
   of output produced.
6. To improve safety performance from 3 to 1.5 recordable incidents per 200,000 hours.

These objectives were the foundation of the maintenance
vision. They would ultimately shape the annual plans and budgets
of the department.

STRATEGY COMPONENTS

Strategy is the basis for your tactical implementation. It provides a
general direction and it need not be complicated or lengthy. It
includes the following components:

- **Mission:** a statement of what you are there to do. This statement should provide a simple common and clear purpose for
  the organization. Most maintenance departments will have
  similar missions, but they will vary with the business needs.
  One company's maintenance mission was "to work with production delivering needed production capacity, consistently
  and safely."
- **Vision:** A simple statement of what you are trying to achieve
  with your maintenance strategy. If you want to improve,
  describe the standard you wish to achieve. Write the statement in the present tense as if you were already there. For
  example, "We are sought after as benchmarking partners of
  choice" indicates that your performance is so good that others want to copy it.
- **Tactics:** A brief statement of the main activities you will
  engage in to achieve your vision. This could be a simple listing of practices you intend to implement like Reliability Centered Maintenance (RCM) or Total Productive Maintenance
  (TPM).
- **Target timing:** A statement of when you plan to achieve your
  vision. This does not need to be a complicated Gantt chart
  with milestones. A single realistic completion date is enough
  for your implementation teams to work towards. For exam-

ple, "All critical production systems will have RCM-derived maintenance programs within 2 years."

- **Rules:** A statement of a few simple rules you will follow in implementing the tactics. These rules will reflect shared corporate values for behavior that will hold when the vision is achieved and guide how things get done along the way to achieving it. Your rules should be easy to remember and follow:
  - Take care of yourself
  - Take care of each other
  - Take care of the equipment
  - Take care of business

Putting a strategy together is a team effort. Don't leave it all to the maintenance manager and his or her people. Operations, supply chain, human resources, training departments, finance, accounting, and plant management will all be affected. Include them in the strategy development team. Because all of them will have their own "agenda," use a third-party facilitator who is completely independent of the result and the various agendas that each party brings to the table. The person who performed the maintenance review for you is the best candidate because he or she will be knowledgeable about your issues and objective. Once a maintenance review has been carried out, the strategy development effort requires only a few days of teamwork. Keep it simple. Avoid overcomplicating the strategy with excessive details. Implementation plan details support the strategy, but there is no need to include them in the strategy document or statement. Manage those separately.

Once you have your strategy in place, you can develop detailed implementation plans and then manage their execution as you would with any other project. Because the overall project could take several years to complete, do not preplan the details for the entire project. Plan for a year at a time, do an annual project review, determine what (if any) alterations to the original plan are needed, and add in the details for the following year.

STRATEGY DEVELOPMENT

Developing a maintenance strategy entails a process that brings the elements of the strategy framework together. Figure 1-5 depicts a highly effective strategy development process: Plan-Do-Check-Act.

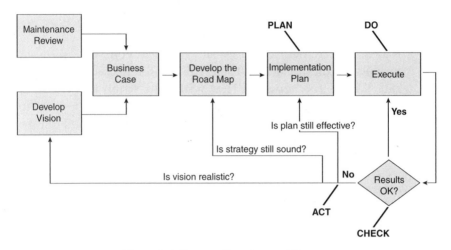

Figure 1-5. Strategy Development Process

If you don't already have a vision of what you would like to achieve, develop one. Brainstorming for ideas after a seminar or workshop on successful practices can be very effective. Another alternative is a "visioning" session.

Next, perform a review of the status quo to give you a sense of what you are doing and how well you are doing it. Compare your present state with your vision and decide if you are there or not. If not, develop a business case that justifies any changes you might wish to make. This will be based on the costs required to bring your practices up to the level that you have chosen in your vision and the return on those costs (your investment) that will be achieved by improved results.

If the business case is sufficiently sound, develop your overall road map that describes what the major changes are going to be and what approximate sequence they will take. A workshop on successful practices will give you a rough idea of what it will take to implement this sequence. The strategy should cover the entire transition from your current state up to the point where you have attained your vision. From this sequential road map, you can work out an implementation plan that describes who will do what and in what time frames. Each part of the vision (e.g., implement TPM) will form a workstream.

Plan the details of those workstreams in one-year increments using a rolling-wave approach. Things can change from one year to the next, so don't get too detailed too far in advance because that can lead to a lot of rework. Once the plan is in place, assign responsibilities to workstream leaders and give them the authority to get things done.

Manage their progress as if it were any other project. Provide the necessary support to get things done while watching both progress and results. If the results are not what you want, then determine whether the problem is with execution, the plan, the strategy, or the vision. Are they realistic? Is the plan detailed enough? Are time frames realistic? Are the goals realistic? Remember that unreasonable goals will serve as demotivators because those responsible for implementing them will realize that they are on a path to failure.

The next sections discuss these steps in more detail. Chapter 2 addresses managing the transformation you are setting out to achieve.

DEVELOPING THE VISION

The difference between the current reality and the vision is what your maintenance improvement plan will address. A shared vision is used to provide the direction needed for future improvements. This vision may be somewhat nebulous at first. It will emerge clearly, however, if you follow the strategic model, base your main goals on the overall business plan, and fully understand the major differences between "best practice" and current reality. Two other items are critical: 1) ensuring that "successful practice" is a realistic vision for your industry sector and your particular operation and 2) setting priorities for the various factors assessed.

Benchmarking is an excellent way to determine successful practices. This technique, discussed more fully in Chapter 6, involves looking at how the leaders in the field achieved their performance targets and will show you what realistic targets really are. Once you know what is realistically achievable and how others achieved realistic targets, you can emulate their approach and work toward achieving your own performance targets.

Consider including a sister plant within your organization in your study, or a successful competitor (an enterprise somewhat related to what you do), or an operation that performs the benchmarked process better than anyone else, regardless of its industrial sector. Some industries carry out regular benchmarking within their own industry organizations. In some countries, for example, oil refineries and pulp and paper mills participate in annual benchmarking studies that rank performance across a broad range of metrics. Each of the participants know exactly where they stand. Finding out how to improve, however, takes more than a numerical comparison of performance.

Obtaining this information, especially from a direct competitor, may be difficult. A published review of maintenance engineering may be an easier option. Technology and management periodicals and newsletters often publish features on innovation and best practice. Another option is a benchmarking best practices Internet database, which is available to participating member companies. The best benchmarking studies entail visits to high performance companies to see and document how they got there. Another option is to rely on the knowledge of third parties. This approach taps into the deep experience of others who have already done the legwork and can be far less expensive than a benchmarking study.

Understand your own strengths and weaknesses before studying how others manage maintenance. When it comes time to compare notes with other operations, be sure to have a list of specifics. What you want to learn from them is how well they are really doing (i.e., the measures and statistics) and how they got their results.

There is a significant difference between stating a vision and having all concerned accept it. Those who will be responsible for achieving the vision are involved in developing the maintenance improvement plan. This usually includes your managers, superintendents, supervisors, influential trades' persons, and union leadership. Include people from departments that will be affected outside of maintenance, like purchasing and human resources. An excellent way to do this is to bring everyone together for an off-site strategic planning session. Try building team decision making with, for example, brainstorming and nominal group technique or prioritization matrices. Giving participants the chance to help create the vision and plan will encourage them to pull together when it comes time to get it all done. Everyone feels more responsible for making it work if it is their baby.

The facilitator of this group session should be a person who has no direct stake in the outcome but has some knowledge of modern maintenance management methods. That way, you will get objective leadership and individual involvement.

THE MAINTENANCE REVIEW

Maintenance improvement fails when there's little understanding of the situation at hand. There may be a strong inclination in the department to retain the status quo, or there could be friction between production and maintenance. Technically, it may boil down to lack of knowledge about automation or how to predict probable failures.

For instance, a city transit company wants to use RCM to become totally proactive so that it will have fewer breakdowns on the road. That goal will fail if the transit company does not establish a solid, systematic maintenance work management program—one that ensures that preventive maintenance gets done on schedule all the time. It doesn't matter whether the goal or the program comes first; both must exist to ensure good results.

Before embarking on an improvement program, assess thoroughly the strengths and weaknesses of the present system and which areas head the list for enhancement. A maintenance review can produce a clear understanding of the shortfalls relative to successful practices and let you see the necessary next steps to achieve the vision. It is comprehensive and covers strategic, procedural, technical, administrative, and cultural issues. Never underestimate the impact of cultural issues. Experience shows that these are usually the biggest hurdle.

Appendix A describes a maintenance management diagnostic review. Major areas of this review are:

1. Overall business context
2. Leadership
      Maintenance strategy and its fit within the business context
      Organization and people management
3. Essential Practices
      Work Management
      Materials Management
      Basic Care
      Performance Management
      Management and Support Systems

4. Methods
    Asset-centric Methods
    Team-based Methods
    Process Optimization
5. Results

The review is best performed by an experienced and unbiased third party. Another way to perform assessment is to distribute a self-administered questionnaire that asks participants to rate various aspects of plant engineering and maintenance. Thus, for example, you may have an independent specialist review the maintenance environment and asset management *or* have participants answer questions about the approach in place—whether it is a three-year improvement plan, annual budgeting process, or maintaining equipment on an ad hoc basis (reactive). The questionnaire should include carefully crafted questions that plant the seeds of knowledge of successful practices while prompting answers that will aid in learning what is actually happening today. (For example, "What is the percentage of your weekly scheduled work that is actually completed within the week? Less than 20 percent? Twenty to 50 percent? Fifty to 75 percent? Greater than 75 percent?") To avoid confusion, different questionnaires should be created for individual departments or participants. (For example, stores and supply chain personnel are not likely to know much about reliability engineering, so their questionnaire should focus on supply chain issues.)

Each response is scored and plotted either on a histogram (Figure 1-6) or on a Bell-Mason type spider diagram (Figure 1-7).

The histogram in Figure 1-6 has ten categories, one for each element of the Pyramid of Excellence. The areas requiring the greatest attention are those that are most important to the business but have the lowest scores: strategy, people, materials management, and asset reliability; however, all areas would benefit from some improvement. In Figure 1-7, the same data are presented in a different format—a spider gram reveals the same areas of concern. In either case, a low score in an area that is not considered important to the business is of little concern. (For example, a company that chooses not to use team-based methods would not be concerned about a low score in this area.)

Maintenance management is often perceived differently throughout an organization. Production, engineering, senior

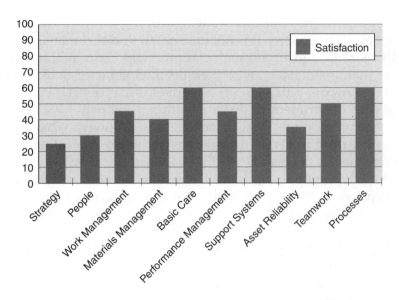

Figure 1-6. Maintenance Self-assessment Results (Histogram)

Figure 1-7. Maintenance Self-assessment Results (Spider Diagram)

management, or a specific trades grouping all have their own needs and perceptions. It is not unusual to find that management, with its high and broad expectations, will score maintenance lower than maintainers, with their detailed knowledge of what is really going on, will score it. Moreover, because each company (and each department or division within a company) is different, there are no absolute "best" practices to be followed. What is best in any organization is what works best for that organization. What matters most is the results, not the practices. The practices are simply tools that help you achieve the results. Because of differences in corporate culture, individual personalities, availability of support resources, and other factors, practices that work well for one company may work poorly in another. For this reason, the rating scales used in diagnostic assessments are relative and not absolute. They should not dictate choices but guide them by reflecting what it would take for your own company in its unique business circumstances to excel. If those circumstances are subject to change, as they often are, you look at worst case scenarios to determine what standards to use.

Comparisons with other companies must be done with caution. Many managers want to see them, but to get value from such comparisons it is imperative that key success factors for the business be sufficiently similar to make the companies truly comparable. Otherwise the comparisons can be misleading. A diagnostic review does not produce a benchmarking comparison. Benchmarking findings are used to show what is achievable and what practices are most widely used, but they may not always be applicable in your situation. The diagnostic review will help to point that out.

A simple grid measuring the elements of the Pyramid of Excellence against the current status can give a qualitative score on a scale from Innocence to Excellence. Figure 1-8 provides an example of the grid. Each block contains an abbreviated description of the characteristics of a typical organization operating at different levels of development for each of the 10 elements of the Pyramid of Excellence.

Comparing the perceptions of one department to another can also be quite revealing. At one base metal extrusion plant, four groups evaluated the status of their maintenance function. Production, maintenance, and front office management all scored their status at approximately the Competence level. Project engineering,

	Strategy	People	Work Management	Materials Management	Basic Care	Performance Management	Support Systems	Asset Reliability	Teamwork	Processes
Excellence	Complete strategy developed with full participation including plans.	Fully developed multi-skilling, autonomous teams in place.	Long-term planning cycles and extensive use of standard job plans.	Stockouts rare. Service level 98% plus. Inventory turns >2 times.	Full regulatory compliance. PM program features extensive CBM. Operators do some minor PM. Equipment condition good.	Fully balanced score cards for teams. Improvement results evident in performance trends.	Full user acceptance and widespread use of management systems. CBM, reliability analysis and decision support systems in use.	PM program fully developed using RCM. RFCA used but not needed very often. MTC inputs to design of new assets.	Autonomous teams of maintainers and operators used extensively. Support by management and specialists. Consistent maintenance standards in use.	Processes are efficient and effective. No work arounds in use. Regular reviews carried out to keep processes fresh. Support systems automate parts of the process.
Competence	Complete strategy developed by key personnel with plans.	Multi-skilling and managed teams of maintainers and operators.	Scheduling and planning well established for most work.	Inventory turns >1. Service level 95% plus. Stockouts less than 5%.	Full regulatory compliance. PM program features some CBM. Operators help with PM. Equipment condition good.	Reliability measures in use and improvement programs monitored, trends being developed.	Extensive management systems used mostly by management. Some CBM, reliability analysis and decision support systems in use.	RCM in use to define PM programs. RCFA in use.	Area- or unit-based teams or maintainers and operators with management. Maintenance standards applied in each area.	Processes are efficient and effective. Some work arounds may be in use. Reviews carried out infrequently.

continued on next page

Figure 1-8. Maintenance Maturity Grid

	Strategy	People	Work Management	Materials Management	Basic Care	Performance Management	Support Systems	Asset Reliability	Teamwork	Processes
Understanding	Management defined strategy & plans.	Some multi-skilling. Mostly distributed maintenance teams with conventional supervision.	Scheduling established, compliance good. Planning for major work and shutdowns as work arises.	Inventory turns >0.7. Service level 90% plus. Inventory analysis being performed.	Partial regulatory compliance. PM program based on fixed interval task with little CBM. Equipment condition fair.	Basic maintenance performance measures in use.	Management systems in use. Some reporting is used. Some CBM support systems in use.	Reliability improvement program in place. RCFA and possible PM Optimization in use.	Maintenance working in area teams under maintenance supervision. Operations separate.	Maintenance processes reviewed. Interfacing processes untouched. Work arounds in use.
Awareness	Documented goals but no plans.	Partly decentralized organization based on trades.	Scheduling with about 50% compliance. Plans for shutdowns only.	Inventory improvement plans in place. Measurement of stores performance started.	Poor regulatory compliance. PM program under development using traditional methods. Equipment condition fair.	Financial measures used to analyze spending patterns. Some downtime records.	Management systems use is spotty and providing little valuable output. Ad hoc systems still in use. CBM support being considered.	Downtime analysis is performed and some improvements are implemented.	Mix of centralized (shop) labor and individuals assigned to production areas. Conventional supervision.	Processed documented but not reviewed. Work arounds in use. Inefficiency evident particularly at functional handoffs.
Innocence	No documented strategy. Maintenance is largely reactive.	Centralized organization based on trades demarcation.	No planning, little scheduling and poor compliance to schedule.	Frequent stockouts. Service level poor. Jobs frequently waiting for parts.	Poor regulatory compliance. Minimal or nonexistent PM program. Equipment condition poor.	Only financial measures being watched but no analysis of costs performed.	Little to no use of management systems. May be using variety of ad hoc systems.	Plenty of downtime but no analysis of causes or attempts to improve.	No teamwork. Conventional supervision.	Processes not documented and inefficient. Plenty of work arounds. Plenty of complaining.

Figure 1-8. Maintenance Maturity Grid

however, rated it well below, at Awareness. When the results were discussed with all groups together, it was clear that the project engineering team was remote from day-to-day activities and their opinion was driven by what they saw relative to other organizations, not relative to results being obtained. This assessment not only shed light on a new strategy for maintenance but also highlighted the need for project engineering to become more involved on the shopfloor and vice versa. Many companies still have well-defined functional boundaries that act as barriers to cross-functional information and experience sharing. A diagnostic review helps to reveal those barriers so that choices can be made about whether or not to keep them in place.

CLOSING THE GAP—PLANNING IMPLEMENTATION

With the maintenance review completed and the vision defined, you can devise a detailed plan for achieving the vision. Consider the following:

- The task and its key activities. For example, implementing Reliability Centered Maintenance entails selection of systems for analysis, selection of analysis teams, training of analysts, training of facilitators, pilot projects, evaluation before and after performance, and more.
- The priority of the initiative, relative to others. If you have several improvement projects, how much senior management time will each receive?
- Estimated resources and level of effort required.
- The "champion" responsible for ensuring successful completion and the "sponsor" to provide the resources.
- The start date, completion date, and milestones along the way.
- The goal to be achieved on successful completion, and what you are going to measure to determine if you are on the right track.
- The challenges you will face that could derail your efforts or cause you to lose focus.

Implementation of these plans is far more than a technical project. It will involve a great deal of human change, and that's the hard part. Don't shortchange yourself by ignoring change management at all levels in your organization.

One business with a solid history of reliability and profitability developed an overall physical asset management strategy that dealt with most of the asset management process described in Figure 1-2 and included companywide objectives for fixed asset accounting, economic evaluation of projects, and maintenance management. Because of the high average age of the company's assets, there was an increasing demand for refurbishment in an environment of cost reduction. One key operating division developed its maintenance strategy based on this companywide strategic direction:

- **The Mission:** "To maintain assets to meet customers' needs cost effectively, to continuously improve skills and processes to optimize asset life, using best-fit methods and technologies; to work safely and be environmentally responsible." Each word was crafted after tedious but heartfelt debate by those who had to live with the finished statement.
- **Objectives:** A vision was set by looking at the current situation—challenges in structure, planning, methods, skills, applied technologies, and measures—and by coming to a consensus of what was possible over a three-year period. Five long-term objectives were selected to fill the gaps between the reality and vision. The focus was on having higher equipment effectiveness than the industry average at a lower maintenance cost based on the replacement value of assets employed.
- **Action:** Each objective was "owned" by the person responsible for ensuring successful completion: a champion who committed resources, developed a timetable, and structured a detailed implementation plan. Orchestration of these plans was key to overall success. Bimonthly progress review meetings were held to share successes and manage frustrations.

The company stuck to its strategy, making measured steps to improvement in a tough business climate, and succeeded at making the desired changes.

CONTRACT MAINTENANCE

Most businesses contract out some form of maintenance, whether specialized technical work, like nondestructive testing, or overflow fabrication and machining work. Some contract out the entire maintenance function while others contract out all operations and maintenance. The practice of outsourcing maintenance is common around the world (more so in Australia, Asia, and Europe than in North America, but it exists everywhere). In fact, several very large contracting firms look after maintenance for hundreds of plants worldwide.

There are many reasons for contracting out or outsourcing maintenance. The most common is that a contractor can do the work more cost-effectively than you can. Some companies use outsourcing to transfer risk. By having a contractor take full responsibility for maintaining lifting equipment, elevators, and hoists, for example, you eliminate (or substantially reduce) an element of risk and potential liability from your business. In other cases, the work requires technical specialties that are not available (or wanted) in house. Heating, ventilation, and air conditioning (HVAC) maintenance is very commonly outsourced for this reason. Occasionally, there is simply not enough work to justify having your own talent do it (e.g., some companies outsource their oil analysis work). Some companies look to outsourcing as a means of alleviating the demographic problem of finding enough skilled tradespeople, not realizing that the outsource service providers may have the same problem.

Contracting maintenance has many benefits, including labor leveling for shutdowns and cost and capability factors. It also has some drawbacks, such as the difficulty in controlling quality and getting the labor experience needed. To answer the strategic questions of whether to consider contracting out significant portions of your planned and preventive maintenance, first understand the concept of competitive advantage. Your business has one or several core products and services that you provide to customers. There are a few core processes and physical assets that allow these processes to happen. Can your cost effectiveness and capabilities in maintaining these assets be considered a competitive advantage, something that allows you to compete and win in the marketplace? If so, contracting out maintenance of these assets may give away or diminish some of your competitive advantage.

Many believe that maintenance is a "core" capability that cannot be contracted out. Rather than think in terms of "core" vs. "noncore" activities, it may be better to think about "uniqueness." If what you do in maintenance is unique to your business, then it is something you probably want to hang on to because no one else is doing it. If it is something that is commonly done by many other companies or service providers, then it can be considered appropriate for outsourcing. Something that is not unique is unlikely to give your company any competitive advantage. In fact, that sort of work may even be done better by another company since that company focuses on the work as a business instead of treating it as a "necessary expense item." For example, an electrical rebuild shop that services several dozen customers may do a better job at rebuilding motors or switchgear than your own electricians, who also have many other, more pressing tasks to perform. The diagram in Figure 1-9 can help you determine whether outsourcing is a good option.

	Strategic	Not Strategic
Competitive Advantage	Keep work in house	Consider outsourcing (evaluate)
No Competitive Advantage	Rework to provide advantage	Outsource

Figure 1-9. Outsourcing Decision Matrix

Ask yourself if the maintenance activity is of strategic value to the business. Is it unique to your business or does having the capability in-house result in some other advantage in the market? For example, if maintenance costs are typically high in your industry, you may want to keep it in-house where you can have better control over those costs. On the other hand, a contractor who is more skilled at maintenance may deliver the greatest uptime. Which is more important, cost or results? Generally, if you can get more uptime, your costs will drop and output will increase.

The competitive dimension row in the diagram helps you determine whether or not you are already providing cost-effective maintenance compared to what is offered at what price by external service providers. If maintenance is of strategic value to your company and you are providing it cost effectively, maintain the status quo. If what you are doing is not cost effective but it is of strategic value, then consider an improvement program for your maintenance function so that you can deliver it more cost effectively.

If you do plan to contract maintenance, your key concerns will be contractor productivity and performance. Ideally, the contractors will be subject to a thorough review, appropriately trained, and not subject to high turnover. Contract out specific, well-defined projects or responsibilities and ensure that performance standards are set and closely monitored. "Service level agreements" based on minimum acceptable standards of performance results have proven successful. Do not specify how to do what you want done; do specify the results or performance outputs you want. Leave the "how" to the service provider but give that provider an incentive to do the work well. Remember that providers expect to make money too; if they save you money, it may mean they are earning less. Successful outsource agreements stipulate that a contractor can earn more if savings are realized.

Clear lines of demarcation should be drawn between in-house and contract involvement. Contracting can bring a lot of flexibility to your business, but it requires assertive management and control. Managing contracts is not the same as managing your own people—it requires a different skill set and approach and may require new people or additional training for your existing staff.

An example that illustrates the broad concept of outsourcing centers on an interesting challenge facing a global mining company that is choosing excellence. The company has chosen Total Productive Maintenance[3] as a preferred method for improving performance at all its global operations. Several of its mines are already using outsourcing under Maintenance and Repair Contract (MARC) agreements. These were originally put in place using manufacturer's recommended maintenance practices as a basis for pricing. There was no provision to encourage reliability and availability improvements, so performance remained relatively flat. There was also no mechanism to encourage teamwork between maintenance, which was outsourced, and operations, which were performed in-house. In one mine, the company chose not to renew the MARC agreement and brought all the work back in-house. Within a year, reliability and availability at the particular mine were up and costs were down dramatically. The company is now seeking to challenge its other MARC service providers in ways that encourage similar improvements by using asset and team-based

---

3. Total Productive Maintenance (TPM) is discussed in detail in Chapter 10.

approaches so that both the customer and the outsource contractor benefit in a win-win arrangement. Service providers not interested in such an arrangement may lose the company's business. An alternative solution is to outsource operations along with maintenance. Another is to perform all the work in-house (as the mining company did). If the work is outsourced, gain sharing[4] provisions in the contracts can be used to encourage reliability and availability improvements using asset-centric methods.[5] This might also work for team-based methods like TPM, although management of a joint program involving employees from two companies could prove challenging. There is no easy answer to this issue, but the onus is on the contractor to influence company decision makers that the work should be outsourced. Because many companies are becoming increasingly more selective about whether and to whom they should outsource, it is up to service providers to come up with attractive proposed solutions for their customers.

UPTIME SUMMARY

In choosing excellence, you will be choosing a path of constant change and improvement, but you need to remember that if you want excellence, you need leadership. Leadership is about strategy, effective execution and your people—without them you accomplish very little. Taking your organization in new directions is a complex process, so you should remember that leaders rock the boat while managers keep it stable.

Maintenance is an important business function. It sustains your productive capacity, and it is part of your fixed and variable costs. Reducing maintenance costs through efficiency gains (doing maintenance the right way) and effectiveness (doing the right things) increases operating margins. Just as it contributes substantially to the company's safety and environmental performance, it also impacts how financially "risky" the business is. Well-maintained assets can meet production commitments more easily and reduce risks, something that lenders and insurers like to see. If you are building a new plant, consider the importance of maintenance and reliability

---

4. Gain Sharing concepts are described more fully in Chapter 2 as related to people, but they can be applied equally well in contracting situations.
5. Asset-centric methods are described more fully in Chapters 8 and 9.

decisions at the design stage when you have the greatest opportunity to reduce life-cycle operating and maintenance costs. All of these are factors to consider in developing maintenance strategy.

Strategy can be as simple or as complex as you like, but simple works best. Your business objectives, the asset environment, its present state, and the state of maintenance management practices are your starting points. Understand what it means to be a high performer and to be using successful practices. What is best for your company is what works best for your company—there are no absolute "best" practices. Decide what you want to achieve—that is your "vision." Compare what you do today with that vision and consider using successful practices, such as those described in *Uptime*, to close any gaps. Plan the improvement activities and manage them as you would any other improvement project. Execution is what matters.

Some companies choose to outsource maintenance. Do it for the right reasons. Transferring your problem to someone else may not be the answer and can even be harmful. If maintenance is of strategic importance or if it is unique to your business, you are probably better off keeping it in-house.

Once you have embarked on making improvements, it is important to sustain them. Excellence as described in this book is a journey, not a destination. Never let up. You will know it is working when you find yourself dealing with new problems every year and not revisiting the same ones.

2

People

*For organizations and employees alike, the only real security
is the ability to grow, change, and adapt.*

A. T. KEARNEY

Increasingly we are being asked to "do more with less," but what we really want is "more result with less effort." Working smarter, more effectively, and more efficiently are keys to success. In the dimension of human resources, we are especially challenged, because increasingly we have less to work with. We need increased productivity from fewer people. As our people adapt to the only constant we can count on, change, we gain security and competitive advantage. Getting the most from your people by adapting to change, responsive organizational structures, multiskilling, having and aligning learning, training, development and compensation schemes with business goals is what this chapter is all about.

PEOPLE REALLY ARE YOUR MOST IMPORTANT ASSET

There are three things that make up any business: its assets (financial, intellectual and physical), its processes (what it does and how it does it), and its people. The business itself is an extension of its people—whatever they bring to the business becomes a part of that business. Change only one person and you change the business. Without your people, nothing will happen. Maintenance is a complex business process with many subprocesses. It exists to ensure that your physical assets do what you want them to do, but it is the people in your maintenance group that makes this happen. Leading companies recognize how important their people are and put them first.

Excellent companies that truly recognize the value of their people keep their turnover costs down and provide consistent service to their customers. When motivated and inspired employees remain with a company, they help it grow and expand. These employees constantly look for ways to improve things and are always adding value. They know what needs to be done and they do it, often delighting the customer in the process. Motivated maintainers keep their customers in operations happy, much like front-line sales staff does when dealing with customers. Employees who are demotivated, uninspired, or unhappy will not expend that level of effort, and many will leave. Employee turnover is expensive—recruitment, replacement, and training costs are measured in multiples of annual salary or wages. A hidden expense is lowered productivity while a new employee learns how to do a job an experienced employee has left.

Today, there are significant changes in the social landscape we inhabit. Fewer young people embrace trades, instead they seek careers in the technology sector, which are perceived to be more challenging and rewarding. Many of these young people have a social awareness about things that did not concern previous generations. They value social responsibility, personal growth, and development. At the same time, they want autonomy and a great degree of self-actualization. Managing them successfully is different from managing baby boomers.

The baby boom generation that makes up the bulk of today's workforce has not been as prolific as its parents, and it is aging. Some boomers have already retired; the rest will soon follow. This will leave business scrambling for fewer available workers to do an ever-increasing amount of work. Replacing the aging baby boomers and capturing their knowledge is going to be one of your most significant strategic challenges.

Demographics have always been a driving force for change in business. Today, the greatest demographic concern is the dwindling number of skilled tradespeople. There simply are not enough qualified tradespeople to do things the way we used to do them, and our most senior (and most experienced) tradespeople are retiring. With them goes considerable "corporate memory." Simply capturing and storing their knowledge isn't enough. You must be able to use it too. (For example, you can easily get hold of your supervisors' contact lists, but can you get their contacts to call you back when you use it?) Replacing these people is difficult because the pool of skilled workers is small. Moreover, those who replace them do not have the same knowledge or skills. Government skills training programs, which were once numerous and reasonably effective, have all but disappeared. Successful companies realize that they must tackle this problem themselves. This, however, is no simple task.

Although the replacement workforce may be highly skilled, the skills younger workers have do not always match what a company might need, and there are far fewer workers. As noted in the previous chapter, immigration is not keeping pace with the demand for new workers, and this presents an additional problem. In some companies, this has already reached a truly critical stage, and work management looks like emergency room triage. Confronting these problems, companies are forced to rethink what it is their people are doing and create viable solutions that are often radically different from the old labor solutions. (Some of these are discussed later in the chapter.)

To deal with the problems of a shrinking labor pool and an environment that is unpredictable and sometimes chaotic, the successful maintenance manager must be far more than a competent technical person. In addition to management skills, this individual must have consummate "people skills." He or she is a coach and a nurturer who enables people to get their jobs done by clearing away barriers and providing resources. The astute maintenance manager does not control people tightly but rather tells them what needs to be done and then gets out of their way. This person encourages reasonable risk-taking, rewards success, and attacks problems, not people. These "soft" skills are the hallmarks of the modern maintenance manager, indeed, of any successful manager. They are critical in dealing with today's biggest challenges.

We all know that the only constant in life is change. Today, change is faster than ever, and it is largely unpredictable. Many businesses are left scrambling, uncertain how to catch up. Mergers, acquisitions, divestitures, strategic alliances, increasingly stringent regulatory requirements, and deregulation are all driving substantial and often unexpected change. Such a charged atmosphere demands quick reflexes and well thought out approaches to remain competitive.

MANAGING CHANGE

In this ever-changing environment, companies and individuals alike are subject to challenge. Even if you think you are static, you are really undergoing some form of change, albeit slowly. Things around you are always in motion—technology, processes, people, etc.—and you must keep up with this motion and these changes to stay ahead of competitors. As the chapter's opening quotation implies, change is necessary for survival in today's business world.

History teaches us that dogmatic approaches to change tend to produce mixed, short-term results at best. Today's workers simply don't buy into this approach—you cannot just direct them to change and expect it will happen. It will not. Even your older employees are likely to balk at such directives. Although they might have responded to them in the past, they are no longer receptive to many changes. Most are looking forward to a smooth and predictable transition into retirement. They do not want change and they especially do not want change by coercion. Today, for both younger and older workers, a different approach works best. Change must be driven from within.

Successful organizations steer their own courses in an organized fashion toward a predetermined goal or vision, navigating among many challenging constraints. Change can be described as a movement from one state to another, through various transitional forms, to some final state. For plant engineering and maintenance, the main objective is usually to boost equipment productivity. Change in maintenance is a little different and a lot more complex. There are many factors involved, all of which can be in a state of change simultaneously:

- Increasingly complex technology in every aspect of work.
- Integrated information and data management systems for employees, fixed assets, costs, performance, and virtually all business activities.
- Advancing process automation and robotics requiring fewer operators but more highly trained technicians.
- Tighter design tolerances for higher quality products and less maintenance intervention.
- Shorter obsolescence cycles and time-to-market for new products, especially in the area of high technology.
- Larger scale of plant with increasing flexibility to serve today's demands for mass-customization.
- Higher targets for return on investment and profit margins in the new global economy with few business boundaries.

- More rigorous health, safety, and environmental standards in all jurisdictions. Failure to meet standards can cost your company dearly, shut it down, or, in some countries, send your executives to jail.
- Increased degree of contracting as businesses stick with their core competencies and contract out the rest.
- Product liability law changes.
- Workers' expectations for self-realization in their jobs, especially among younger members of our workforce. Skills and knowledge are highly portable, workers are highly mobile, and many don't mind moving. If a company provides a terrific working environment and interesting people to work with and for, people will stay. If it does not, they leave.
- Workers' expectations of their bosses. A good boss helps attract and retain good people; a bad one causes them to leave.
- Less emphasis on loyalty both to and from employers and employees alike. The security of having "jobs for life" is largely a thing of the past. Changes like the demise of defined benefit pension plans have made staying in one company for an entire career less attractive.

For maintenance managers, these changes represent a great challenge. It can be met in part by having a strategic direction, as described in Chapter 1. Within this strategic direction is a successful vision, which is embraced by every employee at all levels. This is a tall order. Anyone involved in maintenance management or any management knows that a project can be derailed by employees unwilling to execute it. Thus, achieving your maintenance strategy will require change on the part of everyone in your organization. All employees must understand, accept and, most importantly, internalize the inevitability of change in order to improve.

Organizations are altered by the individuals involved in the change process. Getting them involved requires a compelling case that drives their desire to change and move toward a shared vision of the desired future state. The process also requires the means to make it happen. We cannot expect new processes and methods to happen without investing time, energy and money. The major steps in the process are:

1. Identify the need. What is the business case that calls for a change?

2. Identify a champion for the change initiative. Who is accountable for the results?

3. Enroll the team that will lead the change. Who is going to make it happen?

4. Define the change. What is it you intend to do?

5. Demonstrate that the specific change is really the best option. What are the alternative solutions? Which alternative is best? Who needs to know?

6. Plan the change activities and plan your work. What are the specific objectives or goals, approach, timeline, and boundaries?

7. Communicate the plan. Does everyone affected understand what is going to happen and why?

8. Carry out your plan. What gets done?

9. Measure and communicate results as you implement. What has been done? Did it produce the right results? Who needs to know?

10. Foster continued engagement and development of the people affected to support the change. What will sustain the change?

To ensure success, include detailed change management assessments and plans with your primary plans. Managing the change entails considerable emphasis on the human element that is often overlooked in technical projects. Implementing improvements in maintenance and engineering often entails a number of technically oriented activities. Do not forget that the improvements are carried out by real people who have feelings, judgments, fears, ambitions, and emotions. If they are not fully on-board with your program, it will not work the way you intended.

Change is difficult in any organization. There are several things that make it easier, more successful, and faster.

Have a compelling reason

The most difficult aspect of change is usually convincing those concerned that there is good reason to change. That is not easy, especially when it means destabilizing the entire organization. Any sane person will ask, "Why put ourselves through this pain?" The impetus for organization-wide change can take many forms: the threat of business closure, the desire to remain competitive in a changing market, the desire to avoid being outsourced, or the need to make up for natural attrition in the workforce. These are reactive reasons. There are also proactive reasons to want a program of change. For example, customer satisfaction surveys can provide information on how the organization is perceived by its clients. In maintenance, this can be an internal customer survey.

Regardless of the reason for the change, any change means shaking up the status quo, encouraging employees to think of better alternatives, and allowing the organization to move forward. Unfreezing old thinking is usually the best place to start. New concepts will often clash with old ideas and perceptions. Challenge the old methods, show more logical alternatives that work, and give people a chance to accept those new ideas. Education and training are usually the most effective ways to do this. Do not just train the people who will be directly involved in making the change happen. Train those who are also going to be affected by the change, too. Ideally, the change will make their work more interesting and satisfying. You want your employees to endorse the new methods, but more importantly, you want them to play a large part in designing them. If they are not involved, resistance will be high, ownership will be low, the present situation will not improve much, and the organization may even be harmed. The most successful organizations at making change "stick" are those who involve the entire workforce in the decisions about what and how to do things in the future. These organizations are great at execution because they embrace a culture of change.[1]

Deal with the fears

People resist change for many reasons. Chief among these is fear: fear of the unknown, of losing skills and status, and of not being able to cope in a new environment. Some employees may see a proposed change as implied criticism: "It's been working well for years, what do you mean we had it wrong all along?" Others may criticize those introducing the change: "What do they know about our business?"

---

1. Larry Bossidy and Ram Charan discuss this at length in their book, *Execution: The Discipline of Getting Things Done* (New York: Crown Business, 2002).

or "Our business is unique, how can someone from outside possibly know what's best for us?" (Note: It is never a good idea to have an outsider lead the change for you.) Still others may not agree with the targeted end result, especially if they have had little or no input or they believe the new plan is being foisted upon them from outside—and that includes changes coming from "head office." Managing change requires that these people be allowed to choose. Let them choose to come on board and make the change theirs. All of this is far more difficult to achieve than simply giving orders, but it works.

When introducing significant change in people's lives, it helps to understand what psychologists refer to as the "cycle of loss." Whenever we undergo a radical change, we go through six identifiable stages: Shock, Denial, Anger, Passive Acceptance, Exploration, and Challenge. The cycle of loss depicted in Figure 2-1 was developed to help in counseling people when they have experienced a major setback—the death of a loved one, divorce, or bankruptcy, for instance. It also applies when a major change occurs at the workplace. Any change means some people will lose something with which they are familiar and comfortable. The loss is real and everyone goes through the process at a different pace.

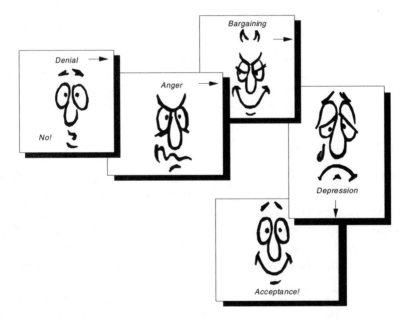

Figure 2-1. Reactions to Radical Change

- **Shock:** This is similar to grief. It generally takes people time to adjust to the news. Not much can be done at this time but wait.
- **Denial:** We commonly react with "this doesn't apply to me" (or my department). Denial is a way of not saying "goodbye" to the old ways of doing things. For example, it is difficult to accept contracting out much of what was perceived for many years as core work. If it is viewed as work that contributes competitive advantage, it is viewed as a good thing that cannot and should not be outsourced.
- **Anger:** This stems from seeing the new way of doing things as somehow worse than the old way. Some people will manifest anger by actively resisting or attacking the change. Anger can engender a mood of self-preservation and get in the way of innovation. It must be dealt with.
- **Bargaining:** Once the anger cools off, it is common to see an attempt to get out of the situation. People will try to change the symptoms but not the underlying causes. For example, in order to avoid outsourcing they might try cutting out contractors and bring work in-house, believing that this will cut costs. Eventually, that work becomes more expensive because the skills are lacking in-house. When they realize this is not going to work there is a period of depression.
- **Passive Acceptance:** Eventually people "give in" to the change and begin to accept it by simply getting on with the new order.
- **Exploration:** Actively seeking ways to make the change work and stick.
- **Challenge:** Once the change is implemented, people start to use it as a way to make other improvements and challenge the status quo in other areas. This is success.

Be aware that this cycle affects everyone, though not at the same pace. Some people go through it quickly, and others never quite make it to the end. Some people embrace new ideas immediately, some accept changes slowly, and some never will. In every population there are innovators, early adopters, a majority that comes along eventually, laggards that come aboard long after everyone else has, and those that simply refuse to budge. Recognize that your workforce comprises all of these. The innovators and early adopters can help bring the majority along. Geoffrey A. Moore[2] describes how to use this concept in marketing and the selling of high-tech products to mainstream customers, but his ideas are just as applicable to entire organizations and to maintenance management.

Figure 2-2 depicts another concept: a force field showing that change occurs only when there is an imbalance between the sum of restraining and driving forces. The premise behind this concept is that there are three basic strategies for achieving change: 1) increase the driving forces, 2) decrease the restraining forces, and 3) a combination of 1 and 2. Another way to look at this is that change will occur when the status quo becomes so uncomfortable that the future state is perceived to be more comfortable. When a steering group, study team, or task force is inaugurated, consider conducting a force field analysis. Document the key drivers and restraints to change in the organization. The challenge, of course, is to estimate the relative strengths of the driving and restraining forces. Recognize that this is not an exact science, but it will provide some interesting insights!

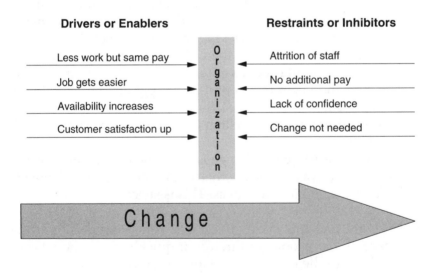

Figure 2-2. Force Field Analysis Example

2. Geoffrey A. Moore, *Crossing the Chasm* (New York: Harper Business, 1999).

As humans, most of us naturally resist change because we want to remain comfortable. Change means facing the unknown, and fear of the unknown is usually greater than our fear of any discomfort associated with the status quo, so people resist change even if they are shown the benefit of change. They tend to evaluate from a present frame of reference, which means staying with what they know. Eventually, however, discomfort with the status quo becomes so great that the change begins to look like a more comfortable option and becomes desirable. That is when people choose to change. Interestingly, discomfort is the mechanism that makes them accept change. Rather than being proactive and choosing to benefit from a changed state, they wait to experience discomfort before accepting change and whatever comes with change. The pattern is to defer the inevitable in hope that the unknown will become known before they are compelled to choose.

Communicate

By providing information through communication, education, and training, you will greatly improve the odds for success by reducing the fear factor. This can help employees understand the driving forces behind complex business imperatives and see the benefits of a proposed change. By providing relevant communication, education, and training, you also enable your employees to participate more meaningfully in the design and implementation of the change process. By trusting them to provide their input, you also empower them. Instead of having to accept a change that is entirely directed from the top, employees can participate in the makeover, be given the time to get used to it, and even have a stake in the process of making it happen. Your chances for success with this kind of participation are high. Successful organizations use all available channels to get through to both their employees and others who are likely to be impacted by any change, including the employees' families.

Show that it works

Nothing succeeds like success. When you plan a change initiative such as improvements in plant maintenance and engineering, you might turn to benchmarking for support. The benchmarking of indicators, processes, and organizational structures can also help you determine the direction and rate of change that has worked elsewhere. That can serve as a useful guide and as a showcase for skeptical employees. It is particularly valuable if the organizations studied are best in their field.

Benchmarking companies that have been successful at transforming themselves reveals some noteworthy patterns of how change came about:

- It was directed strategically and led by a clearly recognized leader.[3]
- It was participatory. Employees understood what was going on and were deeply involved.
- It was well planned.
- It was developed from previously established principles and precedent, not from personal edicts.
- A team approach was used. Teams were used for projects, subprojects, and tasks and were empowered to make decisions. They were also held accountable for results.
- It was balanced in functions, not one-sided or targeted only at one group. For example, a change to plant maintenance performance did not target only the maintenance trades—it included MRO supplies, purchasing, human resources, etc.
- It was flexible—one size does not fit all.
- It was integrated (not simply interfaced). For computer system implementations, tight integration among different systems usually works better than leaving data interfaces to manual and batch processes.
- There was excellent communication; timely and meaningful messages were sent and heard. All communication had content relevant to the audience, not just the sender.
- The participants in the change benefited from its implementation. There was something beneficial for everyone involved, and there was no threat to financial or emotional security.

---

3. John P. Kotter, *Leading Change* (Cambridge: Harvard Business School Press, 1996).

Leadership

"If your actions inspire others to dream more, learn more, do more, and become more, you are a leader."[4] Leadership style is another key to implementing change. If leaders are not fully committed, if they vacillate, subtly or overtly question why they are doing what they are doing, or have more pressing priorities, then chances for success will be severely diminished. On the other hand, if leaders dominate the change process with a personal vision or agenda, others can resent it and become inflexible. Leadership is often walking a fine line between too much and too little. Micromanaging is not leadership and neither is allowing others to do whatever they want. The trick is to find a balance and that means motivating without browbeating, nurturing without excusing, and giving direction without hamstringing.

Leaders will lead by example. They communicate through their actions as well as their words. People will follow the way they are led, so it is important to set the example of the behavior you want to achieve. Ideally, you want people you are leading through change to want the change. As Dwight Eisenhower said, "Leadership is the art of getting someone else to do something you want done because he wants to do it." Change your own way of doing things and you will change the way that others around you work. Say one thing yet do another and you'll get results that match your actions.

In organizations where change is embraced, it is often implemented quickly and the changes stick. A culture that focuses on execution[5] is successful. A corollary to this is that when organizations make significant changes, one of the things that must change is the organizational structure. If you set out to do things differently, you often find that the current structure simply won't work or even gets in the way of execution. Structure follows function.

ORGANIZING THE MAINTENANCE STRUCTURE

Today's maintenance organization has abandoned industrial age command-and-control concepts and replaced them with looser, self-organizing structures that allow autonomy for small but effective

---

4. John Quincy Adams, sixth president of the United States, 1825–1829.
5. Larry Bossidy and Ram Charan, *Execution: The Discipline of Getting Things Done* (New York: Crown Business, 2002).

service delivery teams. Highly successful organizations depend on such autonomous teams to meet or exceed agreed-upon expectations for performance. These organizations are tapping into the power and creativity of motivated and inspired individuals to truly add value to the companies for which they work.

Traditionally many maintenance organizations were centralized through the maintenance manager, who was often an experienced tradesman with good management skills. Typically, this person was responsible for management and centralized dispatch of all aspects of plant and facility support and services while all spares and materials were regulated from the main or central stores.

The strength of this system was threefold: 1) it ensured control over policy, procedures, systems, quality, and training, 2) leveling of the workload across the operation was guaranteed, and 3) it worked well when decision making was needed at the top. The major disadvantage was inflexibility, and this was felt in many ways, particularly in larger organizations:

- Sluggish response time to production requests
- Workers' lack of familiarity with specific equipment in the plant and difficulty matching the skills to the job.
- Workers who felt unappreciated.
- Rigidity in approach, procedures, and policies (what worked in the past was expected to work today and for the foreseeable future).
- High charge-out rates reflecting bloated management infrastructure and bureaucratic processes.
- Customer dissatisfaction over allocation of resources.
- Strict demarcation among trades, which complicated even simple jobs and often created turf wars.
- Focus on process efficiency rather than process effectiveness. Emphasis was on doing things right, not on doing the right things.

Today, only small maintenance organizations (i.e., those with fewer than fifty people) seem to be able to overcome these drawbacks, and successful centralized maintenance organizations are found only in small companies. Elsewhere, different approaches emerged.

Production became the responsibility of area or product managers, who had to react quickly as economic conditions changed. Management participation and job enrichment for front-line workers improved productivity and effectiveness. Especially in larger organizations, structure shifted towards decentralization and maintenance moved into the mainstream of operations. In some organizations the maintenance manager completely disappeared and was replaced by production area superintendents. In Japan in the 1970s, the Toyota Production System emerged and was followed by the teamwork concepts embodied in Total Productive Maintenance.

Despite its popularity, decentralization was not a panacea either. It was difficult to manage risk and maintenance engineering consistently from one production department to another. Often neither was handled very well. Some production areas ignored proactive maintenance and pockets of chaos coexisted with plant areas that were well run. Standardization became attractive to senior management, but decentralized groups preferred to go their own way and, in the absence of standards, conditions often deteriorated. When standards were applied, decentralized organizations worked very well. Total Productive Maintenance builds on this concept very successfully, but does not work well everywhere. Clearly, there is no one approach that is best for all.

Maintenance strategy—its mission, vision, policies, key objectives, and resultant organizational structure—must fit the business that it serves. It is important not to lose sight of the enterprise business plan and the environment in which the maintenance function performs.

There is no one correct organizational structure that can be transferred from a book to a real-life situation. There are only strategy options that can be applied in specific situations. Usually the best solution in larger organizations is to restructure for maintenance as a hybrid of centralized and local area functions that have close, regular, and formal liaison with operations and engineering. This hybrid model was implemented in a plant in the Midwestern region of the United States. A brief look at what was done and why is in order.

The 2-million-square-foot plant of a microelectronics operation was divided into four focused factories producing different products: chemicals, components, hybrid electronic circuits, and capacitors.

After the introduction of the just-in-time manufacturing philosophy, these focused factories were further divided into sixty production cells. This new arrangement caused unacceptably long response times and less than satisfactory customer service. Within the focused factories it was rare to have the same maintenance technician dispatched to the same cell on different days, so the learning curve for technicians exacerbated the delay time. After much soul-searching and debate, maintenance and production managers agreed to try a new structure for maintenance:

- Central maintenance for facility maintenance (HVAC, etc.), stores inventory warehousing and control, fabrication and machine shops, tooling, information database control, and specialized trades training.
- Focused factory maintenance for workshops, planning and scheduling, operator training in maintenance, and maintenance engineering.
- Cell maintenance for multiskilled teams (sometimes covering several cells), urgent maintenance, preventive maintenance, and consumable and free issue parts and supplies.

Before investing time and resources into the change in structure, plant management considered the implications and weighed costs and benefits. The new, hybrid model satisfied the ultimate objective of the maintenance function admirably, providing equipment uptime safely and at a reasonable cost.

In the twenty-first century we are now focused sharply on corporate responsibility to various company stakeholders as well as to society at large. As a result, another organizational shift has begun and has precipitated an increasing awareness of the importance of physical assets to business. Compared with past changes, this shift is rather subtle. At the shopfloor level, for example, it is almost imperceptible because most of the changes are happening at the most senior management levels where physical asset management is becoming a hot topic.

In highly automated systems, poor design, poor execution, unsafe practices, and equipment failures of all kinds can result in safety and environmental problems and severe business losses. These events are bad enough, but their consequences are worse. Because executives are increasingly being held liable for these consequences, they have begun to take a hard look at how to fix the underlying causes. What they have discovered is that businesses need competent professional support in managing the technology and physical assets for which senior executives are ultimately responsible.

In large global organizations, there is a trend towards standardized models for maintenance and engineering that requires corporate level leadership but allows for execution at the local level. At the same time, as businesses automate more and rely more heavily on computerized controls and systems, they put less emphasis on the operator and more on the maintainer. And while maintenance is still viewed as an engineering function, in most organizations, it is often located in a separate department. All of this points to the real nature of the current shift—the emergence of Physical Asset Management as a new paradigm.

With so much efficiency already built into management processes and systems with complex networks connecting suppliers and customers, it is apparent that meeting today's standards and demands means working smarter, not just harder and better. Physical Asset Management encompasses the entire spectrum of asset life-cycle management from conceptual design to disposal. It includes traditional engineering and maintenance functions and recognizes that operations contribute to asset integrity by operating the assets correctly.

Slowly but steadily, maintenance management, once relegated to a corner of the shopfloor or the warehouse, is being elevated to the executive suite. Many companies now have vice presidents or directors responsible for Physical Asset Management, and standards are being set and applied to maintenance, engineering, and operations in much the same way as they are applied to any manager who incurs expenses or any manager who hires and fires employees. Like the hybrid organization, the physical asset management organization manages some services centrally and others at a local level. Responsibility for execution of the work is separated from the responsibility for creating and maintaining the standards. The VP manages the latter and focuses on compliance. The maintenance, engineering, and operations managers are responsible for doing the work and for complying with those standards. Figure 2-3 shows a typical organization chart for this model.

What this figure and the previous historical analysis of organizational infrastructure suggest is a shift away from dogmatism and

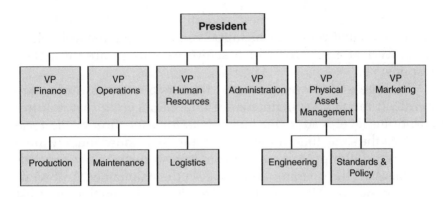

Figure 2-3. Physical Asset Management Organization

toward a more flexible approach better suited to the behavioral complexities of today's workplace. As previously noted, industrial age solutions do not work for children of the information age. Margaret J. Wheatley[6] points out that command-and-control structures don't work well anymore—they hold us back from progress. Particularly in dealing with the challenges of replacing an aging workforce, anything that holds us back is clearly unwelcome. The new model to embrace involves greater reliance on people who are free to choose their own paths and respond to their environment within a self-organizing system. Although this may sound chaotic, this model has the potential to unleash latent talent and capability that can solve some of our most pressing problems. Studies[7] show that productivity gains in truly self-managed work environments are on the order of 35 percent greater than gains possible in traditional organizations. These concepts are certainly worth examining and are discussed further in Chapter 10. One proven practice that unleashes some of the latent talent in a workforce and illustrates the ability of individuals to expand is multiskilling.

MULTISKILLING

As decentralization took hold and flexibility increased, it became essential to improve labor skills, planning, and scheduling. Man-

---

6. Margaret J. Wheatley, *Finding Our Way: Leadership for an Uncertain Time* (San Francisco: Berrett-Koehler Publishers, 2005).

7. Wheatley.

agers had to offset the inevitable duplication of talent that arises in a decentralized system with higher asset performance and labor productivity. One highly successful option was to train workers in multiple skills or multiple trades. Today, multiskilling has become a staple of many organizations and is one of the solutions to the current problem of reduced availability of skilled trades. It is a viable option, but not always easy to implement. Multiskilled employees possess all the skills necessary to do their tasks safely across traditional disciplinary boundaries. In some companies, tradespeople hold more than one recognized trade certification or are "ticketed" in more than one trade. Generally, the multiskilled worker may not necessarily have all the skills to qualify in multiple trades but does have the skills needed for his or her particular job. Multiskilling works best where jobs are relatively simple and of short duration. For example, it is ideal for jobs like changing out a small motor but is not as well suited for calibration of a direct current speed control. The objective of multiskilling is not to have everyone do everything, eliminate specialist skills, or loosen the standards for quality work. Specialists are still important. A secondary, but equally important, function of multiskilling is flexibility. Multiskilling can help reduce costs because increased flexibility reduces the number of jobs for which you will need multiple people with multiple skill sets. A cautionary note to this is to avoid approaching multiskilling simply as a method to slash costs, because its most significant long-term benefit is improved productivity.

In organizations in which multiskilling was used primarily to reduce workforce size, it has failed, sometimes miserably. Usually those organizations had more to do than they could handle and reducing the workforce through multiskilling failed to address the basic problem of too much work. One example serves to illustrate what can occur if multiskilling is implemented with the sole intent of reducing the workforce in a facility overburdened with too much work. Multiskilling was instituted over a three-year period by an aluminum industrial products manufacturer in central Canada. In the first year, training was provided to increase workforce skills. The excessive backlogs of work were gradually reduced. Late in year 2, following a downturn in the business, the workforce was cut. Backlogs gradually returned to previous levels, and the workers who survived the cuts, now demoralized, gradually stopped using their multiple skills. By the end of year 3, the backlog exceeded previous levels and multiskilling was all but forgotten. The workload required more people than ever before, but there were fewer to do it. The situation deteriorated, and a once proactive maintenance organization became reactive.

In all cases, introducing multiskilling has its challenges: boundary disputes and communication difficulties, workload leveling among the various distributed work areas, demands for job enrichment and variety, unequal opportunities for overtime and general management career path planning, and trade union resistance. Some organizations contract work out in order to smooth workload peaks. Others have centralized floating teams for shutdowns and major overhauls. Maintenance and production duties are sometimes shared, increasing the know-how of the decentralized maintenance and operations teams.

Multiticketing, where a tradesman is fully qualified and recognized (ticketed) in more than one trade, is an excellent way to introduce multiskilling. Union resistance to this approach is usually less strident than it is to the less formal multiskilled approach, probably because multiticketed tradesmen are very well compensated with premium wages. In some cases, unions actually support the practice as it has clear benefits for their members.

On the other hand, organized labor's resistance to multiskilling in general remains rather strong. There are several legitimate concerns about the practice:

- There is normally no marketable, generally recognized skill certification that can be transferred to other organizations or jurisdictions. Multiskilling programs can lock employees into an organization because their skills are unique to that organization. This is becoming less of a concern as more companies are seeing the value in multiskilled as well as multiticketed workers.
- Training programs can be poorly conceived or inadequate. Often a lack of up-front definition of the work is the culprit. Simply throwing together a training program without adequate analysis and without training follow-up does not work.
- Multiskilling ignores traditional career patterns, in which long or valuable specialist experience often leads to promotions into management. With multiskilling, those who are the most capable can now move forward more quickly.

Seniority or tenure is no longer enough to ensure advancement or promotion, and older workers understandably resist the shift.

- Some organizations attempt to generalize skills to meet immediate needs. This reduces mobility and is a shortsighted approach that unions are right to challenge. Over time, workers become bored and turnover rates increase. This presents a new, high-cost problem. Turnover results in lost knowledge (equipment history, organizational issues, human issues and technical knowledge), additional recruiting requirements, the costs of getting recruiting wrong, and lost time associated with learning curves and errors that occur while new employees learn and gain proficiency in their new jobs.
- Multiskilling is sometimes viewed as a precursor to contract maintenance, making the workforce more attractive to a potential contract service provider under an outsourcing agreement.
- Often, organizations introduce multiskilling programs with staff reductions and inappropriate compensation schemes. The desire to cut costs quickly leads to rapid cuts, usually before the payback of multiskilling is realized. As in the example above, it harms the very people needed to pull it off successfully.

To foster employee commitment to multiskilling, it is important to encourage their involvement in addressing these issues openly and early in the process. If the process is thrust upon them without adequate notice and preparation, you have a recipe for disaster.

Planning and training for multiskilling centers on a "training needs and task analysis." What tasks are currently being carried out and by which tradespeople? Is the current skill level appropriate? What are the most frequently performed tasks of some typical jobs or work orders? What tasks will be performed in future? The concept of "natural work" applies here. Tasks that may entail a variety of different trade skills that are relatively simple are appropriate for multiskilled workers. Tasks with very complex skills in one or more trade areas will demand a multiskilled worker with a great deal of training in several trades. It is often not cost-effective to provide all that training. Moreover, multiskilling does not replace truly unique specialists.

To perform the training needs and task analysis you can search for task requirements in work-order histories, industrial engineering studies, maintenance manuals, or employee questionnaires and surveys. Organizations that use Reliability-Centered Maintenance have an excellent source of defined task requirements. Figure 2-4 shows an example of the relationship between various trades and some of the tasks performed.

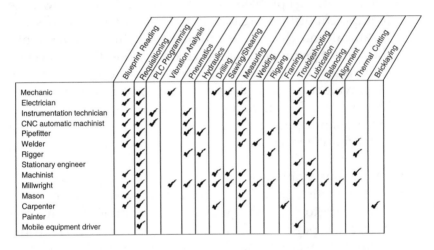

Figure 2-4. Trades-Tasks Relationship

Through the "needs and task analysis," you can develop an overall education and training approach. Because high school dropout rates remain high, and schools have deemphasized basic and trade skills, many organizations find that this process requires basic education before skill training can start. In some cases, new employees are actually less educated than their predecessors. In other cases, employees who have "learned on the job" but have failed to keep up with developments in computing technology are being replaced by younger and more highly educated engineers and information technology professionals. Depending on your workforce demographics, the first priority may be upgrading employees' literacy, facility with numbers, and basic computer skills. All employees will benefit from a clear description of the company's markets, customers, products, services, and overall strategy for success. Never assume that just because people have worked in your organization for many years they really know the business. Recognize that employees who understand the basics of your business are more likely to make meaningful and rewarding contributions to its success.[8]

Other general knowledge that will benefit employees includes basic statistics, modern concepts and methods in maintenance management, and quality management. Try alternating classroom and on-the-job experience, including job rotation. Remember, too, to make use of the various training media that are available today: CD-ROM, the Internet, old-fashioned chalk and talk, case studies, etc. Games are an excellent training tool—they combine classroom learning with hands-on practice, often using simulation techniques that appeal to the visual and tactile learning styles common among maintainers and operators. The results of the detailed needs and tasks analysis will, of course, set the agenda.

It may help to segment the many tasks performed by maintenance into skill modules. Clusters of these modules are then linked for logical multiskilled groupings and progression. Common groupings are fairly obvious: mechanical, electrical, control. For example, the new "industrial mechanic" skill set includes the traditional skills of fitting, pipe-fitting, rigging, welding, millwright, and mechanics.

Implementing multiskill training in tandem with changes in compensation works best. Employee representatives can help design pay-for-knowledge systems, in which workers are paid for learning and using new skills. To be eligible for the extra pay, they will use a skill when and where called for. Make sure you can measure the output and reward improved performance and teamwork with bonuses and other benefits. Setting up a pay-for-knowledge system can necessitate changes to existing collective agreements and to the less formal but traditional expectations that make up your corporate culture.

If you need to hire new employees and train them to become multiskilled workers, you will need to be picky even though the available talent is limited. A recent study of candidates for multiskilled positions in the United States revealed that only 37 percent had multiskill aptitude. Only 6 percent of electrical trade applicants

---

8. This concept is described as "Open-Book Management" in *The Great Game of Business* by Jack Stack with Bo Burlingham (New York: Currency Doubleday, 1992).

met entry requirements, 18 percent of mechanical trade applicants met entry requirements, and less than 1 percent were able to perform multiskill tasks.

Multiskilling has its costs and it helps to be aware of these before you begin multiskill programs. To the direct cost of increased compensation, add significant investment in training and facilities, management time and changes to existing systems, methods and labor agreements. The company will also pay, at least initially, for some of the time used for training, either directly (paying for your employees' training time) or indirectly (a larger workforce to get the work done while your core workers are out being trained).

Many colleges and trades schools are now producing mult-skilled graduates, and many of today's new hires are already multiskilled. What they lack, however, is job-specific experience. Apprentice programs ensure this experience is gained while the knowledge is fresh—avoid the traditional approach of starting too slowly because a new hire needs to "get adjusted." The best adjustment comes with appropriate training. Do not use your most junior tradespeople for predominantly menial tasks. You will lose them. Younger workers today want to be challenged intellectually, not just physically. They have invested in their own education up to this point and expect you to continue the process. Minimize their value and they will go somewhere else.

The long-term benefits of multiskilling are worth the investment you make. You can expect:

- Increased flexibility in scheduling workers.
- Shorter response times.
- Reduced supervision.
- Greater labor and asset productivity.
- Higher morale among workers.
- Improved scheduling, communication, and integration among departments.
- More stable employment.
- Greater job satisfaction.

Case Study

The following case study shows how one consumer goods company, Lever, dealt with severe business challenges by using an extensive multiskilling program. Lever, a Unilever company, manufactures soaps, detergents, and other laundry and personal hygiene products, and operates several plants in the United States and Canada, one of which is located in Toronto. The North American Free Trade Agreement (NAFTA), signed by the United States, Canada, and Mexico in January 1994, was about to increase the competition for the rights to manufacture various products among the various Lever plants. Unless the Toronto plant could find a way to produce at lower costs, all of its products could be manufactured at other plants and imported as tariffs began to fall. Responding to this perceived threat, the Toronto plant increased the productivity and flexibility of its maintenance workforce through multiskilling. The overarching philosophy was to achieve "one-job—one person," and the overall objectives were to:

- Broaden the scope of skills for each tradesperson.
- Reduce the complexity of trade demarcations.
- Provide new career paths.
- Increase the skill level of key tradesmen.

Working closely with two local community colleges, Lever designed a series of courses that enabled millwrights to acquire basic electrical skills and electricians to become skilled at alignment and vibration. A career progression plan was developed so that millwrights and electricians could achieve a super-trade category, earning skill-based incremental pay as they progressed. Figure 2-5 summarizes the training modules required for the multi-skilled trade designation at Lever.

During the first round of training, about 80 percent of the tradespeople participated in upgrading or expanding their skills, with 95 percent of these eventually passing their courses. Each participant's record of the various modules completed and those yet to be achieved was documented. The company is continuing its multi-skilling process, with management and the local Teamsters union negotiating the fine points and implications for workers.

The provincial government approved the trade of "multi-skilled industrial mechanic," with the requisite skills and training requirements. This recognition increased the marketability of participants. Lever and the union worked toward the development of a super multiskilled technician, with expanded troubleshooting

Module/Skill	Millwright/Industrial Mechanic	Packing Mechanic	Electricians	Instrumentation	Supertrade
1. Safety	✓	✓	✓	✓	✓
2. Communications	✓	✓	✓	✓	✓
3. Trade science	✓	✓	✓	✓	✓
4. Blueprints	✓	✓	✓	✓	✓
5. Hand and power tools	✓	✓	✓	✓	✓
6. Machine tools	✓	✓	✓	✓	✓
7. Measurement	✓	✓	✓	✓	✓
8. Fasteners	✓	✓	✓	✓	✓
9. Lubricants	✓	✓		✓	✓
10. Rigging	✓				✓
11. Materials handling	✓	✓		✓	✓
12. Power transmission	✓	✓	✓	✓	✓
13. Compressors & pumps	✓	✓			✓
14. Prime movers	✓	✓	✓	✓	✓
15. Weld, braze, solder	✓	✓	✓	✓	✓
16. Bearings, seals, packing	✓				✓
17. Valves, piping	✓			✓	✓
18. Fans & blowers	✓				✓
19. Electrical controls	✓	✓	✓	✓	✓
20. Pneumatics	✓	✓		✓	✓
21. Hydraulic	✓	✓	✓	✓	✓
22. Predictive maintenance	✓	✓	✓	✓	✓
23. Milling, grinding	✓	✓			✓
24. Lathe work		✓			✓
25. Packing machines		✓			✓
26. Electrical circuits		✓	✓	✓	✓
27. Electronic systems		✓	✓	✓	✓
28. Electric power distribution			✓		✓
29. PLCs			✓		✓
30. Drive systems			✓		✓
31. Microprocessors			✓		✓
32. Process equipment				✓	✓
33. Process control systems				✓	✓

Figure 2-5. Multiskilled Trades at Lever (Toronto)

and technical training skills. Multiskilling has been a major factor in the decentralization of the Toronto plant's maintenance organization structure. Now the multiskilled tradespeople are an integral part of the area operation teams. The plant survived its NAFTA challenge and is thriving despite a change in ownership in 2002, ample proof that the approach was sustainable. Central to Lever's success with multiskilling was their commitment to learning, training, and employee development.

LEARNING, TRAINING, AND DEVELOPMENT

Learning is constant, a way of life. Those who value knowledge do not hesitate to investigate what they suspect is a more productive way of completing a task. If they find their assumption was correct, they adopt the practice and let others know about it.

Despite the trend toward continuous learning within companies, there are variations in performance from plant to plant and even within plants and among departments. Productivity can vary greatly from one plant to another, even when factors such as size, age, and environment are discounted. Even in large plants, an innovative practice that has been skillfully adopted by one department is often ignored by another. Inconsistencies occur in integrating operations and maintenance, cross-training or multiskilling tradespeople, and empowering supervisors. Making employees (whether they are salaried or paid hourly or on a contract basis) responsible for productivity and profits will not necessarily produce the desired results.

Finding the most productive methods has a great deal to do with access to information of several kinds and sharing ideas and innovations. Having an open pipeline to the best practices in other, similar industries is also important. Much also depends on the attitude, knowledge, and skills of employees. People have to want it or it won't happen.

In *The Age of Unreason*,[9] Handy describes the learning process as a wheel divided into four parts. It starts with a *question* or problem to be solved. Then it moves on to *speculation* or theory. Next comes *testing* the theory, and finally, *reflection*. This sequence is used extensively in setting up benchmarking studies—formalized learning by the corporation. The learning wheel runs on the "lubricants" of self-responsibility, perspective, and forgiveness. A well-oiled attitude includes accepting ownership for the future, being able to view events from many angles, and being capable of living with uncertainty and mistakes. The underlying premise is that people learn from their mistakes and improve. If they are not making mistakes, they are not trying hard enough.

---

9. Charles B. Handy, *The Age of Unreason* (Boston, Harvard Business School Press, 1991).

Employee education and training is the starting point for fostering a learning environment. A good education and training strategy includes:

- A clear objective.
- A review of the training requirements.
- An understanding of the unique work culture.
- An implementation plan addressing both training and the work culture.
- A budget for the associated costs and expectations of where the benefits will be captured.
- A method for continual assessment of whether the objectives are being met.

Training can range from basic literacy (so employees can at least read the employee suggestion form) to the latest methods of managing technical people, and just about everything in between. (See Figure 2-6.)

Here it is important to point out the distinction between education and training and examine why each is important in a different way. A simple example explains. Most people would probably agree that teenaged children benefit from some form of sex education; education, after all, enables intelligent decisions. A more debatable subject, however, is the benefit of training in sex—does any parent really want them to become sexually competent at their age?

As the example above suggests, the objective of education is to expand knowledge of a topic, to bring an uninformed individual through stages of awareness to understanding and to enable the right decisions. The aim of training is to upgrade a person's skills so that he or she acquires proficiency in a given job or task.

To define education and training requirements, you match tasks with the skills required to execute them. Taking a bottom-up approach, basing plant and equipment maintenance requirements on the manufacturers' recommendations and equipment history records can be overwhelming unless you are designing a facility from scratch. (In this case, the bottom-up approach works best.) The definition of training and education can also be based on the results of Reliability-Centered Maintenance analysis where the work required is already thoroughly defined.

For an existing operation, you should look from the top down and review plant and equipment performance against performance

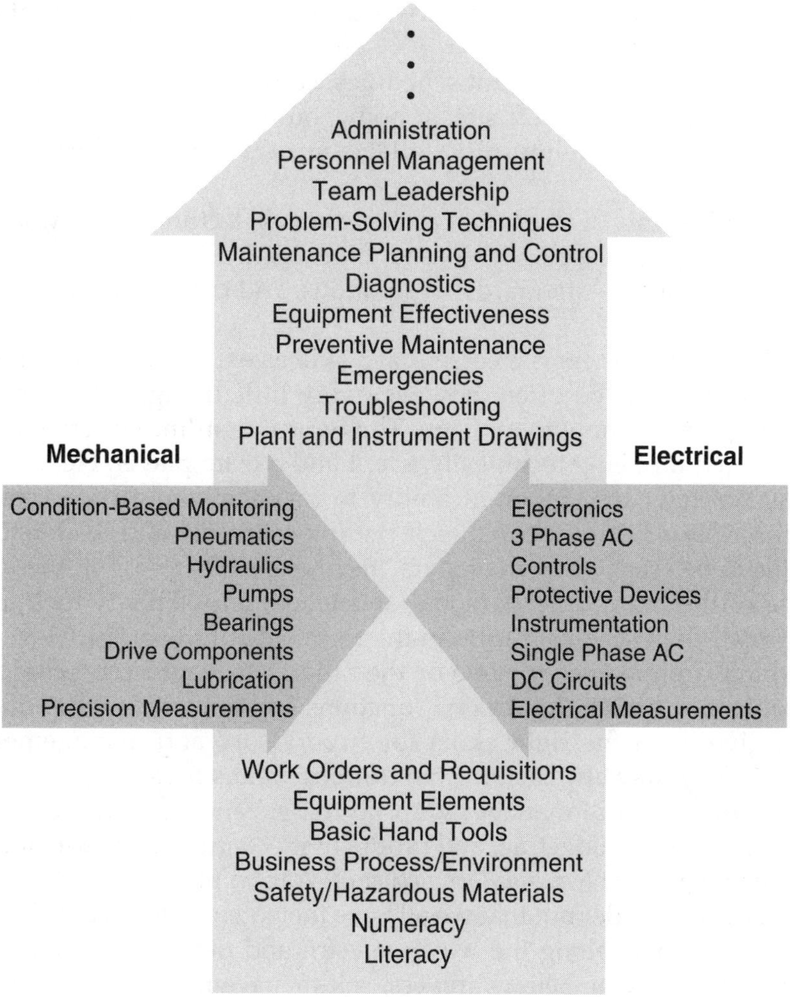

Administration
Personnel Management
Team Leadership
Problem-Solving Techniques
Maintenance Planning and Control
Diagnostics
Equipment Effectiveness
Preventive Maintenance
Emergencies
Troubleshooting
Plant and Instrument Drawings

Mechanical

Condition-Based Monitoring
Pneumatics
Hydraulics
Pumps
Bearings
Drive Components
Lubrication
Precision Measurements

Electrical

Electronics
3 Phase AC
Controls
Protective Devices
Instrumentation
Single Phase AC
DC Circuits
Electrical Measurements

Work Orders and Requisitions
Equipment Elements
Basic Hand Tools
Business Process/Environment
Safety/Hazardous Materials
Numeracy
Literacy

Figure 2-6. Scope of Training Requirements

and output requirements or expectations. You will invariably see thorny areas. Many of these are caused by gaps in knowledge or skills. Recognize what work can be done and the skills required to do it. Then look at the training needed to deliver the necessary skills and competencies and provide it. When planning a training program, you should obviously factor in the skills and competencies that need to be learned, but you should also give some thought to the following:

- *Who*—to optimize the costs and impact on the available workforce.
- *When*—consider plant schedules, cultural issues, after hours.
- *Where*—on-site, off-site, at home, out-of-town.
- *By whom*—community college, supervisors, vendors, consultants.
- *How*—mix of classroom and on-the-job, lecture, audio-visual, computer-based, web-based, home study.
- *How much*—standards, evaluations, and certifications.

Managing others is as essential a skill as expertise in the maintenance trades. Too often, however, very little thought is given to training people how to manage. The typical first-line supervisor is promoted for being technically adept and a team player. He or she may not have any inherent ability to manage, and all too often, technically oriented people lack the interpersonal and leadership skills to be effective as managers. Technical skills reside in the left side of the brain; interpersonal and leadership skills (which are more art than science) reside in the right side of the brain. Most of us have a preference for one or the other, and your best technical people may prefer "left brain" functions and knowledge that does not give them the right skills for supervisory and management roles. They may also lack formal training in business.

A maintenance manager with no understanding of leadership, administration, budgeting, and productivity control can be a liability. In *The 108 Skills of Natural Born Leaders*,[10] Warren Blank writes that no one is a born leader but that we all have the potential to become leaders. Somewhere along the way, we learn and develop the skills to make this happen. Self-awareness, self-management, social awareness (empathy), and relationship management are skills required to be "Emotionally Intelligent," and they are key to leadership.[11]

Many planners act solely as parts chasers, clerks, or data entry personnel. Because they sometimes have little shopfloor experience, their credibility is seriously questioned by the tradespeople and supervisors they serve. They end up dissatisfied with their

---

10. Warren Blank, *The 108 Skills of Natural Born Leaders* (AMACOM, 2001).
11. Daniel Goleman, Richard Boyatzis, and Annie McKee, *Primal Leadership: Realizing the Power of Emotional Intelligence* (Boston: Harvard Business School Press, 2002).

roles and rarely make the valuable contribution that planning can make if it is executed well. Planning is a valuable skill, and a well-trained planner is probably the most highly leveraged employee in maintenance. A good planner can keep up to 40 tradespeople very busy, but planner training, like management training, is often inadequate (in some cases, nonexistent).

When change in an organization occurs, old paradigms are shattered or unfrozen; new ideas are planted and allowed to grow. For people to learn to handle change, education is key. Encouragement is also important and the best way to encourage people is to acknowledge and share positive results, ensuring more of the same. Nothing succeeds like success, and public recognition will motivate others while expanding and extending knowledge.

Another element in Lever's success was their tying of compensation to the demonstrated use of new skills. Compensation in a variety of forms is important if you are to attract and retain the best workers.

COMPENSATION AND REWARDS

The younger generation of workers has a different set of motives than their predecessors and money is not always at the top of their list. Money, in fact, is a motivator with hidden defects. If you pay only by the hour plus overtime, you encourage inefficiency. If you pay a straight salary, you discourage overtime and do little to encourage efficiency. Various schemes exist for compensating the workforce, but the bottom line is that money is only one of many rewards that make people want to work in any given company.

The best way to *attract* qualified, enthusiastic technical employees to challenging careers is to offer generous financial incentives. If you don't pay well or provide attractive benefits, the talent you want will go elsewhere. Even the prospect of a major commitment to education and training will pale without a direct payoff because even though increased skills can bring long-term rewards, most people want to see something more immediate. The best way to *retain* employees is to create an environment that they want to work in. Without such an environment, people turn off their brains or go elsewhere. If they stay, they do so only for the money.

One major supplier of industrial equipment had about twenty apprentices in one of its maintenance shops. The manager went to

extraordinary lengths to get them the required field experience so
they could become ticketed quickly. The apprentices appreciated
the effort—the maintenance shop had the best employee retention
record in the company.

Your compensation program is best linked to your organization's overall objectives as well as to your maintenance strategy.
One or more approaches may be appropriate. The following categories of compensation can be mixed and matched to make up the
total compensation package:

1. **Base pay**. In any compensation system, base pay is competitive and guaranteed. The technical trades employed in maintenance work are in great demand and the supply is
   shrinking. If you want low turnover, begin with an appropriate base pay. It is normally related to an employee's position, grade or seniority, skills and the tasks or duties required
   in the job description. In the case of multiskilling, tie base
   pay to the knowledge or skill level demonstrated and
   applied by the employee. Ideally your base pay is sufficient,
   precluding the need for overtime payment.

2. **Overtime**. Base pay often covers only a specified number of
   working hours per day. If more effort is required, overtime is
   paid. Unfortunately, overtime provides a disincentive to getting work done during the normal working day. It puts more
   pay in the employee's pocket, and increases maintenance
   costs. Overtime pay can also become addictive to employees,
   especially if it forms a substantial part of their compensation.
   It encourages reactive working environments and provides a
   disincentive to do any proactive maintenance. This results in
   plenty of extra overtime, call-ins, and unplanned shutdowns. If you have a situation where overtime pay is creating this situation, consider making the average overtime
   payment a part of the base pay and eliminating the overtime
   altogether. It does not raise labor costs and it provides plenty
   of incentive for the workforce to become proactive. Workers
   are paid as much as they were paid when they were working
   less, and you get improved reliability and performance.

3. **Profit-based incentive pay**. Incentive schemes can be
   designed for either individuals or groups. These schemes
   pay out a share of profits based on gains made by the com-

pany, equity, or stock options. Incentive pay can be decided at the discretion of the manager using some formula based on time worked or piecework achieved. Some programs offer incentives for suggestions that are implemented or compensate for sick and vacation time not taken. With increasing emphasis on teamwork, there is a trend toward group rewards as opposed to individual awards. Such plans reinforce desirable team behavior and employee involvement. Individuals in these schemes are under pressure from their peers to perform for the benefit of the entire team. Productivity gains are shared between the company and the employees, according to a predetermined schedule. These schemes are often very effective at achieving their goals.

4. **Gain Sharing.** This is a form of incentive pay that is not tied to profits. Incentive payments are based on the attainment of specific goals, regardless of profit. The goals might be related to production levels, availability or reliability targets. This has an advantage over profit-sharing schemes because payout is not tied to profits that employees often feel are beyond their control. It also avoids the inevitable disappointment and disillusionment with the profit-sharing program that arise when goals are met but profits expectations are not.

5. **Benefits.** Traditionally, benefits have comprised a social safety net and basic life and disability insurance. In many jurisdictions, some of the basics, such as unemployment insurance and pensions, are legislated. Beyond those, however, most companies provide additional paid benefits. These packages have become expensive and in some cases (e.g., the steel and automotive industries in most of North America) they have led to severe financial hardship for companies. With cost cutting aimed at remaining competitive with offshore companies, there is a trend to contracting with insurance and other providers for the management of these benefit packages. Some enterprises are offering a menu of benefits, usually grouped into packages that are carefully tailored to cater to various employee desires (e.g., single employees vs. married vs. married with children vs. nearing retirement, etc.). Each is priced so employees can select the most appropriate cluster of benefits up to a preset dollar limit. These can include participation in pension programs,

savings programs, medical and dental programs, drug programs, etc. The best packages offer a lot of variety and individual choice.

6. **Perquisites.** Perks are popular when the economy is expanding and competition for highly qualified employees is keen. In maintenance management, the most common perks are subsidized personal work tools and equipment, education leave, and financial assistance. Other perks include car allowances, free parking, cell phones, work clothing, education and day care, fitness clubs, social clubs, cultural and recreational activities, and employee discounts on purchases of company products or shares. Beware of the temptation to pull the perks when times get tough. Companies tend to view perks as a privilege, but employees tend to view them as an entitlement. Eliminating these perks, once they are established, can be a challenge. If a perk is "lost" by the workforce and is not replaced with something else, workers are likely to resent it. (Overtime is a good example of a business requirement that has become a perk and an entitlement.)

Nonmonetary rewards are another way to compensate employees. Besides base and incentive pay, you can recognize individuals and groups for a job well done. There is usually no set pattern for these rewards, which vary greatly depending on the organization. Most companies that offer such rewards began to do so as a form of thanks to employees for their achievements in throughput, safety, project management, or for completing formal training courses. Now, they are also offered for significant contributions in quality service, cost and time improvements, and for advances in job-based knowledge or competence. Awards can range from certificates, medals, and trophies, to dinners and get-away weekends. Make sure you reward the desired behavior. Avoid the temptation to reward the "white knight"—the one who rescues you from a major failure situation—while ignoring those whose efforts helped to prevent other such situations. Also be aware that some individuals do not want public attention drawn to them. In such cases, public recognition would be counterproductive, so keep it private and personal.

Today's trend in compensation is moving away from pay for a single trade skill toward pay for demonstrated knowledge and multiple skills. An excellent practice is to have all employees on salary with specified annual hourly contracts. Incentives are paid based on business results or outputs rather than individual or departmental results alone. (For example, increasing production levels by x% or reducing unit production costs, which include maintenance costs, by y%.) This encourages interdepartmental cooperation and helps break down the old maintenance/operations barriers. Additional incentives based on individual or departmental results are kept to a minimum to encourage teamwork. Incentives are paid regardless of profits because profits can be impacted by market conditions that are completely out of employees' control. This also shows that management appreciates employees' efforts to improve the business, even if external factors negate their efforts.

This chapter began with a look at the extent of change in the marketplace and the business imperative to respond quickly and effectively. Handling change really boils down to managing people well. Doing that is not something you teach now and again; it is a lifelong learning process. Your own workplace version of the three R's—reassess, recognize, and reward—will earn you top marks for your efforts. Best of all, you will make change work for you.

Managing people is a huge challenge, but an astute leader will have a workforce motivated by free will and people who choose to work toward common goals. People make all the difference between companies that are good and those that are great. If you get the people part wrong, other goals will suffer.

UPTIME SUMMARY

An organization is nothing more than an extension of its people. It stands to reason that we need to focus on people if we want our organizations to thrive and change. Without your people, nothing happens. They are the most important part of your business. If you want excellence, your people need to choose it with you.

When you choose excellence, you are choosing to make changes. Remember that managing the changes is critical to success. Managing change should not be a separate project workstream running in parallel with your improvement efforts. It is an integral part of all you do. Excellence is a journey and change will be constant, so managing that change will also become a constant.

Purely technical approaches, long-time favorites of engineers and technical people, no longer work well on their own. Today, an effective manager is unlikely to be a purely technical person who has risen through the ranks on the basis of technical merit alone. He or she needs a balance of technical, managerial, and human skills. Your managers, superintendents, and supervisors will be most effective if they are true "people persons."

Organizational designs continue to evolve. Centralized, military style organizations have given way to more responsive decentralized structures. To deliver maximum business benefits today, traditional maintenance, engineering and operations departments are working together. Increasingly, they are becoming single delivery organizations. Traditional departmental boundaries are blurring, and focus is shifting to the delivery of business results, not departmental results.

The "self-organizing team" that combines disciplines is emerging as a highly successful model. It already exists on a small scale, but it will proliferate as its merits become fully appreciated. It requires less management and supervision than conventional "industrial age" command-and-control organizational designs, which have long stifled initiative and improvements. Self-organizing teams outperform other structures and deliver high levels of employee and team productivity, but they require managers to give up control—something that many find extremely difficult to do. As the benefits of doing so become more apparent, the learning curve will become less steep.

Multiskilling continues to grow in popularity as a means of developing workforce flexibility and enabling more efficient deployment of maintenance resources. Learning, training, and development are critical to companies that strive for excellence. Our educational systems are no longer geared towards industrial careers, and the onus is shifting to companies to foster their own talent. Without a focus on developing people, companies will become victims of the demographic realities of our times. Obviously, attracting, retaining, and rewarding talent is equally critical. There is no point spending a great deal on recruiting and developing people in-house if you do not retain them through a competitive and attractive compensation program that recognizes their individual and team contributions and successes.

PART II

Essentials

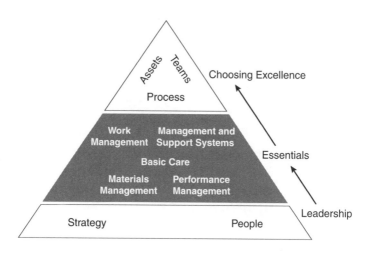

This part of the book describes the core elements of Maintenance Management, which all companies use albeit with varying degrees of competence. Excellent companies make it look easy, but even those companies that perform poorly find that they provide at least some level of consistency and stability. For companies that are underperforming in maintenance, building a conscious awareness of strategy and managing people more effectively (as discussed in Chapter 1) will help spark improvement. For companies that are performing well, these issues may be less of a concern and the greater focus may be on moving from good to great (as discussed in Part III). In either case, mastering the essential core elements discussed in this chapter is a step on the road to success.

3

Work Management

So much of what we call management consists in making it difficult for people to work.

PETER DRUCKER

THE WORK MANAGEMENT CYCLE

Drucker's observation doesn't apply to those few companies that are truly high performing in maintenance. Making it easy to do the right work the right way and in a timely manner is what work management is all about. At the heart of the maintenance function are work planning and work scheduling, but these tell only part of a complex story. Work management includes planning and scheduling, but it also extends to other activities that together comprise the six-step work management cycle depicted below:

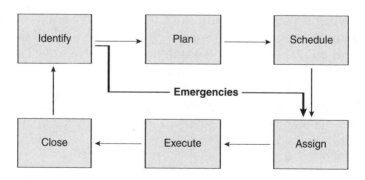

Figure 3-1. The Work Management Cycle

As Figure 3-1 illustrates, planning and scheduling are two important steps in the cycle. Planning defines what gets done and how; scheduling defines when. The problem with focusing only on these two segments of work management is that this presumes that operations always proceed without problems or variations, and that is rarely the case. For this reason, the material presented in this chapter deals with the entire work management process, including an emphasis on shutdowns and on managing a mobile workforce.

What every plant or fleet manager wants most is to sleep soundly—to turn off the office light at night confident that the equipment will be running reliably and efficiently the next morning. Unfortunately, such peace of mind is rare. Breakdowns, emergency repairs, unplanned and unscheduled downtime, overtime, and maintenance stores stock-outs all rob a business of capacity and profits. Avoiding these pitfalls requires effort in four areas:

1. Having the materials you want available at the time you want them. (Materials Management is covered in Chapter 5.)
2. Doing the right proactive work that eliminates or at least minimizes the disruptive consequences of equipment breakdowns. (Reliability Centered Maintenance is a technique for identifying the most appropriate work in a systematic way and is covered in Chapter 8.)
3. Having the skills and abilities available to do the right work efficiently. (This has been covered in Chapter 2 on People.)
4. Getting maintenance work done the right way through effective Work Management practices.

Let's begin with the assumptions that you have good materials management support, you have the right people with all the right skills and abilities at your disposal, and you have a well-defined maintenance program. It is the maintenance work management process that pulls these elements together so that the right work gets done by the right people using the right materials at the right time. The six-step work management process depicted above is the framework that enables that to happen:

- **Identify.** Preventive, predictive, and failure-finding work orders are usually generated from your proactive maintenance program schedules. Repair work arises as a result of failures that are reported, usually by operators, using your work management support system.

- **Plan.** This describes what work is to be done and how. A sequenced, documented plan is made, with descriptions and drawings of what has to be done for each job. All materials are made available and repair manuals are reviewed to get any needed relevant information. The job is not scheduled to start until all the right parts are onsite.
- **Schedule.** Once materials and labor availability has been confirmed, the job can be put on a schedule for execution. Jobs are scheduled for the best production window with the least disruption to customers. Scheduling is best performed for a weekly cycle, which means identifying next week's work before the end of this week. The schedule should be revised daily to accommodate emergencies and every effort should be made to complete all work within the week it is scheduled. A successful practice is to allow a portion of the schedule for "break-in" work in order to minimize schedule disruption. The amount of time allowed can be reduced as your proactive maintenance program takes effect and reduces the number of "emergency" and "urgent" work situations you experience.
- **Assign.** Maintenance supervisors assign the various tradespeople under their direction to the various scheduled jobs, given the planned work package and any additional instructions the supervisor deems appropriate. Unless you are training less experienced workers, use the most highly skilled people rather than whoever is available or whoever will stay on overtime.
- **Execute.** In successful companies, work crews do the work the right way the first time, and this is where trade skills, multiskilling, and training pay off. Do not rush the work. If something does not go exactly as planned, correct it. Do not try to work around it just to meet the schedule.
- **Close.** When the work is completed, inform operations. If operations is satisfied that the work is indeed ready, the equipment will be deemed ready for production. The parts used, materials used, and other relevant data is recorded on the work order along with any feedback to the planners from the work crews. The work order is closed and the job history data are made available for reliability analysis and standard job plan improvement.

As with every complex business specialty, maintenance has a language of its own—terminology that describes conditions, processes, tasks, and practice. A few definitions will facilitate comprehension of maintenance management concepts and protocol:

- **Break-in Work.** Work that is added to a schedule for execution after the schedule has been finalized.
- **Corrective Maintenance.** More commonly known as "repairs," this is work done to correct a defect or restore a failed device to working order.
- **Detective Maintenance.** Also known as "failure finding tasks," This form of proactive maintenance is work done to detect failures that have already occurred but remain undetected because the functionality that has been lost is normally not used or is dormant. This work is most often done on backup, stand-by, protective, or safety systems.
- **Emergency Maintenance.** Work that is treated as if it were truly an emergency, whether or not that treatment was warranted. Emergency work gets top priority regardless of other work that is being executed. Emergency work always "breaks into" an existing schedule and displaces other scheduled work. Every effort is made to hasten work execution, including but not limited to expediting missing parts, use of overtime, use of contractors on call-outs, etc.
- **Planned Maintenance.** Work that is planned in detail in advance of being scheduled and assigned to work crews for execution. Planning is used to increase work effectiveness, ensuring that the right work is done. Work is not "planned" unless the plan included all the details necessary for effective execution of the job and the work was carried out according to the plan. If some work around was needed, the plan was obviously deficient in some way, usually increasing the cost of doing the work and defeating the very reason for planning.
- **Planned Job.** A single maintenance job that is fully planned as described above.
- **Planned Work.** Planned jobs that are completed on schedule (i.e., work that is both planned and scheduled).
- **Predictive Maintenance.** Also known as "condition-based maintenance" or "on-condition maintenance," this form of proactive maintenance is work done to look for signs of

impending failure so that corrective maintenance can be done before equipment functionality is lost. There are two stages to predictive maintenance: "condition monitoring" or "inspections" (also known collectively as "condition-based monitoring"). These are used to determine the condition of the equipment followed by corrective maintenance performed only when that condition is deemed to be unsatisfactory. High-performing companies monitor the success of their "condition-based monitoring" closely by tracking the corrective work that arises from it on separate work orders.

- **Preventive Maintenance.** This form of proactive maintenance is work that is scheduled and executed to replace components or restore them to original condition regardless of their apparent condition at the time. This work is done for failures that are age or usage related and it is done before the failures manifest.
- **Proactive Maintenance.** Work that is done with the intent of avoiding the consequences of failures. This includes preventive, predictive, and detective (failure finding) work.
- **Reactive Maintenance.** Repair or corrective work that is done when something fails.
- **Scheduled Maintenance.** Any work that is committed to a time schedule for execution before the scheduling cycle in which it is to be executed. Work added to a schedule after it has been committed is known as "break-in" work. Scheduling is done proactively to increase the efficiency of use of the workforce and materials. Work is scheduled if it is carried out or started within the scheduling window as scheduled. If scheduled work is started outside the intended scheduling window, it is effectively unscheduled.
- **Unplanned Maintenance.** Work that is not planned; it may be scheduled, but it is always issued to work crews for execution without a detailed plan.
- **Urgent Maintenance.** Work that may require break-in to schedule but the situation is not so serious as to demand the work be done immediately. There is some time for preparation before the job is executed.

Studies done by several research teams, including Alcan, General Motors, and the authors' own consulting team, have shown a clear link between planned maintenance and reduced costs. When work is planned, it is easier and cheaper to execute than work that is unplanned. This is not only logical but also statistically sound. A conservative "rule of thumb" is that unplanned running repair work will cost at least 50 percent more than fully planned and scheduled work and that emergency work will cost 3 or more times as much. A ratio of 1 to 1.5 to 3 times can be used to estimate the breakdown of work costs if you know the ratios of planned and scheduled, unplanned, and emergency work. Estimates of 1 to 3 to 9 to 14 are also fairly common—the actual ratio will vary considerably from industry to industry and from plant to plant. One underground mining manager estimated his emergency repair costs to be 14 times the cost of planned work. A large nickel refining operation had estimated ratios of 1 to 3 to 5.

When measuring your planned work and schedule compliance, consider that the percentage of planned jobs multiplied by the percentage of schedule compliance results in the percentage of planned and scheduled work. For example, if you plan 90 percent of your job and comply with 90 percent of your schedule, you are achieving 81 percent of "planned work."

Planned and scheduled work is both effective and efficient. Planned work may be effective from the perspective of those carrying it out, but it is not cost-effective unless it was scheduled as well. It is possible to carry out planned work using parts that were flown in from far away at great expense in order to meet a hastily prepared or ill-conceived schedule. It is more cost-effective to get both planning and scheduling right.

Some work is very simple to execute, requires no parts, and needs only minor hand tools to be completed by a single, trained tradesperson. Clearly, not every running repair warrants detailed planning and scheduling—that would be going overboard. But it is clear that jobs involving complex procedures, specialized skills, multiple trades, replacement components, and parts certainly do. Under most circumstances, leaving the work planning to the tradesperson who will also execute the work is inefficient.

THE SIX KEY STEPS

Effective maintenance work management comes down to six key steps that are the same regardless of industry or circumstances. The process starts with identifying what has to be done and ends with analyzing why you had to do it in the first place (see Figure 3-1).

Identify

Maintenance work can spring from something as simple as a noisy bearing or pushing a "test" button to something as complex as interpreting trends in vibration signatures. These are examples of using equipment condition to trigger the repair work and are considered to be "proactive." Random observations have a low probability of catching a problem before its condition becomes unacceptable. The most effective observations are those that are both disciplined and regular. It is also much better to program inspections by operators or maintainers who are equipment sensitive and know what they are looking for. It is not good enough to tell someone to "check it"—you must specify what to look for, what is acceptable, and what is not.

Like your family car, your equipment will benefit from regular cleaning, lubrication, adjustment, and observation for signs of abnormal performance. These are important checks that give us early signs of problems, and they can help you decide where in the "repair queue" a job might be positioned. Work prioritization determines what gets repaired soonest.

Waiting for equipment to fail is one way to be certain you are repairing it without wasting "useful running life." However, this may also bring unacceptable consequences, such as loss of production or interruption to customer services. This approach of waiting for failures is known as "reactive maintenance." Organizations that are highly reactive plan less of their work than proactive organizations—some even plan none of their work in advance. Unfortunately, the cost ratios still apply to them, and they are choosing the most expensive approach. These organizations are also easy to spot but not so easy to change.

Plan

Planning is ensuring that all the resources necessary to do a job are accounted for and available. Scheduling (discussed later) is a matter of when to do the job. In many organizations, people refer to "planned maintenance" when what they are actually doing is scheduling their work. The two are quite different.

The most obvious planning tasks are to determine what has to be done, in what sequence, and with what skills. Parts, materials, and components are usually necessary and often not immediately at hand. Sometimes, extraordinary items or resources may be needed, including engineering drawings, outside contractors, special tools, or mobile equipment. Safety reminders or regulatory direction may also be required. Some tasks will need work permits, lock, and tag-out of equipment. All of these should be identified and included in your job plans. Miss even one item, and the tradespeople who are trying to do the work will be spending their time looking for whatever is missing—and driving up the costs.

Getting the plan right requires a planner. Benchmarking results show that a planner can plan work for 25 to as many as 80 tradespeople, with the more proactive organizations having well-established practices at the upper end. The planner, of course, is someone who has the technical skills and plant-specific experience to be credible to those executing the plan. The planner uses field inspections, his or her own knowledge of the equipment and systems, and all additional available information to lay out a job and estimate how long it will take. Finally, the planner often estimates the overall cost, which facilitates cash-flow projections and repair-or-replace decisions. The estimated time to do the job is used together with "Net Capacity" in the scheduling process.

It is worth noting that not every job requires planning in detail. There are many jobs that can be done in just a few minutes by one tradesperson, using standard-issue hand tools and no parts. These simple jobs are well within the tradesperson's skill set and require little to no preparation in advance. One mining operation estimated that up to 60 percent of its work fit that description. Obviously, it makes no sense to plan such simple work. The cost of executing them will not be increased by the absence of a plan, and the planner will have more time to work on more challenging jobs.

Schedule

Scheduling determines *when* the work will get done and is a matter of resource and asset availability. When is the equipment available to be worked on? When can you coordinate the people who have the right skills? Do you have the parts? Do you have the agreement of the production department to release the equipment?

Only when all of these conditions are all in place can the work progress smoothly. If your tradespeople have to wait for any of these, they are being paid but underutilized.

To schedule skilled people, first look to see who is scheduled to be at work, who is sick, on vacation, or on a training course. This gives you a pool of labor to draw from. Then determine who has the best skills for the job—is it a millwright, a rigger, an electrician, an instrument technician, or someone else?

Bear in mind that the estimated time to do a job often considers only productive working time. There is also a lot of nonproductive working time, including time spent on breaks, waiting for parts, waiting for instructions and permits, travel time between the shops and the job site, and clean-up time. When you take away all of this nonproductive (but paid) time you are left with "Net Capacity." In most organizations, net capacity is less than 60 percent of the time you actually pay the workforce; in extreme cases it is as little as 30 percent. Up to half of your lost capacity is used in vacations, sick time, and mandatory meetings. That time reduces availability of the workforce to perform work. Planning eliminates many of the delays and helps to increase your net capacity. If you have 50 tradespeople and an estimated net capacity of 40 percent, you are getting the productive effort of the equivalent of only 20 tradespeople full time, taking no breaks and wasting no time in unproductive activities like waiting. Increasing the net capacity to 60 percent (a realistic target) will add another 50 percent to your equivalent labor effort—you will have the equivalent of 30 tradespersons' productive effort full time. You will still be paying 50 tradespersons because you cannot eliminate all the nonproductive time (breaks, lunch, etc.), but you will be getting more value from your workforce.

There are also mandatory jobs that will have priority. These include regulatory compliance work, proactive maintenance, the normal load of emergency work, and other planned work already started. These jobs are done first. Work priority schemes are used along with knowledge of your available net capacity to help determine the exact sequence.

Parts availability is a matter of checking the on-hand status of the maintenance stores or the lead-time of any items ordered directly from suppliers. In many cases there is a gap between what the stock records indicate and what is actually there. "Open stores," where there are few controls on issues and returns, are usually the worst, especially if they are in a reactive maintenance environment. Maintainers in a hurry are not usually good record keepers. Visual confirmation of parts availability is highly recommended until you gain confidence in your stores and your inventory control system. Most maintenance management systems will do this check for you using their integrated inventory and planning modules. Of course, the data they supply must be accurate and you want to ensure that they stay accurate, or you will find yourself resorting to manual checks.

It is essential to make sure that equipment is available before it is scheduled for maintenance and that production knows when the work will be performed. Coordinating maintenance and production schedules is a must as is a close working relationship among maintenance planners, production planners, and shopfloor leaders.

Except for emergency work, no job escapes scheduling. As discussed above, even jobs that require no planning can and should be scheduled.

In one large paper mill with a highly reactive culture and an almost chronic state of chaos, one remedial activity used by the authors' team was to schedule all work. Using rough time-slot estimates, the team even scheduled work that was not planned. The schedules were posted where the work crews, shops, materials people, and production people could see them. At the end of each week, the team marked up the schedules to show which jobs were done and which were outstanding and then posted the following week's schedule. Initially, slack time was built into the schedule to allow for 20 percent break-in work. The graphic depiction of performance inspired the workers involved to improve schedule compliance, even in the absence of planning. Within a few weeks, they achieved 75 percent schedule compliance. Furthermore, they maintained this percentage and even increased it once they introduced planning and were able to reduce their break-in work. Their backlogs began to drop and most of the chaos dissipated.

Assign

The assignment of a job depends heavily on organizational structure. Autonomous, self-directed work teams do all but the most specialized maintenance diagnostics and repair work themselves.

More traditional organizations usually delegate the day-to-day work assignment for a particular area to the area foreperson or to a supervisor. In either case, it is usually helpful if the team or foreperson has a few days of work planned and ready in advance. This allows for the flexibility to deal with emergencies, unplanned work, or crew changes. The job of work assignment falls to the first-line supervisor or the self-directed work team. These are the people who know the skills and abilities of the tradespeople the best. A few organizations leave work assignment to planners. This is not a recommended practice because the planners provide the most value to your company if they are focused on future work—not today's. Getting the planner involved in today's problems detracts from the proactive approach you are creating by having planners. Planners are not supervisors and they are not parts chasers.

Execute

This is where "the rubber hits the road." Well-trained, motivated team players keep the maintenance process revolving. They add real value: quality and service that is cost-effective and timely. They reduce risk by getting the job done right the first time. All if this happens if the maintenance team is supported by effective management systems, treated fairly, and allowed to proceed with proactive and planned work.

Effective work execution requires that the skills and abilities of the tradespeople be matched to the work at hand. That, in turn, requires that qualified people be hired, trained, retained, and moti-vated. Your work crews have to want to do what they are assigned to do. A poorly motivated crew is more error prone and less effi-cient. Not only can that cost you more, it can result in rework or in equipment that is not maintained at the "as good as new" standard.

Close

Closing the job entails far more than changing the status of a work order from "pending" to "completed." Of course, no job is truly fin-ished until the paperwork is done, but thoughtful analysis of the failure, your response to it, and whether or not it could have been avoided will lessen the chance of repeating the same mistakes. Clo-sure is a process, not an event.

Careful collection of information: parts used, the condition of parts removed, tools used (if different from what was indicated in the plan), skills used (if different from what was indicated in the plan) and the amount of time the work took keeps the quality of maintenance job plans high. This feedback enables the planner to do his or her job most effectively. Feedback about whether the equipment failed in service or not is also very important. This information may be obvious to you today, but it will not be obvious to the reliability engineer who may be looking at the repair history two years from now, so it must be documented. It is quite common for equipment to be removed from service for repair work only to discover that nothing was really wrong with it. But if the records do not reflect that, decisions made later may be compromised. The reliability engineer depends on your accurate and complete maintenance records to preclude future problems.

At the very least, the maintenance work should be part of equipment history. At its best, it is work that leads to improvements. If maintenance work was significant, for example, consider redesigning preventive maintenance and operating procedures so that the related failure does not recur.

The six steps presented above are the core maintenance management process. Many enterprises, however, seem to be programmed to hit only the Execute button (shown as the shortcut line from Identify to Assign in Figure 3-1). Firefighting is certainly exciting, and people feel a tremendous sense of accomplishment when the fire is put out. But this method of managing maintenance leaves less and less time for sober thought and careful planning. People get hooked on the adrenaline rush while the fire rages and some enjoy the "dragon slayer" status of getting it under control. See this behavior for what it is. Give praise to those who prevent the problems and counseling to those addicted to the crises.

Organizations that choose not to deal with this addiction to firefighting are inadvertently choosing high maintenance costs along with unreliable operation and the business consequences that arise as a result. Failure to get this under control can result in unreliable delivery to customers, and that can result in contract penalties that can sometimes be fatal to a business. In one large tissue paper converting plant in the eastern United States, this kind of reactive maintenance was leading to delivery problems with a major retail customer that was buying up to 80 percent of the company's production. The result was a new supply agreement with that customer, which included a penalty scheme for late deliveries. After the first late delivery, the plant received a warning. After the second late delivery, the plant lost $100,000. After the third, it lost the contract. Eight hundred people were laid off and the plant was sold.

PLANNING HORIZONS

Issuing a work order to repair a faulty circuit breaker is clearly a different undertaking from maintaining the civic-run power scheme that supplies it with electricity, yet these are related. All types of fixed assets, from a switch to a power station, require at least three kinds of planning: 1) life-cycle and long-range plans, 2) annual plan and budget, which includes projects and major shutdown work, and 3) work orders for specific jobs (see Figure 3-2).

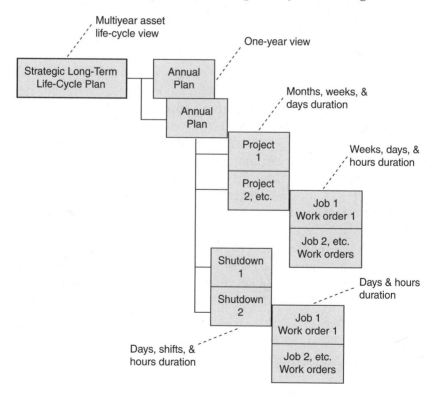

Figure 3-2. Planning Horizons

Life-cycle and Long-range Plans

This type of planning is closely associated with strategic planning for maintenance as discussed in Chapter 1. The planning process involves creating a vision of future performance, including human, financial, and physical resources. It also includes action plans to achieve the vision.

Life-cycle planning for the physical plant, equipment, and fleet means getting the most from maintenance and operating activities and doing it economically. Because most failures are caused by random events, age is not the best indicator of pending failures in most complex equipment systems. It is usually helpful to develop a long-range forecast of major project and maintenance costs, based on past experience and/or the output of a thorough Reliability Centered Maintenance analysis. Besides studying history, scheduled work for age-related failures, such as painting (to avoid corrosion); restoration of deteriorated roads; civil structures and roofing; restoration of worn mining equipment working surfaces; and replacement of fatigued cyclically loaded components like aircraft landing gear all contribute to the plan.

Equipment and system life-cycle plans are geared for major or significant work. They can fit neatly into the operation's overall business strategy. For example, aircraft have long-term overhaul schedules based on flying hours; naval ships have 4- to 6-year refit cycles to accomplish major restoration and replacement work; metal presses have a fixed number of cycles between die changes; steel mills have scheduled furnace relines; and buildings have a roof replacement schedule based on age. Keep in mind that any new or replacement capital purchases will have a direct bottom-line impact on maintenance requirements of all kinds. There is an optimum age at which replacement achieves the lowest equivalent annual cost of ownership for any asset.

Long-term plans help your finance department arrange for suitable funding for big-ticket items. They also facilitate decisions about other significant expenditures, such as those associated with plant expansions.

Annual Plan and Budget

If you do not plan and budget, you jeopardize all of your efforts to improve maintenance quality. A poorly crafted budget will be scrutinized by finance and plant management and is likely to lead to demands for cuts. Sadly, those cuts usually impact training, equipment upgrade funds, and, in extreme cases, your workforce.

The maintenance budget is created from your next year's maintenance plan. This plan includes all the elements from your long-range plan that are coming due along with anything that has arisen and been deferred this year. It also includes all your planned maintenance with allowance for breakdown work and improvements. Inputs to this plan include accurate equipment histories, results of periodic inspections, condition-based monitoring, and an emphasis on continuous improvement. Plant shutdowns, equipment overhauls, and major inspections are forecast by month, priced, and incorporated in the plan. New technology, systems, procedures, and organizational changes that affect capability are also factored in. The plan is then converted to dollars, item by item, to create the budget.

This type of zero-based budgeting and planning is more challenging than relying on last year's budget, plus or minus 5 percent; but it is far more useful for planning for staff, long lead-time parts, and materials and cash flow. It commits everyone to the concept of planned maintenance throughout the year. In addition, a zero-based budget sets the expenditures to match resources required to deal with specific events both planned and reasonably likely to occur. Items can be deferred or excluded if the consequences of doing so are fully appreciated and accepted. Knowledge of the cost of downtime and the total costs of maintenance are essential to this process.

Budgeting solely on the basis of historical costs is a mistake. Like most organizations, yours is probably adding equipment, controls, and more automation to address demands for greater environmental integrity, safety, production capacity, customer service, and quality. That new equipment means there is more to fail and that drives more maintenance. Allow for it—failure to plan is planning to fail.

If you have used the zero-based approach, defending your budget from the inevitable attacks and request for cuts becomes much simpler. Remember that those requests often come from accounting and financial people who do not really appreciate what you are trying to accomplish. Answer requests for cuts with, "What don't you want me to do next year?" Recognize that giving up budget is also giving up work scope that you can execute—customers who would have received the benefit of that work may want to be involved in the decision to cut it out. Making the pain theirs will help fend off these requests for cuts so you can achieve your long-range vision. Perhaps they won't mind the rain and melt water ingress in their administration building when their roof replacement is deferred!

Work Orders and Specific Jobs

Top performing organizations use work orders for all their maintenance work, regardless of who does the work: their own maintainers or contractors. Maintenance work, like purchases and sales, comprises a large number of separate "job" transactions that can be tracked. Similar to the purchase orders used by purchasing and order-fulfillment functions, the record of these maintenance transactions is called a "work order." The basic maintenance work order specifies what work is to be done, authorizes its execution, and serves to collect information about the work. Today, most work orders are computerized documents. Paper copies are sometimes used by maintenance supervisors assigning work to their crews and by tradespeople recording information in the field. The various functions of a work order are:

- To identify and authorize work to be done.
- To facilitate planning and scheduling for complex jobs.
- To record what work is assigned to individuals, contractors, work centers, etc., for execution.
- To collect cost information for labor, stores requisitions, purchase orders, and services to charge against a piece of equipment or production cost center.
- To record the "sign off" or approval of work that has been done, accepting the equipment for production use.
- To capture information about work duration and maintenance-related delays to use in measuring productivity.
- To provide work estimates to determine and manage work backlogs.
- To provide a means of acquiring equipment history data to be used in analyzing failures and the effectiveness of preventive maintenance efforts.

Without work orders your maintenance records are incomplete, and your maintenance work will not be managed as well as it could be. Without records you will never know for sure.

There are hundreds of different computerized maintenance management software packages available on the market today. These packages range in scope and price from simple and inexpensive to complex and expensive. They can range in scale from single-purpose work-order systems to highly integrated systems that provide other enterprise management functions like human resources, accounting, purchasing, and timekeeping. The trend today is towards large integrated enterprise management systems, but even companies with these massive computer systems often rely on simpler maintenance-specific software packages that are easy to use. These are discussed further in Chapter 7.

Projects and Shutdowns

Maintenance departments are often involved in capital projects: improvements to plant and equipment. Strictly speaking, these are not maintenance jobs because they are not maintaining existing capability or capacity; they are extending, enhancing, or expanding it in some way. Usually, these jobs are overseen by a project engineer who is not otherwise associated with maintenance work. Maintenance tradespersons have most, if not all, the skills needed to execute many projects successfully. Top performers segregate capital work from maintenance work, even though they manage it all using work orders. They know how much real maintenance work is being done and how much project work. Knowing this allows them to measure maintenance productivity without clouding their figures with project workloads.

What maintenance departments lack in capability or capacity can be contracted. Contractors can be less expensive, but when contracting project work, take care not to violate any agreements with your trade unions or employee associations. Many of these agreements prohibit the use of contractors except in very specific circumstances.

Shutdowns are disruptive major maintenance activities that are normally characterized by many small jobs being done at the same time while a production unit is out of operation. They are similar to projects in how they are managed, but they are purely maintenance work.

Both projects and shutdowns are labor intensive and entail some shutdown of production capacity. Fortunately, most of the work in many projects can be done without disrupting existing operations, but the final tie-ins and connections to any existing plant will normally require shutdown of at least part of an operation. Shutdowns, being major maintenance jobs, inherently take production down. They cost a great deal, and as they are executed, your capacity to generate revenue is zero. That is a great incentive to end shutdowns as quickly as possible. Like it or not, however, shutdowns are a normal part of most plants' operations. They are needed to clean, overhaul, or inspect equipment at predictable intervals. In successful operations they are forecast in both the long-range and annual plans and budgeted accordingly.

Projects are also part of long-range plans, but those plans are generally managed by engineering rather than maintenance. Successful organizations coordinate the budget activities of maintenance and engineering and operations to ensure that everyone is aware of the need for downtime and project-specific resources. For example, maintenance needs to know if a project is going to require 100 tradespeople during a planned maintenance shutdown to ensure that enough skilled people are available for all of the work to be done.

Projects can arise as a result of changing market demands that are not always predictable over the very long term, so they may not be part of an overall strategic capital plan. If projects are not planned as far in advance as practical, they can be very disruptive to normal operations and the normal maintenance function. Successful organizations maintain regular communication about project, shutdown, and production requirements among engineering, maintenance, and operations groups.

SHUTDOWN MANAGEMENT

Top performers avoid shutdowns whenever possible; if a shutdown occurs, they minimize the downtime required to handle what caused it. From the perspective of the production manager, downtime for any reason is a bad thing because it detracts from the ability to produce and generate revenue. Shutdowns come in two flavors: planned and unplanned. It is best to avoid the latter as much as possible and that is a major reason to perform proactive maintenance. Planned shutdowns are useful from time to time. They can, for instance, facilitate planned maintenance activities or allow for cleaning of process equipment to maintain product quality standards. Regardless of the reasons for the shutdown, there is much that can be done to minimize the downtimes and maximize the time between them.

Unscheduled shutdowns are a result of failures of critical equipment that an organization has failed to prevent, predict, or design out. When a shutdown occurs, it creates a business emergency. Production is down and revenue is not being generated, yet many of the operating costs of labor are still being paid. Moreover, maintenance will probably be working overtime to fix the problem. In any case, costs are up but revenue is zero. The best way to avoid this situation is to institute an effective proactive maintenance program, and that is what successful organizations do.

Even the most successful enterprises cannot always prevent unplanned outages. They do not, however, allow these events to become crises. Instead, they see unplanned outages as a window of opportunity for other planned but unscheduled work to be done. Top performers never extend these unplanned outages to get other work done; they squeeze in what they can without lengthening the downtime period. This opportunity allows them to clear at least some backlog, but this is not done haphazardly. For it to work well, jobs that are squeezed in must have been fully planned and all necessary resources must be available for execution on very short notice. If you expect such opportunities to arise, use a separate work-order classification to make identification of those opportunity jobs easy.

One plant called these planned and unscheduled jobs that require shutdown "If-Down-Do" jobs, or IDD. The maintenance and production shifts always knew what jobs were on the IDD list so they could be done during production changeovers or setup adjustment times when the equipment was down anyway. However, it is never a good idea to stay down any longer than you have to, so avoid the temptation of trying to get too much done. Do not add any workload that will extend downtime. Avoid adding big jobs to your unplanned shutdown and avoid adding jobs that could possibly interfere with the critical path job. Always remember that top performers have all the needed materials and other resources available at short notice for these IDD jobs. If you do not follow suit, you run the risk of lengthening the duration of the downtime and increasing your costs.

If your critical path job is missing materials or a plan or other resources, there is little you can do besides get them—expeditiously and at any cost necessary. If you are already "down," you are in an emergency situation; inaction hurts business. The best you can do is to minimize the damage. Noncritical jobs, jobs that are not yet planned or for which parts or materials are missing, should not get priority during a shutdown. Do not create an opportunity for some logistical glitch on a noncritical or secondary job to extend shutdown time.

Today's maintenance management systems can quickly pull up a list of outstanding work from a backlog file. A quick check of work-order status to identify the planned and ready for scheduling jobs will tell you which can be executed with materials that are available or near to hand. Those jobs are planned already so you can move to scheduling them within the anticipated shutdown window. Allocate your net capacity available in a way that allows you to deal with critical path job first; then execute secondary shutdown jobs as expeditiously as you can.

Successful organizations plan shutdowns beginning with forecasts years in advance so that a window of time is planned into the production schedule and the financial resources are available when needed. That shutdown window is your planning and scheduling constraint. Avoid jobs that will take longer.

Preparing for a planned shutdown requires lead-time and industries that deal with planned shutdowns exceptionally well have long lead-times. In oil refining for example, preparation can take up to 18 months. Needless to say, budgeting for a planned shutdown can easily span two budget years. Because of the nature of shutdown work (the jobs are usually large and complex, the materials are rarely held in stock and may take a long time to procure), preparatory lead-time is essential. This lead-time, in fact, is the primary reason for the long planning cycle. In successful organizations, work scope for the shutdown is fixed or "locked down" well in advance of the shutdown date to allow for long lead-time items to be procured. Remember to allow time for your normal procurement approval processes, vendor lead-time, and, if the materials fit your criteria for capitalization, enough time for your capital expenditure approval process.

Well-planned shutdowns focus only on those jobs that absolutely require equipment shutdown. Each of the jobs approved for the shutdown period is planned in detail as described earlier. All job plans are then integrated into a master schedule for the shutdown. That schedule is essentially a project plan, and it is managed the same way. For top performers, break-in work is not added after the official "lock down" date for work scope without careful consideration of the ramifications and very senior level approval. The plan also includes all the work that will be required of any contractors as well as operators to shut down, isolate, lock out, drain and prepare equipment for work and their start-up activities.

Minimizing downtime entails doing as much work outside the down period as you can. Successful companies prepare the work areas prior to the shutdown (as long as this does not interfere with normal operations) by erecting scaffolding; removing roofing or wall panels to facilitate equipment access; renting cranes and other lifting equipment and moving them into position; staging and prepositioning parts near targeted equipment; prepositioning tools; and rehearsing procedures for critical jobs that will be performed. Rehearsing the work steps is particularly important because practice improves job performance. (A good example of this is the planned and practiced work execution performed by racetrack pit crews.) Generally, the more you can do in advance, the less you risk extending your downtime.

When the shutdown begins, your plans are put into motion. If there is a great deal of work to be done, as is often the case, you will probably have contractors supplementing your workforce. They will require supervision by knowledgeable supervisors or senior tradespeople from your own staff. If the shutdown is extensive, you may even have all of your own staff, supervisors, and tradespeople serve in supervisory roles for teams of contractors. By this time, you have a plan for all the work; all you do now is work the plan.

When machines are opened up for inspection, there are often surprises and these lead to new work. If there is a likelihood of this happening, it is best to anticipate this contingency and to plan for it. Top performers, for example, predict what may happen and keep relevant parts on hand and other resources available so they are not caught off-guard. They rarely have surprises because they have done an excellent job of forecasting all maintenance requirements that might be associated with a shutdown.

But even this level of preparation is not foolproof, and despite rigorous efforts, some surprises do arise. Some may require emergency measures. Others may not be critical in nature. If this is the case, deferring the work until the next shutdown may be the best option. You must determine whether the "surprise" is critical or not and decided what to do about it quickly.

Throughout the shutdown, have a series of shutdown management meetings to update status, discuss problems that have arisen and how to resolve them while maintaining tight coordination over needed resources. Keep track of work completed, work in progress, and its status. Use checklists to ensure that everything is done— don't forget to inspect the job for completion, de-isolate the equipment, remove locks and tags, close work permits, etc. As work is completed, close it off just as you would for running repair work orders. Do not waste time moving work crews to their next jobs. If they are done, send them home. Extra people get in the way of those who are still working.

When all of the work is completed, turn the plant back over to operations for start up. It is an excellent practice to keep a maintenance crew on hand during start up to handle any failures or surprises that crop up while equipment is coming back on line. Your plan should also include the time it takes to ramp production back up to normal once the maintenance work is completed. Another successful practice is to plan production output at reduced but gradually increasing levels to allow for glitches during start up. (For example, a company may expect 25 percent of normal rates from the first shift, 50 percent from the second, 75 percent from the third, and full production by the fourth.)

Progressive Shutdowns

Most production processes[1] can tolerate some minor production disruptions, and the operators are usually very good at managing those. These often occur due to loss of feedstock or other non-equipment related causes and contribute to less than ideal pro-

---

1. This technique was developed in and works very well in nonproduction environments. It is commonplace in building, railway, and other infrastructure maintenance programs. It has also been adapted to batch and continuous production processes.

duction rates. In a progressive shutdown, you can make use of the ability of the operators to handle minor disruptions to create windows of opportunity on parts of the production line while it is still operational.

In a batch process where you have the capability of building up some work-in-process (WIP) between the batch steps, you can take parts of the process down fairly easily without disrupting overall process flow. The duration of the downtime window is dictated by the time it takes for downstream processes to draw down the WIP between the steps. Needless to say, this takes careful planning and preparation. The advantage of this highly successful technique over a full shutdown is that production only slows down for a period of time—it does not come to a complete stop. Production levels are sustained, albeit at slightly lower levels. Avoiding a complete shutdown also avoids the time it takes to ramp back up and the inevitable start-up glitches that occur.

In a continuous process, production flows don't normally stop, and there is often little or no capacity to store WIP between process steps. In these processes, feed is shut down to a part of the process, and the production line downstream is allowed to empty. Areas where equipment is empty can be shut down for work for a short duration. When the work is completed, the feed is turned back on and the empty portion of the production line moves downstream. In this way the portion of the production line that is down for work moves in the direction of production flow. The next section can then be shut down for work, and the maintenance crew moves to that area. The process requires careful coordination of activities, but the payoff is that you do not need to take production all the way down and incur only minor slowdowns. Operators are very good at handling these situations and can ramp-up shutdown sections to full production without difficulty. It is simpler and far less than disruptive than restarting the entire plant after a complete shutdown.

A good example of progressive shutdown in practice is Molson Breweries in Toronto, which is using this technique successfully on sections of its high-speed bottling lines. The decision to go with a two-hour time frame for this was based on the resources the company had available to work on line sections and a realistic assessment of how much work could be managed in a single fixed window. Molson gets 50 percent more productive effort from the maintenance workforce using this system because those involved are fully engaged during the shutdown windows on those sections of production line. The company has also experienced improved compliance with its proactive maintenance schedule, enhanced operator involvement in doing "soft maintenance"[2] tasks, and increased levels of production.

PLANNING AND SCHEDULING TOOLS

The most effective tool for managing work orders is the computerized maintenance management system. Most commercially available systems have comprehensive modules that include work-order management, equipment records and history, preventive maintenance tasks, interfaces to external scheduling systems, costing and budgeting, materials management and labor skills capacity planning. Because of its importance, Chapter 7 deals with this tool in detail. This chapter provides an overview.

The Gantt Chart

Successful shutdown and project managers use the Gantt chart to manage activities, sequences, duration, and dependencies among the various jobs that make up the total work scope. It is a useful yet simple tool for planning and scheduling, first introduced by Henry T. Gantt at the beginning of the twentieth century (see Figure 3-3). Gantt charts list key steps and activities required to complete a job in a vertical column and depict the time to accomplish these activities with corresponding horizontal bars. When properly constructed, a Gantt chart shows in graphic format:

- The sequence of tasks (events).
- The duration of each task.
- The start and end times of each task.
- The overall shutdown or project start time and end time.
- The dependencies among tasks (e.g., showing that a machine must be disassembled before it can be repaired).

---

2. Soft maintenance includes work that requires little training, the use of no parts and few tools, such as lubrication, cleaning, and minor adjustments.

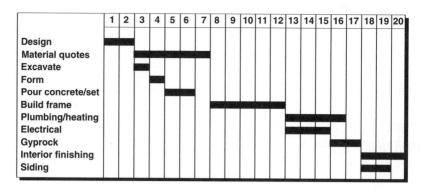

Figure 3-3. A Gantt Chart

The chart also provides information (for each task), such as the resources required, costs, and any interdependencies among the tasks that make up the entire job. The "job" being planned can be a single repair to a piece of plant equipment, it can be a major plant shutdown with many jobs, or it can be a capital project that uses contractors as well as maintenance and operating personnel. It is highly versatile and, because it is a visual tool, it can make the job of planning and scheduling quite easy.

It is particularly useful for events that are either strictly sequential or are independent. It does not, however, clearly show interdependence among different projects unless it is linked with the other projects where the dependencies exist. Today's improved-computerized project planning tools enable this complex integration of multiple projects. They include features that allow individual resource calendars to be considered so that holidays can be avoided and calculate cost automatically. They are easy to use once the planner understands the project management basics on which they are developed. Successful planning organizations use the Gantt chart, usually in computerized form, to plan, schedule and manage shutdowns, projects and large single jobs.

The Critical Path Method

A critical path is the sequence of tasks that must be completed when working through a project or shutdown and determines the length of the overall shutdown. Any job that is on this path is known as a "critical path job." Organizations that successfully stay on schedule in their shutdowns and projects are very good at managing these critical path jobs. They are also very good at managing work arising during the shutdown—they avoid adding anything to the overall plan that would increase the duration of any critical path job, add to the critical path, or change the critical path.

Critical path jobs can be shown on a Gantt chart, often in a different color from other jobs. As Figure 3-4 illustrates, critical paths are usually shown as a network of activities that resembles a flowchart.

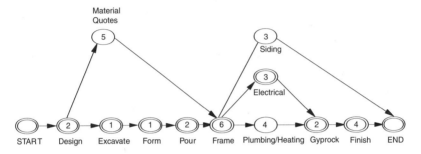

Figure 3-4. A Critical Path

Once the entire network of jobs is plotted, the path with the longest duration is highlighted on the critical path, usually in a different color or different style. In the figure the jobs in double "bubbles" are on the critical path. This path is the sequence of tasks that are related to each other that requires the closest scrutiny during work execution in order to ensure that the entire plan is accomplished on time. Other jobs can generally tolerate a small amount of schedule overrun if it occurs without lengthening the overall duration. However, large schedule overruns on other jobs can change the critical path. For example, if the material quotes took much longer than expected, they may become a critical path job and lengthen the whole project duration. In that case, excavate, form, and pour would no longer be critical path jobs. There are several software packages of varying sophistication available to help determine the critical path. They can also plan and schedule the resources necessary to execute the plan. These packages can often switch back and forth between Gantt Chart and Critical Path views to suit the user's preference.

PLANNING STANDARDS

The term "time standards" is not well received in maintenance. It conjures up images of a dogmatic, authoritative organizational culture with everything being measured and tightly controlled. It is a reminder of the days when techniques such as Universal Maintenance Standards, Methods-Time-Measurement, and Engineered Performance Standards kept employees on a tight leash. These methods were almost universally despised by the workforces being managed. The lesson learned from that experience is that you can't motivate people to do better if you are constantly irritating them. As Dwight D. Eisenhower said, "You do not lead by hitting people over the head—that's assault, not leadership." Frederick Herzberg's *Motivation Hygiene Theory* recognizes that unsatisfied "hygiene factors" can act as demotivators. Recognize that people work first and foremost for their own self-enlightened interests—they are truly happy and mentally healthy through work accomplishment. Because Draconian management techniques demotivated the workforce, they undercut improvement efforts.

Consequently, these techniques are of little value in today's workplace. If you believe in a team approach to continuous improvement and in an environment that truly values the total employee, you will see no benefit in time standards that measure and control individual productivity. These techniques attempt to cure a symptom, not root causes. A motivated individual will perform; an unmovitated individual will not. And in the best of all worlds, the ideal workforce is not only motivated but self-motivated.

Planning standards, then, begins with the understanding that the people affected by those standards and related processes will not respond well to "time standards" like those described above. Nonetheless, it is still important to know approximately how long a job will take in order to schedule it. To do this, you estimate its cost, schedule it along with other jobs, and determine the equipment downtime necessary to complete the work. In a broader sense, you can apply useful standard quality operating and maintenance procedures, as well as benchmarks for equipment performance and cost. Then you seek the input of the workforce in refining these with the objective of improving scheduling, not with the objective of making them "work better."

The Pareto Diagram

The Pareto Diagram (discussed in more detail in Chapter 10) is a simple tool for determining what work should have the highest priority. In successful organizations, it is used by planners, maintenance engineers, and TPM teams to determine what equipment merits the most attention. Planners use it to determine where they should put their planning efforts. By determining what equipment requires the most downtime for repair, planners can look for innovative ways to shorten the duration of downtime by modifying the job plan. They can also use Pareto to determine which equipment causes the greatest downtime or greatest maintenance cost in order to identify improvement effort priorities for maintenance engineers. Another technique, known as log-scatterplots[3] can be used to highlight failure frequency and mean time to repair as well as the downtime and cost factors, making prioritization of the problems to be tackled even easier.

Backlog Time Standards

When maintenance work is planned, successful organizations will estimate the duration of the job to facilitate effective scheduling of the work. For complex jobs requiring more than one trade skill, the task duration is also estimated to facilitate coordination of arrival and departure times for tradespeople involved in the job. This helps supervisors assign work more efficiently and increase actual hands-on-tools time.

Two of the most practical methods for estimating how long a job will take are equipment history work-order file times and timeslotting. Top organizations record the work completion time on their work orders, which can be used to determine the average time it takes to do any job. This average time, in turn, can be used as a standard.

If you do not have such records, or if the plant or equipment is relatively new, timeslotting may be a better solution. Timeslotting is a simple comparison method. For example, it takes less time to

---

3. Knights, P.F. (2001) "Rethinking Pareto Analysis: Maintenance Applications of Logarithmic Scatterplots," *Journal of Quality in Maintenance Engineering*, Vol. 7, No. 4, pp. 252–263.

change a tire than brake pads and less time to change the pads than the master cylinder. Standard time duration ranges are assigned to these tasks. The tire and brake pad jobs may fit in the 1- to 2-hour range while the master cylinder fits in the 2- to 3-hour range.

Typical time slots used in industry are 2 hours or less (the time between subsequent breaks), 4 hours or less (half a day or shift), 8 hours or less (a single shift or day), and number of days. One major newspaper uses a 2/4/7 concept—jobs are slotted into 2, 4, or 7 working hour periods. All of those fit into a normal working shift. An integrated steel mill used operational time windows: 30 minutes to change a work roll, 4 hours for a backup roll, and 12 hours for a shutdown. The mill used 30-minute, 4-hour, and 12-hour slots for any work requiring equipment downtime.

The planner selects several common jobs of varying duration and complexity, then times them, using observation, time cards, or expert opinion of those performing the work. The timed jobs are grouped into categories and used as benchmarks for similar jobs (see Figure 3-5).

Slot	Time Range	Plan Time	Actual Average (6-month moving)
A	0–3	1.5	2.2
B	3–6	4.5	3.8
C	6–12	9	9.1
D	12–24	18	21.7
E	24–48	36	35.4

Figure 3-5. Timeslotting Method

If an average of the actual time taken is kept, that number can be used for the planned time. For example, the jobs slotted in D will likely be of the same repetitive type in that particular area over which the planner has responsibility. Organizations using computerized maintenance management systems often use the average times, but, for ease of scheduling, slot them into convenient time slots. This usually allows for a little bit of extra time in case something goes wrong or allows tradespersons to move on to the next job a bit early.

Quality Standards

It seems ironic that while the quality standards on products and the techniques used to produce them are becoming more uniform and precise, the work environment from which such standards spring has become less rigid. There is, however, a logical underpinning to this irony.

Many successful companies, in their relentless quest for lower costs, are reinventing themselves into lean, flat organizational structures. Often, employees now operate in autonomous, self-directed work teams. There are many examples of this throughout the automotive industry and its suppliers, where cost cutting has become an art form. Working in teams has freed people up to develop the best processes and procedures to achieve near-perfect conformance in their work area. The now-popular Six-Sigma method is aimed at eliminating defects through fundamental process knowledge. It integrates business, statistics, and engineering to achieve its results. This self-directed, integrated move toward leanness can also be applied to maintenance procedures, particularly to repetitive tasks such as preventive care and tool-and-die maintenance. Overall, there is little reason today for getting these wrong.

Quality standards are not a matter of employees having the freedom to do what they want. It is rather a matter of excellence that results when everyone involved is responsible for developing the delineated best practice and is accountable for carrying it out. Six Sigma is implemented through extensive education and then facilitated through design experiments to identify factors that cause waste, which are then eliminated in a controlled environment. Once the best practice is determined, the time standard can be determined using actual time averages or the timeslotting techniques.

MOBILE WORKFORCE MANAGEMENT

Industries with physical assets or service points spread over a large geographic area are likely to have mobile workforces. These pose unique challenges for work management. The crews, once dispatched to their initial jobs, can be away from their supervisors for an entire shift. In some cases, mobile workers may not go into their depots or shops or see their supervisors for days. Work management practices for the mobile workforce are basically the same as for workers in a plant, but there are a few exceptions:

- Communications with your workforce during the day may be challenging; however, today's communication technology is rapidly making this a problem of the past.
- The net capacity of your mobile workforce to get work done will be much lower than it is in a fixed plant environment because of the travel time between jobs. Scheduling must consider this travel time. To maximize workforce efficiency, schedule jobs geographically close together.
- Balancing that lowered net capacity is a tendency of mobile workers to be more efficient than their plant counterparts. They do not have many distractions while working on-site and they often prefer to get the work done quickly to avoid overtime or having to return to the same site the next day.
- The provision of parts and materials can be handled differently because the mobile workforce is usually deployed in light trucks that can carry many of their own supplies. This can actually simplify the planning required for many jobs.

Mobile workers have a special need to have their work assigned and to communicate job status back to the dispatch office while they are in remote locations. There are many ways to handle this:

- The worker can phone or radio in at the end of a job to get his next work assignment,
- The supervisor can visit the work sites of all crews and assign work personally,
- Enough work can be assigned for an entire shift. This can minimize communication throughout the shift unless there is an emergency that requires you to break into the mobile worker's schedule for the day. Pagers can be used for that purpose. The work orders assigned can be tracked using paper documents or portable computing devices that store data collected throughout the day and download it when the crew returns to the shop.
- Handheld computers with built-in communication systems can be used to receive, update, and close work orders while remote from the office. Some of these are very sophisticated

and can access databases of repair information such as spec sheets and drawings.

Communications used to be a great time waster for mobile work crews, but today that is no longer the case. Technology today has resolved many of the problems associated with communication. Cell phones, pagers, personal digital assistants, handheld computers, data-logging devices, global positioning systems, geographic information systems, etc., have all come to the rescue.

Travelling between jobs reduces the net capacity of the mobile workforce, but this is balanced by efficiency. The key to increasing the net capacity of mobile workers is to schedule the work so they do the least amount of travelling. Linking asset locations to a Geographic Information System (GIS) will help the scheduler to pick jobs that are physically close to each other and balance relative job priorities, locations, and duration of work.

Global Positioning Systems (GPS) can be used in the mobile trucks to pinpoint and report their location. This enables dispatchers to see, on a map, where their work crews are located relative to the assets that require work. When work arises, this location information is useful in selecting which mobile crew to dispatch to the job.

Parts and materials are often stored and carried around in the vehicles used by mobile work crews. Materials that are commonly used are usually in stock on the truck, so the work crew can simply pick what they want for any given job directly from the truck. Trucks can be restocked during the off shifts. Often times, mobile crews do more or less standard jobs, so provisioning their vehicles for those jobs is relatively straightforward. Odd jobs or jobs requiring parts and materials that are too large to be carried or manhandled off a truck by the work crew will require special handling. Special vehicles provisioned for transporting and unloading these materials can be dispatched as needed. These jobs will require the same degree of work planning that would normally be applied in a fixed plant; the more common jobs won't.

Some mobile work crews are assigned to specialized vehicles, for instance, cable vehicles in municipal utilities. These vehicles and their crews may be required in conjunction with other crews for some jobs. One electrical distribution utility was engaged in jobs such as underground vault transformer replacements that required upwards of six separate crews to cover all the skills, materials, special purpose, and lifting requirements. Coordinating those crews required excellent planning. Timing the arrival of the various crews so that they arrived when wanted and spent as little time as practical waiting for their role was a challenge for the schedulers. This difficulty is what usually accounts for the times when you see several vehicles from the same company at the same location with workers standing around idly—they are usually waiting for their turn to work.

UPTIME SUMMARY

At the core of the maintenance function is work management: a six-step process for getting maintenance work done. Without it, workforce deployment becomes reactive to emergencies and maintenance costs are high. Work done in those reactive situations is anywhere from 1.5 to 3 times as expensive as work that is fully planned and executed on schedule. In some industries the cost of emergency work is even higher. Choosing excellence means mastering the work management process.

The simple cycle of identifying what work must be done, how to do it, what resources are required, when to do it, who should do it, doing the work and, finally, learning from the experience is what good maintenance departments do. Getting this basic process right drives improved efficiency and opens the door to enhanced effectiveness through a variety of reliability improvement initiatives.

There are planning and budgeting cycles to consider. These range from detailed job plans through project, shutdown, and annual cycles, to strategic multiyear and asset life-cycle focus. The basics of planning and scheduling apply to all work. Individual jobs, projects, and shutdowns are all managed the same way, the only difference being scale and scope of work. Shutdowns in particular are high-cost, intensive activities that occur when revenue generation through production is zero. It is important to get it right and avoid the temptations to do too much unplanned or poorly planned work in the available time windows. There are many tools and standards that assist the planner to deliver high workforce productivity consistently and keep costs down.

Mobile workforce management differs from fixed-plant management. Communications are more challenging and have led to the development of a variety of technologies. Scheduling plays a big role in efficiency because of the need for travel from job to job. Technologies like Global Positioning Systems coupled with Geographic Information Systems help keep mobile workforces productive while meeting the demands of far-flung customers. Mobile work crews are autonomous by nature and carry much of their own support parts and materials with them, but those must be replenished regularly or excessive travel time will result. Planning and scheduling to accommodate geographic considerations is a key to success in managing a mobile workforce.

Work management is the most important maintenance process. Paying attention to it provides substantial benefits.

4

Basic Care

"Institutional Paralysis" and "Lamentable failure."
Two of Lord William Douglas Cullen's comments in his report on the
Ladbroke Grove rail crash that killed 31 people in 2001.

IT'S THE LEAST WE CAN DO

Many business-related regulations that exist today are the result of past failures by companies to do the minimum to protect their workers, the public, or the environment. The proliferation of process safety management regulations since the 1984 accident at Bhopal, India, and the widespread acceptance of Lord Cullen's far-reaching safety recommendations following investigations into the 1988 explosion of the offshore rig "Piper Alpha," are good examples of how regulations are spawned by disasters. Australia, Britain, Canada, the United States, and other countries now have laws that hold employees, supervisors, managers, executives, and directors of their companies liable for accidents that seriously injure or kill people. All these laws and regulations have one thing in common—they were put in place after the fact. After mistakes were made and after lives were lost, regulators stepped in to protect the public or the workforce or the environment. These regulators, usually representatives of governments or government agencies, appeared on the scene because businesses were remiss in protecting people or the environment and were deemed not competent to regulate themselves. Today, most businesses complain about over-regulation, sometimes with good reason. The volumes of regulations we are asked to follow are almost impossible to digest, let alone adhere to. In some cases, regulators have probably gone too far and their noble intentions have sometimes led to regulations that are unduly restrictive, overwhelming, and costly to implement. At the same time, it can be argued that without the regulations they imposed, many companies would not have done enough to reduce risks and consequences on their own and some would have failed to take even minimum precautionary measures.

Regulations are society's way of defining minimum expectations that citizens and business must comply with. Regulationscan be a good thing because they do intend to protect the common good. But they are often written in vague terminology that leaves room for misinterpretation and error. Violating these regulations, however, is not a good option. It is bad for business and bad for people. Few companies violate these regulations intentionally. Doing so might kill or hurt people, harm the environment, cause major loss of production, and drive up operating costs. Violations can also result in fines or lawsuits or even the end of the business.

But even when companies are scrupulous about following regulations, bad things do happen. In most cases they happen inadvertently, but this does not make the consequences less harmful. Recognizing potential risks and their consequences and preventing them from occurring is the most important function of the maintenance manager. It is a great responsibility and requires consummate attention. One example of how this works in practice illustrates how significant the maintenance manager's decisions can be.

Running equipment to failure is a legitimate maintenance strategy when used where the consequences of failure can be tolerated. If safety is not compromised, if the environment is not compromised, if the business can tolerate the costs, if the choice is made consciously and with adequate deliberation, then run to failure works well. But this choice must also be a selective choice. Allowing everything to run to failure is an unacceptable choice that will inevitably increase risks and produce unpleasant or harmful consequences. Most companies lie somewhere between these two extremes, consciously allowing some failures, preventing some, and all the while remaining unaware of the potential consequences of others that have not been examined. In our increasingly litigious and heavily regulated social environment, however, errors of omission are seldom tolerated. We all pay the price for others' errors with increased regulation, higher workers' compensation insurance premiums, high liability insurance premiums, environmental taxes, and loss of business. Those who are not diligent invite litigation, more regulations, punitive fines, and worse.

Lord Cullen, one of Britain's most respected judges, has led formal inquiries into several disasters, among them Piper Alpha (July 6, 1988) and the Ladbroke Grove train tragedy in (October 5, 1999). His criticism of management, particularly in the case of Ladbroke Grove, was especially bitter and included the quotation at the start of this chapter. No business wants to be the subject of such a report. No manager wants to be held responsible for environmental disasters or for business failure. Nonetheless, accidents happen because not everything can be predicted. So how do companies prevent this?

The simple answer is to do everything possible to avoid endangering people, the environment, and the businesses. Be aware of the risks, take conscious steps to avoid the dangers, and mitigate the damages. Basic care is all about following the rules and taking small, incremental steps to improve what needs to be improved. It is not about doing all you can; it is about getting started.

BEYOND THE MINIMUM: BASIC CARE

The minimum your business must do is to comply with regulatory requirements. But in a recent benchmark study, some 17 percent of respondents indicated that they did not meet regulatory requirements for their equipment and processes.

Let's assume that your business does not fall into that percentile and that you are in compliance with the minimum levels of protection. If your industry is heavily regulated, you probably feel that you have already done a lot. If your business is in a less regulated industry, you may feel that some of the regulations are a nuisance, but you operate within the law—probably to the minimum standard required. The question here is whether there is more that you can choose to do? The answer is easy: Of course! And the corollary to this is that doing so will benefit your business.

Basic care is all about taking care of equipment at a very basic level. It will not take care of everything, but it will keep you running in reasonably good order and this will provide more uptime.

Think of your plant or fleet of vehicles as if they were your brand new family car. You make sure the oil and fluid levels are maintained, the windshield wipers are in good working order, the brakes work, the tires (including the spare) are fully inflated, the upholstery is clean, the seat belts are working, the child restraints are secure, and the lights work. Periodically, you will also wash the new car. When you wash it, you may find chips in the paint, small cracks in the windshield, or leaks in the door sealing systems. You may also notice oil or transmission fluid leaks on your driveway. When you find those minor defects, you are fairly likely to correct them, especially if they are items that are still under warranty. As the car ages, you are less likely to look after the aesthetic features of the car and focus only on the safety-related features. However, if the car is a vintage classic or your favorite "toy," you will look after it very well, regardless of its age.

Sadly, many companies treat their physical plants as they would treat an old car. The older the physical assets are, the less overall attention they get. Yet these physical assets generate revenue, keep people employed, and produce products that are used by customers. If the family car breaks down, you can always take a bus or a taxi or hitch a ride with a friend. If the plant breaks down, the problem is not as easy to fix and business suffers.

Basic care is all about doing the things that will keep the plant running reliably and safely. There are a variety of things you can do and many sources of information about what to do. Reliability Centered Maintenance and optimization techniques that will move you from mere compliance to truly doing all that you can do are discussed in Chapter 8 and are the most comprehensive approach to analyzing all of your equipment to determine the safe minimum maintenance program. If you are not ready to go that far, there are several basic approaches that will serve you well in the interim. These will help you design a basic maintenance program that works for you in your operating environment.

Maintenance practices recommended by your equipment manufacturers are a good place to start, but be cautious about following them. The manufacturers may not know your operating environment, nor do they know how you are operating their equipment. Their recommendations may not always be entirely appropriate. Your past operating experience may reveal areas of weakness that can be addressed. Your existing maintenance program (if you have one) may already be preventing some failures. On the other hand, it may also be causing some. Regardless of the source of your ideas about what to do, your basic care program will comprise the maintenance work (and sometimes operator work) that makes the most sense to you. Some examples of basic programs that you might choose are listed below.

- Operators to do regular checks of oil levels and to top up lubricants.
- Checklists for use when operators take over operation of equipment.
- A regular set of maintenance "rounds" during which an experienced maintenance supervisor or tradesperson walks around and visually looks for signs of trouble.
- A vibration analysis program for critical and general-purpose rotating equipment.
- An oil sampling and analysis program to look for lubricant deterioration in major equipment.
- A thermal imaging program to look for loose electrical connection "hot spots" and signs of deterioration in thermal insulation on static equipment.
- A cleaning program (with instructions for how to clean specific equipment) that is used to clean up spills, to remove contamination sources, to reveal where leaks are before they get out of hand, and to keep heat transfer surfaces clean.
- Permanently installed monitoring equipment for vibrations, temperatures, and other equipment condition parameters on critical process equipment.

This is not an extensive list, but it covers many of the activities that companies use to go beyond the minimum required by regulations. In striving for higher reliability, these companies ensure that equipment runs longer (more uptime) so it can generate revenue. These activities are all relatively easy to put in place without a great deal of analysis work to justify them. They go a long way but are sometimes overdone.

Some companies follow manufacturers' recommendations a bit too closely. In those cases there is a very good chance that they are doing more work than the minimum needed and doing work that can even create problems. After all, manufacturers do not pay for maintenance costs. Because they do pay for your warranty claims, it is to their advantage to have you do more than necessary after you purchase equipment if this saves them from paying claims. In addition, many manufacturers' recommendations are grounded on little more than "We've always done it this way."

For example, recommendations to overhaul equipment are based on the assumption that after so many running hours or kilometers of use, equipment will be worn out and require restoration. Most equipment, particularly more complex equipment, does not actually wear out—it suffers mostly random failures. Worse still, if you disturb it, you run the risk of inducing a failure. Statistically, this is the most common type of failure, yet many manufacturers still recommend overhauls. Be careful, however, not to dismiss overhaul recommendations entirely because there may be specific failure modes that do respond well to the fixed interval approach. On the other hand, be aware that a complete overhaul may be overkill. The next section on Tactical Options provides guidance on making those decisions.

TACTICAL OPTIONS

Do you replace your car headlights at regular intervals of six months? Do you wait to replace your tires until they wear through? Do you check your car engine oil using spectro-chemical analysis before replacing it? Each component or system in your car has a function that is prone to failure, a consequence that has greater or lesser economic implications. If you run headlights to failure, for example, you can replace them. You cannot tell when they are going to fail; they give you no warning of imminent failure and the consequences of their failure are usually not severe. Running tires to failure, on the other hand, is a different matter altogether. Wear on tires is more obvious and failure can be more easily predicted. The consequences of not replacing worn tires can be fatal.

Similarly, you benefit from knowing the maintenance options available (and necessary) for fleet or plant equipment and machinery because this knowledge helps you decide which actions are the most appropriate. Just as in risk management, your range of options runs the gamut from accepting to avoiding to transferring to reducing whatever the problem or failure may be. The actions you take can be grouped as follows: reactive (accepting the risks), proactive (avoiding, minimizing, or transferring the risks), engineering to design out failures (avoiding or transferring the risks), or consequence reduction (reducing the risks). For each decision you make about what to do, you must also decide when to do it.

Many maintenance actions are repetitive, but "how often?" is an important consideration. Timing maintenance tactics can be

- Scheduled (rigid adherence to some time or usage-based frequency or fixed interval).
- Unscheduled (no fixed interval used at all. This only applies to the reactive approach.)
- Flexibly scheduled (which entails the shifting of scheduled or unscheduled work to convenient "windows of opportunity" when the work can be done with minimal disruption to production. This, of course, implies that the work is something that can be deferred or advanced with minimal consequences.)

Reactive Maintenance

Run–to-failure. Maintenance is performed only after the equipment fails. This is typical for electronic circuit boards and light bulbs. Generally, the equipment that is allowed to run to failure is noncritical to operations, and its failure is tolerable from the perspective of safety, environmental, and business loss consequences. By default, most reactive maintenance will be done on an unscheduled basis, although some repairs can be deferred to a suitable window of opportunity.

Proactive Maintenance

Preventive maintenance. This is based typically on either time or use factors, such as kilometers, cycles, throughput, fuel consumption, and running hours. It is carried out by conducting inspections, cleaning lubrication, minor adjustments, and other failure prevention actions. Often, records of observed condition are kept for trend analysis. This type of maintenance is common in processing sectors (food, pulp and paper, minerals, and chemicals) where there are visual signs of wear and corrosion. Scheduled replacements and overhauls are types of "preventive maintenance."

- *Scheduled component replacement.* At a predetermined point, based on either elapsed time or use, a particular assembly, component, or part is replaced, regardless of its condition. Electric wheel motors in large diesel electric haul trucks are usually replaced on an hours-operated basis, for instance, because the repair expense skyrockets if they are run to failure.

- *Scheduled overhaul.* As with scheduled replacement, the plant or equipment is stripped and overhauled, based on a predetermined plan such as the annual shutdown. This is standard industry practice for petrochemical plants, which take shutdowns on frequencies that vary from one to four years, and in the pulp and paper industry, where machines are often taken down at monthly or quarterly intervals. The schedule itself is driven by a few dominant-failure mechanisms that require periodic action (for example, cleaning filters).

Predictive maintenance. Maintenance consists of two distinct activities, the first of which is recognizing that the equipment is failing and the second of which is correcting the defects. The former is "condition-based monitoring"; the latter is "condition-based maintenance." (Often both are lumped under the heading of "condition-based monitoring," which can be somewhat confusing both in theory and in practice.) In either case, maintaining plant and equipment is based on measured conditions. When the condition being measured falls outside acceptable limits, corrective repairs are made.

Maintaining plant and equipment is based on measured conditions.

Engineering Approach (Design-out Maintenance)

Redundancy. Redundancy is built into an equipment system. If the primary unit fails, the secondary unit is available. All maintenance managers know that having a spare is an excellent way to guard against loss of service. Unfortunately, this is also an expensive option that is (or should be) limited to situations where failure is absolutely unacceptable. Note that redundancy does not eliminate the failures or maintenance action; it merely allows service to continue even when failures occur. Adding redundancy adds assets and cost as well as the potential for additional failure modes and maintenance.

Redesign. Designing out maintenance is used particularly for critical equipment where it is difficult to measure the condition or detect imminent failure. A good example of effective redesign is the automobile industry. In the 1940s, sedans had a practical speed limit of about 60 km/h. Roads were rough and the cars often had loose nuts and bolts, marginal suspension systems, and inefficient power trains. Engine oil and the cable controlled braking system had to be checked frequently. Today, the top speeds are whatever you can get away with, the car bodies are unitized, and the suspensions are robust. The "information center" on the dashboard monitors the condition of everything from the engine to the door locks. Hydraulic disc brakes last longer than the engines did in the 1940s, and maintenance intervals are now being measured in the tens of thousands of kilometers. Redesign entails identification of the cause of recurring or otherwise unacceptable problems that result from defects and then changing the design to eliminate the defects.

The redesign approach fits very well within the modern quality concepts of Six Sigma, but it is important to remember that it is a "fallback" option that has a root cause. Unless you design your systems right from the outset, the engineering approach to maintenance improvement is almost always the most expensive. Fittingly, the analysis that is used for redesign purposes is often called "Root Cause Failure Analysis" or simply "Root Cause Analysis."

Equipment Upgrade. This is a form of "redesign" that is often performed to increase equipment capacity. In aging plants where capacity increases are being considered, there is an opportunity to enhance reliability and maintainability. During the redesign effort it is common to perform improvements that also enhance maintainability and reliability. Of course, equipment upgrade should only be used to address known problems; don't use capacity increase as an excuse to fiddle needlessly.

Selecting Tactics

Selecting the correct maintenance tactic has its own challenges, which can be somewhat offset by RCM and Preventive Maintenance Optimization (PMO). In the absence of these tools, however, you still have to determine which action and schedule is most appropriate when considering costs, plant downtime, and other risks. From a technical viewpoint, you should always understand how failure happens and if there is any way you can predict or prevent it. If not, decide on whether or not you can live with it (reactive) or to design it out (usually the most expensive option).

Maintenance is usually time-based for a car, but very few car components actually fail simply because of elapsed time. Body finish and corrosion to the chassis and aging elastomers are exceptions. Nonetheless, it is hard to shake the notion that something is more likely to fail the older it is and the more it has been used. It is more likely that a car will fail as it gets older (cumulative probability of failure), but it is not more likely that it will fail at any given age (conditional probability of failure). As this analogy suggests, time-based or usage-based maintenance generally assumes that there is some identifiable "end of useful life." While this is certainly true some of the time, it is not always the case. For this approach to work at all, it is first necessary to identify a distinct "end of useful life." Often this applies only to cases with a very limited number of dominant failure mechanisms at work.

When is it economical to replace an asset? For assets that we repair in an effort to restore original condition there is an age effect due to the repairs. The cumulative effects of past repairs, none of which return the asset (e.g., your car) all the way to its "as new" condition, will be to allow its overall condition to degrade gradually as it ages. This gradually reduces its resistance to failure so the time between failures decreases with age and the car becomes less economical to repair. Eventually it is replaced and the cycle starts again. Where you are repairing assets watch the costs closely and specifically the rate of spending on repairs for that point at which replacement becomes more economic than continuing to repair.

Another common view of age-related failure is what is commonly known as the biological model or the "bathtub curve." This thinking contends that equipment has a greater chance of failing when very "young" and then goes through a stable period until it becomes unreliable because it is very "old" and has passed its "useful life." The chance of equipment failing at any given time is known as "conditional probability of failure." This happens in only a few cases.

Detailed research[1] into equipment failures has produced some interesting findings. The most significant finding is that there is

1. F. S. Nowlan and H. Heap, *Reliability-centered Maintenance* (Springfield, Virginia: National Technical Information Service, U.S. Department of Commerce, 1978).

rarely a strong link between age and failure. Another is that there are six broad relationships of conditional probability of failure to time, not just one or two. These are illustrated in Figure 4-1, adapted from the Nowlan and Heap report, where operating age is the basis for initiating repair or overhaul. The vertical axis represents conditional probability of failure. The percentages represent the proportion of aircraft components that exhibited these patterns. Note that the first two (A & B) have a point at the right-hand end of the curves where conditional probability of failure increases dramatically. That point effectively delineates the useful life of the component. Pattern C is also age-related but does not have a clearly defined end of useful life, however it has a point at which resistance to failure is no longer tolerable. The final three patterns show no relationship of conditional probability of failure to age at all.

With increased operating age, the cumulative probability of failure increases and eventually all items in the population will fail. The six broad relationships of conditional probability of failure to time are defined on the following page.

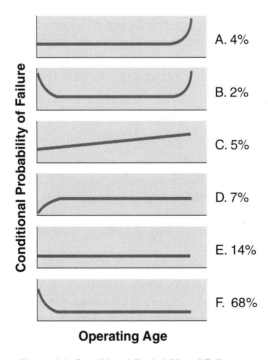

Operating Age

Figure 4-1. Conditional Probability of Failure

A—Worst old

This is a wear-out pattern and applies to simple components where the dominant failure mode is that of wearing out. Items that are in contact with each other, with a product (rocks, slurries, powders, resins, etc.), or with another surface (a roadbed) tend to wear out over time.

B—Bathtub

This occurs in systems or devices with more than one dominant failure mode. One will have pattern A (wear out) and another may be more random in nature (pattern F). An example of this would be home electronic devices, such as VCRs and DVD players. The electronics tend to suffer in a random mode with a tendency to higher infant mortality (hence the need for manufacturers' warranties), but the mechanical drive components will gradually deteriorate due to dirt and wear as the equipment ages. This is also representative of biological systems like the human body. There is a high risk of death near birth and again much later in life. In between, death results from a great number of random effects and events.

For patterns A and B, fixed interval maintenance based on operating age or usage is appropriate as is condition monitoring for random failures that occur prior to that fixed interval replacement age.

C—Slow aging

This also occurs in simple components with a single dominant failure mode and is typified by fatigue, corrosion, or erosion failures. A device gradually deteriorates at a steady rate; eventually, it is no longer useful or it breaks. Pipes, refractory materials, rubber tires, paints, surface coatings, and structural elements all exhibit this gradual deterioration.

Fixed interval maintenance based on operating age or usage is appropriate here as is condition monitoring for random failures that occur prior to fixed interval replacement age. Note, however, that the replacement age should be based on the age to which cumulative probability of failure remains tolerable, as there is no obvious end of useful life point.

D—Best new

This occurs in complex systems that are assembled by highly qualified technicians in a carefully controlled environment and then turned over to less qualified operators in a less controlled production environment. Hydraulic and pneumatic systems are examples.

E—Constant

This pattern, which is common in more complex devices and systems, shows no relationship between conditional probability of failure and operating age. The failure causes are all random. This pattern is also exhibited in systems that have pattern F characteristics when they have been run-in for a period of time before being put into service. Many rolling element bearings and electronic systems commonly exhibit this pattern, although caution should be exercised in assuming they all do. Some rolling element bearings also fail with pattern B.

F—Worst new

This is the most common failure pattern for complex equipment and systems. For most of the life of the system, failures are random; there is, however, a period of time when infant mortality is common. This is common in plants, systems, or vehicles that have been shutdown for overhaul work. They often experience some start-up problems that must be corrected before they settle down to a relatively long period of reliable operation in which purely random events take their toll.

Age or usage-based interventions are of limited value for patterns D, E, and F. Condition monitoring will be most effective at revealing failures that have already begun but not yet progressed to the point of loss of function.

This study was the result of work performed over 30 years ago and is confined to failures in aircraft components. Since then, far more complex control systems, computerization and extensive automation, and mechanization in virtually all of our equipment and systems have been introduced. The change has been driven by advancing technology and by rising labor rates. Since much of this new technology exhibits random failure characteristics, it adds even more randomness to the behavior of equipment and systems. It makes sense to adjust maintenance practices to suit. Although the statistical distributions of these failure patterns may have shifted *slightly* with time and from industry to industry, the 30-year-old study remains remarkably relevant and provides some important tips about equipment maintenance:

- Failure is not usually related directly to age or use; fixed interval maintenance intervention will not always work.
- Failure is not easily predicted, so restorative or replacement maintenance based on time or use will not normally help to improve the failure odds.
- Major overhauls can be a bad idea because you can end up at a higher failure probability in the most dominant patterns. Random events are more common than age-related events.

It is also important to understand that many failure mechanisms (both random and otherwise) provide some warning that failure has been initiated and is progressing (e.g., bearing vibrations increase, temperatures increase). These signals can be used as the basis for a condition-monitoring program that allows time to respond with planned intervention.

Determining the correct failure pattern is enabled by careful scrutiny of the available failure data. Weibull analysis is a statistical technique that is useful in determining if a failure is age related, random, or the result of infant mortality. Unfortunately, while most maintenance management systems use some form of database for this purpose, the data are often corrupt or incomplete. Brainstorming with an experienced operator (the mechanic or electrician), the service representative for the original equipment manufacturer, the area planner, or the clerk who manages the equipment histories can reveal a great deal. In the absence of solid statistical data this "tribal knowledge" is the best indicator you are likely to find. Never underestimate its value.

If you can live with the consequences of a failure, try statistical sampling studies over several months. You will end up with some useful information, particularly if there are several similar units in operation. If you cannot accept the consequences of a failure, use a proactive method for identifying failures before they occur—Reliability-Centered Maintenance or PM Optimization are the best options.

Knowing the failure pattern does not necessarily tell you what maintenance tactic will be the best to use and you should always consider the economic implications of tactics you are weighing. When the steering clutch on a tracked dozer was analyzed, age-related failure patterns were found. But an economic study revealed that it was actually more cost-effective to allow the clutch to run to failure than to replace it, despite good prospects of predicting a PM replacement schedule because the failure pattern was age-related. Similarly, one major electric utility opted to systematically operate hundreds of 3-phase ganged switches on its distribution systems in order to catch failures before they occurred. Managers eventually realized that there were far fewer failures to deal with per year than the number of overhauls that would have to be performed if manufacturer's recommendations were followed. By performing scheduled switching operations in an orderly manner, the utility avoided customer interruptions and dramatically reduced incidents of "stuck" switches. Remember that although some activities are technically doable, they may not be economically justified. It is always a good idea to check the costs of your proposed maintenance tactics against the costs of doing nothing and allowing the devices to fail.

CONDITION-BASED MAINTENANCE

Condition-based maintenance is usually the most effective option because it uses the early warning signs of a failure in progress. This allows time to act before the failure mechanism progresses to complete loss of function (see Figure 4-2). Checking for those warning signs is condition-based monitoring (or condition monitoring); correcting the problems you find is condition-based maintenance (or on-condition maintenance). The warning signs of failure may be subtle or give you very little time to react. However, when they are more obvious and there is more warning time, you will have more opportunity to intervene without affecting the equipment excessively.

Key equipment with components that fail in a progressive manner, rather than without warning, is a good candidate for condition monitoring. Typical components that benefit are dynamic (moving) mechanical units or connecting devices (like electrical connectors). Those components that do not benefit include integrated electronic

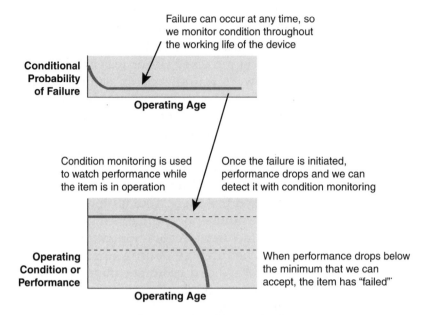

Failure can occur at any time, so we monitor condition throughout the working life of the device

Conditional Probability of Failure

Operating Age

Condition monitoring is used to watch performance while the item is in operation

Once the failure is initiated, performance drops and we can detect it with condition monitoring

Operating Condition or Performance

When performance drops below the minimum that we can accept, the item has "failed'"

Operating Age

Figure 4-2. Condition Monitoring

circuits, which usually fail suddenly and without warning. Selecting the most appropriate method or measurement depends on several factors:

- The failure mechanism itself.
- The reliability of the method chosen.
- The warning time it gives.
- The cost of monitoring (both initial and ongoing) and the cost of repair once the fault is found.
- The skill level required to monitor and interpret the measure.
- The cost of the failure and its consequences if you allow it to run to failure.

It is easier to manage cost and skill level if you can use two or three common methods to monitor critical components of important equipment. To illustrate, most small- to medium-sized businesses concentrate on fluid and wear particle monitoring from lubricating and hydraulic fluid systems. They also tend to have some basic methods of vibration analysis for dynamic devices and thermography for static devices and most electrical equipment. Obviously, this is dependent on the type of equipment in use—

high power, high temperature, high speed, etc. One technical solution does not fit for all failures, so tailoring of your condition-monitoring program is essential.

Vibration

Vibration analysis monitors the mechanical movement of a machine. Based on a regular schedule, you watch for vibration levels that exceed a predetermined range or baseline. The vibration signal can also be used to diagnose the location of the problem. The most common vibration sources are misalignment, imbalance, and the imminent failure in rolling element bearings. Defining the problem usually involves looking at the amplitude (how much movement), frequency (how fast), and phase (how a machine is vibrating). Vibration analysis is commonly applied to compressors, pumps, turbines, fans, paper machines, and other large rotating equipment. The accuracy of the readings and hence the value of the diagnosis you can derive from them, is heavily influenced by background vibration or noise levels, equipment loads, speeds, and temperature. These environmental factors should be controlled it you want to obtain useful data on which to base your equipment condition decisions.

For example, the pasteurization area of a brewery had a fixed-time overhaul schedule on the pumps for its 30 units each year. At a cost of five tradesperson days and $1,200 in parts and materials per pump, this added up to over $60,000 per year and about 75 days with at least one of the pumps out of service for overhaul. A fixed-time vibration analysis schedule was set. Consequently, only one pump per year was overhauled based on the readings obtained. The cost for that was $2,000, an increase that resulted from finding defects that required more parts usage. The brewery also considered the ongoing monitoring cost of an additional $2,000 and 2.5 down days for the one pump. The condition monitoring was indeed worthwhile doing.

Lubricants

Lubricant analysis (spectrographic, ferrographic, chemical, etc.) involves lubricating oil condition, wear particle count, and physical observation. Physical and chemical analysis of the oil—the viscosity and acidity, for example—are periodically compared to a baseline to check for deterioration. The size and shape, as well as a chemical analysis, of the wear particles can indicate the suitability of the oil, the component that is wearing, and the likely wear mechanism. One railway uses lubricant analysis coupled with an expert system that helped interpret the analysis results to schedule all of its PM routines, component replacements, and locomotive overhauls. This practice has become widespread in many industries including mining, petrochemical, refining, pulp and paper, and metals processing. Airlines have been using this technique for years.

Temperature

Thermography—mapping the surface temperature using an infrared camera or other imaging device—is useful when it can be related to the condition of the equipment. Corona discharge, hot electrical connections, refractory lining defects, insulation on static electrical equipment, roofing and its insulation, misaligned and overheating machinery couplings, and even inflamed human and animal tissue are prime candidates for this condition-monitoring tool. One example is a typical infrared survey of power lines, substations, main disconnects, and breakers carrying high currents. Problems such as loose connections, deteriorated splices, cracked insulators, and tarnished or charred connections increase current density and cause temperature increases that can be detected. One of North America's largest electrical distribution utilities has a contractor who drives along all of its overhead power lines annually, scanning them with infrared detectors to identify defects for corrective action. A large nickel smelting operation in Southeast Asia introduced infrared scans of its electrical equipment and quickly identified loose connections in switchgear and overhead switchyard apparatus that were quickly repaired. Those actions avoided what most certainly would have led to severe power outages and major plant shutdowns. The infrared monitoring equipment (and the related training) paid for itself from the first day it was used.

System Performance

Condition monitoring also looks at equipment and system performance for signs of problems. Precision or quality of the product produced and its cycle time can also be observed. An increase in rejects can indicate problems. At breweries, for example, optical monitoring of fluid level in beer bottles is used to determine if the bottles are over- or underfilled. If the reject rate increases, there is clearly a problem with the filling line. Pressure, temperature, flow, amperage, resistance, voltage, and other factors are also observed. A recent study[2] performed for the electronics industry shows that electronic "noise" generated by solid state micro-electronic components as they deteriorate through surface electromigration can be detected by using discrete smoothed pseudo-Wiger Ville distribution (DSPWVD) technology. This brings electronics, previously thought to be unresponsive to condition monitoring, into the realm of what can be monitored, although more work is needed to make these methods practical for industrial use. All of these parameters lend themselves to monitoring long-term trends in equipment performance and degradation.

Condition monitoring is usually very cost-effective. Typically it requires little training to do properly, and it is nonintrusive—the equipment can be monitoring while it is running. In fact, most condition monitoring can be done only while equipment is running under its normal operating conditions. Depending on the method, it can be done by a semiskilled operator and often indicates both equipment condition and product quality. In fact, the equipment operator using his five senses is your most versatile and valuable condition monitor. Of course, this individual is subject to human limitations—not everyone will sense the same problems or signals the same way or interpret what is sensed the same way every time. For critical applications, specialized monitoring devices and equipment are often easily justified.

There are more than 100 condition monitoring and nondestructive testing techniques, with more sophisticated ones being developed each year. A discussion of these is beyond the scope of this book.[3] However, for specialized, critical equipment, all associated data should be reliable and precise because of safety, environmental,

---

2. Cher Min Tan and Shin Yeh Lim, "Application of Wiger-Ville Distribution in Electromigration Noise Analysis," IEEE Transaction on Device and Materials Reliability, Vol. 2, No. 2, June 2002.
3. Refer to Appendix 4 of *Reliability-Centered Maintenance* by John M. Moubray for a more extensive listing and explanation of these methods.

or economic risks. A sophisticated condition-monitoring approach is worth the investigation and investment.

PREVENTIVE MAINTENANCE

Preventive maintenance can reduce failures and emergency repairs. It promotes equipment awareness and disciplined inspection. It also works well for simple components that become less reliable as they age. In these cases, failures can be reduced by a logical overhaul or replacement schedule.

The first step in developing a PM program is to classify equipment and key components by failure pattern. They are either age-related or they are not. For those that are not, consider condition monitoring. For those that are:

- Set a standard condition, range, or function.
- Prepare inspection, overhaul, change-out, adjustment routines, and schedules.
- Establish record-keeping, histories, and trending statistics.
- Organize for analysis and periodic updating, based on the results of the routines and schedules.

In all cases, make sure that the cost of the monitoring or preventive action is warranted when compared with the costs (or other risks) of allowing the equipment to run to failure.

THE COST OF THE TACTICS

It is almost irrelevant to discuss the cost of maintenance without considering what you are buying. The job of maintenance is to keep equipment running so that it continues to do what we want it to do. If it is done only in a reactive way, after breakdowns occur, downtime and subsequent repair bills will most likely be high. Remember that unplanned work, especially work done under "emergency" conditions, tends to be the most expensive. Being proactive is usually less expensive, but be aware that there is a point of diminishing returns. Like any other business problem, this requires analysis in order to make the most informed decision that maximizes value to your company.

When you start using preventive maintenance, even simple tasks like checking lubrication and changing out badly worn components can reduce the number of unexpected failures. Production losses also decline. A preventive approach will mean more shut-downs to inspect, adjust, overhaul, replace, and test. These delays can cost you money in lost production time, but at the same time, emergency repairs will taper off.

At some point there is a minimum on the total cost curve that represents the optimum balance between the cost of emergencies and that of proactive maintenance. This is shown in Figure 4-3.

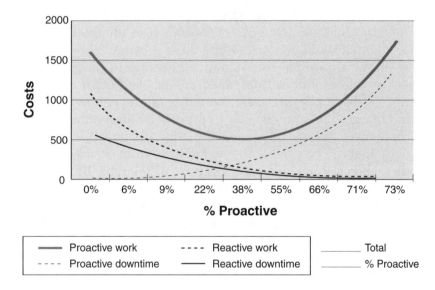

Figure 4-3. Total Cost of Maintenance

To take care of your equipment truly well, use a combination of experience, proper data collection and analysis, good engineering, and teamwork. When combined, these will help you begin your advance toward the minimum point in the total-cost-of-maintenance curve and truly add value to your business.

UPTIME SUMMARY

Like the human body, our plant and mobile equipment will break down if they are not looked after. They will tolerate some abuse but they won't do it forever and they won't do it if you don't take care of them at a basic level. Basic care is all about taking care of our physical assets so they continue to do what we need them to do. To choose excellence, it is essential to master the basics. They keep you compliant with regulations and keep you operating. Go beyond the basics and you expand in the direction of excellence.

Physical assets are needed, first and foremost, to deliver uptime for production and other operational uses like service delivery. More uptime produces greater revenue generating potential. While operating, physical assets must comply with various regulations regarding safety and environmental emissions; ideally they should also be efficient so they do not consume excessive amounts of energy (i.e., fuel, electric power). Basic care is all about meeting these minimal standards. Exceeding them is better.

Without a minimal maintenance program in place you can expect to suffer failures, unplanned outages and other disruptive events. As the old saying goes, "an ounce of prevention is worth a pound of cure." It is far cheaper to prevent a failure than to repair it. There are a variety of proactive maintenance tactics and technologies that can be used to prevent failures from occurring and to predict when failures will progress beyond tolerable limits. These buy time to plan contingency action to minimize the consequences of those pending failures. There are also the options of redesigning the asset to eliminate the failures or doing nothing and letting the asset run to failure. All of these are acceptable under the right circumstances.

Understanding the nature of failure mechanisms, their consequences, and the available failure management tactics enables maintenance managers to make intelligent decisions about the best course of action. Basic care includes making these decisions so you get reliable service from your assets. Methods for doing this in an orderly fashion are covered in Chapter 8.

5

Materials Management

Bitter experience in war has taught the maxim that the
art of war is the art of the logistically feasible.
ADMIRAL HYMAN RICKOVER, USN

Although no one is actually fighting a war in our maintenance departments, there are certainly times when it feels that way. Almost always, the worst battles are over critical parts or materials that are needed immediately but are not where they need to be. Maintenance managers tangle with suppliers to find out about material availability, with their own purchasing departments to get the paperwork done, with plant managers to get the approval for premium pricing, and so on. It is no fun and it almost never has to happen.

Planning efforts are for naught if maintenance schedules work without having materials available, so it is critical to have the right materials available when they are needed. At the same time, it is critical to keep costs under control and balanced. Excessive investment in parts and materials ties up working capital. Too little investment will fail to serve maintenance and business needs when failures occur. Moreover, to ensure that their accounting statements are accurate, accountants want to book the investment in material inventories as visible assets, not as hidden costs. With today's tight financial controls, managing inventory becomes more important than ever; however, if that inventory is properly managed, it will be used two or three times a year and help keep maintenance costs down.

THE MATERIALS MANAGEMENT PROCESS

A key to success in work management is the timely provision of the materials and parts for maintenance work. The lack of even one part can delay the job, add to the cost, increase total downtime for the asset itself and possibly for the process it belongs to. It increases business risk even if the item being repaired has a backup.

The consumption of maintenance, repair and overhaul (MRO) supplies—spare parts, components, consumables, lubricants, fasteners and all other maintenance materials—typically accounts for about one-half of most companies' maintenance budgets. As more and more of our industrial equipment and fleets are designed for increasingly more expensive modular parts replacement, material costs devour an increasing portion of the budget. In many companies this is neglected. If the processes are not working, maintenance supervisors often react by creating their own unofficial stockpiles of inventory—off the books. If the stores-keepers are not getting input from maintenance, they start decreasing inventories based on the aging of the parts in inventory; the longer inventory sits collecting dust, the more likely it is to be scrapped or sold off. Of course these two reactions set up the conditions for a downward spiral which satisfies no one.

In one very large North American integrated steel mill, there was an estimated $108 million in spares and materials on site, but only about $18 million could actually be accounted for in controlled inventories. The rest was hidden, squirreled away by maintenance supervisors and tradespeople. This inventory was not on the books and generated a big accounting headache when eventually auditors found it. Parts that are hidden away like this are rarely available to anyone but the person who has hidden them and that leads to duplication of parts among various stashes and with the stores. The practice of keeping stashed parts inflates operating expenses, bloats inventory, and ties up working capital—none of which is good for business. Maintenance managers, supervisors, and tradespersons will argue with some validity that if they do not keep these stashes, they cannot do their jobs. If this is indeed the case, the materials management system has let them down. What they often fail to see, however, is that they have had a hand in creating the problem by working around the system instead of working with it or fixing it. They have also exacerbated their own materials headaches!

Often, if there's a problem with maintenance getting its job done there is also an underlying problem with MRO materials management. To get it "right" requires:

- Good communication between maintenance and materials people,
- Well-defined and working linkages between Work Management and MRO Management processes,
- Discipline to follow the processes and not to work around them, and
- A clear delineation of who is responsible for what work when it comes to materials procurement (maintenance and engineering provide the specifications, and materials management handles the supply chain).

The basic processes of purchasing, stores, and inventory control are shown on the right-hand side of Figure 5-1. As the figure shows, this process has several links with the Work Management process. If one or both of those two processes is not working properly or if any of the links are not working properly, then maintenance and materials costs go up. The following sections describe each of the materials management process steps.

Specify

This first step is simply defining what is required, and the best people to do this are maintainers and engineers because they know what they want. Specifying the correct parts is facilitated if there is an equipment register—an accurate, updated record of the equipment configuration. In the register, each major equipment assembly or system is broken down into the smallest component or part that can be bought as a unit. For older equipment you may have lists of all the individual parts. Newer equipment, particularly electronic or instrumentation, tends to have several integrated components that are changed out and returned to the manufacturer for repair or simply discarded and replaced. If your records are accurate, the rest of the materials process will be simplified.

Of course, not all the materials are found on parts lists. Bar stock, fasteners, lubricants, adhesives, and a host of other materials are generally not listed, but should be considered necessary materials. In either case, specifying precisely what you want is a critical

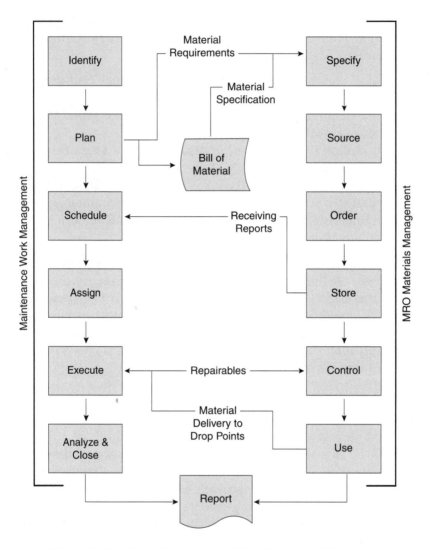

Figure 5-1. The Linked Materials and Work Management Processes

first step. If you specify the wrong or substandard materials, you are likely to shorten the useful life of the equipment.

The specifications for parts and materials should be clear and unambiguous so that your supply chain staff (buyers, stock clerks, and suppliers) will know what it is you really want. Specifying a "drive end bearing for motor M-33" will only invite questions. If you want a certain part or material from a specific supplier because of quality requirements or unique tolerances, then make sure your buyers are aware of that. If you do not, buyers will tend to shop around for the best deal and end up buying the wrong parts. If equivalent parts from various suppliers are acceptable, use the words "or equal" when specifying any particular vendor's part identification—a sign to your buyers that it is OK to shop around.

Your MRO inventory contains the parts and materials you anticipate using at some time. That includes fast-moving parts and materials as well as some slow-moving but critical items. Over time, inventory holdings go "stale." This happens when the equipment certain parts are used for has been removed and the parts for it remain in stores. In the interests of keeping inventory holdings (and their costs) down you want to eliminate those items from stores and minimize the slow-moving inventory. That inventory, however, will often also include hard-to-get parts that are being held as "insurance" against major failures. Some of those parts may be critical to your operation but are no longer being produced. It is important that those items be identified to the inventory management staff so they are not discarded or sold during regular inventory "clean-up" efforts.

Source

Once maintenance and engineering have specified the materials they want, the request is turned over to your supply chain to handle the acquisition process. Supply chain staff will get what you asked for and attempt to get the best pricing available.

Vendor management used to be a win-lose situation, and confrontations between buyer and seller were the order of the day. Buying strategy often dictated going for the lowest price of three or more bids for each purchase. Today, this can be an expensive process, especially when you consider that maintenance supplies typically generate a large volume of small value orders. In most production plants, MRO inventory accounts for less than 20 percent of the spending but 80 percent or more of the buying activity. An example of how costly this can be is what occurred when a purchasing agent at a public board of education was required by policy to send out a request for proposal for a $2,000 project to all qualified vendors—sixty-three of them! The cost of the "politically correct" bidding process far exceeded the cost of the project. This is a flagrant waste that few companies can afford. Fortunately most owners and shareholders, unlike taxpayers, generally have the option of refusing to engage in such practices.

A much more productive approach is to develop a supplier partnership. You lock yourself in with a trustworthy supplier for one, two, or more years, and work together to try to improve the overall value of the transaction to both. You gain lower cost overall, higher quality and better service, while your supplier gains a relatively long-term arrangement with a stable business. In many of these relationships the price you pay for some parts may not be the lowest possible price, but don't forget that this is offset by the overall value of the contract and its administration. High service levels from your suppliers will reduce your order lead-times. In turn, this reduces the inventory levels needed to obtain the same level of spares availability, your inventory and carrying costs, and ties up less working capital. A supplier that has a strategic supply partnership with a major customer will be willing to carry the inventory levels necessary to maintain that relationship and service.

This approach has been highly successful for many North American industries. Today, for example, North American automotive companies compete globally on a cost, quality, and time-to-market basis with Japanese and European manufacturers. A great deal of manufacturing has been moving offshore to low-cost labor markets in order to drive costs down. Many automotive parts for U.S. and Canadian built cars are supplied from plants in Mexico. Electronic components are increasingly being manufactured at lower costs throughout Asia. Your own MRO materials are a significant part of your operating costs so, just like your overseas competitors, you will want to keep those costs down.

Utilizing a few major suppliers who provide most of your MRO supplies is known as "Strategic Sourcing." With this approach, you have a relatively small number of contracts with those strategic suppliers. Today's enterprise management systems can get tremendous value from these arrangements. A global pharmaceutical company, for example, cut 17 percent from its materials costs by using this approach. The company aggregated many of its material requirements from several production facilities in the United States and Puerto Rico and purchased them from only a few key suppliers through a central purchasing group. Some items were indeed more expensive than those available locally, but the overall savings were substantial. Not only did materials costs drop, but the cost to purchase them dropped, as there were fewer transactions and fewer buyers to manage.

Order

Once the specifications and the supplier are known, the part can be ordered. Items kept in an inventory holding account (a balance sheet account as opposed to an income statement account) are normally ordered once the minimum or order point has been reached. The final user is not involved because the inventory management system creates the order automatically as soon as the stock holding drops to a preset level. Because the authority to order was established when the order point was approved, circulating paper order forms for approval signatures becomes redundant.

Many maintainers make the mistake of assuming that catalogue items are also stock items—they are not. Inventory items are stock items that are actually held in stores. Catalogue items are items that you probably purchase, or anticipate purchasing, on a regular basis. They are specified and given stock numbers; their suppliers are known and possibly even under contract so that purchasing can acquire them easily. For catalogue items, most of the buying paperwork is already done so they are quicker to acquire than noncatalogue items. Stock items are always catalogue items, but catalogue items are not necessarily stock items. For example, items you want for planned shutdowns may be catalogue items but not held in stock as inventory because your shutdowns have long lead times that are sufficient for the ordering and delivery cycle.

Items not kept in the maintenance stores can be ordered by the user and are known as direct purchase items. Some of those will be catalogue items and some will not. Your buyers will often ask for approval before adding noncatalogue direct purchase items to their catalogue. If you anticipate ordering these items again, it is a good idea to say "yes." To simplify ordering, many businesses have only one or two maintenance people (often your planners) placing requisitions with the buyers to avoid duplication and to allow for grouping of requests. Today's integrated enterprise management systems have direct links from maintenance planning to requisitioning from stores and from suppliers (via the purchasing process) to facilitate this sometimes complicated process.

The need for maintainers and planners to do "direct purchase" of materials usually reveals flaws in the inventory management system. Direct purchase items effectively bypass inventory management, going directly from source to user. Watch the volume of direct purchases. If it is high, you probably have an inventory management problem.

Some organizations resort to purchasing cards, also known as P-cards, for purchases by maintenance supervisors or tradespersons. This seems convenient and it does help if unplanned material requirements arise at odd hours, but it is a result of errors in planning, or worse, no planning at all. These transactions are usually difficult to trace back to a work order so the history of materials used for these jobs is lost. That is unfortunate because these jobs were probably important enough to justify the use of the P-card in the first place. Generally the widespread use of P-cards is a symptom of underlying problems in the basic maintenance management processes.

A practice that fortunately is becoming increasingly rare is to allow maintenance supervisors to buy directly from suppliers, bypassing the purchasing process. This is very convenient for maintenance but is not recommended. Although it can be a big help in emergency situations, it can easily lead to the same sort of problems that arise with P-cards. This practice requires a high degree of cooperation between vendors and maintainers because they are supplying goods on the basis of a handshake. Again, it is a clear signal that other problems exist.

Store

The core job of maintenance stores is to receive stock and issue MRO materials for use. They also receive returns of unused materials, dispose of scrap, arrange for the repair of repairable items, and, in some cases, even maintain inventory items on the shelves. Numerous factors affect the efficiency of the stores, from layout to the use of enabling technologies. Many storerooms have quarantine areas where newly received materials and parts await receipt inspection. If the sourcing step in this process is done correctly, much of the receiving inspection work can be eliminated. One company's solution to a 35 percent rejection rate of incoming maintenance supplies (by maintenance) was to add receiving inspectors in stores. That dealt very well with the problem as maintenance saw it, but it did not deal with the source of the problem—poor specification and poor compliance with specifications by suppliers.

In addition to normal receiving, there is also a direct-order receiving area, for parts ordered by the users from suppliers. As previously noted, direct orders reveal potential flaws in your inventory management processes and keep inventory off the books. These special receiving areas only serve to institutionalize the problems rather than solve them. Paradoxically, the area is normally managed aggressively to ensure that direct purchase items are given to those who ordered them for imminent use. Without this sort of aggressive management, parts and materials can become obsolete before they are unwrapped.

Many poorly run stores have shelves full of direct order materials with no work-order tag or other identifying information. That information is used to ensure that parts get used and to avoid the risk of double ordering by the maintenance planners. In some organizations, these materials make their way to the maintenance shops or some other plant area where they end up being stored for use "just-in-case." They are often forgotten or discovered only after they have been reordered. In one steel mill, a large roll intended for use in a press during an upcoming shutdown was received and left outside in a large materials lay-down area without proper documentation. Winter came and the roll was buried in snow. Several weeks before the shutdown, someone in maintenance noticed that the roll was missing and the mill rush-ordered a new one at a cost of $250,000. A couple of months later the snow melted and the stores people, wanting to make space in their lay-down area, decided to scrap the original roll. One alert mechanic, who just happened to be in the area on the day it was being lifted onto a flatbed, recognized it and asked the stores people what they were doing with it. His inquiry saved the roll, but it still sat for another year and half, tying up working capital, before it was used. The take-home message here is that parts, even very expensive parts, that sit long enough in direct purchase receiving areas may be thrown out as scrap. These materials are not controlled, and as this example illustrates, they drive up costs.

Storage conditions are also important for many items. Items in stores should always be stored properly in a clean location. In some cases, temperature, humidity, and exposure to light must be controlled to ensure a long shelf life. In addition, some items received are not shipped the same way they should be stored, and this must be dealt with so that the items remain in usable condition. Storage conditions should be specified for all inventory items, and the specifications should be rigorously applied.

Control

Companies often tie their maintenance stores inventory to the number of active tradespeople they employ and may spend from $30,000 to $80,000 per person. As a rule of thumb, the value of your material usage will be roughly equal to the unburdened cost of your labor. The prime issue with this investment is its efficiency and productivity. If it is fast moving, turning over at a reasonable rate (say, twice per year or better), your inventory level (not including capital or insurance spares) will be about half your unburdened annual labor budget. On the other hand, your inventory may comprise mostly "insurance spares," with one-third or more of the investment still parked (no issues) after 24 months. Because depreciation rules vary widely, there is no rule of thumb for insurance spares value. Moreover, they are a sunk cost and their book value is irrelevant anyway. Their value to the company is driven by their potential operational value (as insurance), the cost of carrying them vs. their salvage value. Consider these facts before you decide whether you really want them in your inventory.

Your inventory of spares and materials is normally measured and managed rigorously. It deserves the same scrutiny as your raw materials, work-in-process, and finished goods inventory. Although shrinkage is not normally a major issue, free access to the storeroom, something the maintainers will want, is not advantageous. It is easy to lose track of what is actually in the stores. Maintainers are often in a hurry to do their jobs so accurate reporting of issues and returns is not their priority. If they can walk in, grab what they want, and walk out with it, they often will. The paperwork gets ignored and the result is invariably a high level of stock adjustments and stockouts. Your inventory records won't accurately reflect what you actually have in stores, and faith in the entire system may be shattered. Free access should be granted only to fast-moving, low-value, common items such as fasteners, piping, steel fittings, and the like, and ideally at the workplace where they are used. The cost of managing these items closely often exceeds the cost of losses such as shrinkage due to spoilage (dirt accumulation, rust, aging of elastomers), so free issue management is warranted. Note that spoilage of some items (e.g., elastomeric o-rings) can result in hazardous consequences if the items are used in a critical service. Be especially wary of managing these items as "free issue." Many companies today are having success with vendors managing these ready-use inventories for them. They pay for what they actually use on one monthly invoice and let the vendor worry about the details. Some companies have concerns about their vendors, fearing that they will be "ripped off" by overinvoicing and inflated reports of actual usage. In most cases, your vendors are highly unlikely to cheat. Fear of getting caught and having the word spread is a good incentive to avoid such practices because it can destroy a business overnight. If you do not trust a particular vendor for some reason, the best solution is to find a vendor you do trust. There is little value in entering into "vendor-managed inventory" contracts to save your own stores and administration time if you end up spending time checking up on the vendors. Observe too, that if you are afraid of attracting vendors that would cheat you, it is because you know that if the opportunity arose, you too might take advantage of them. Change that willingness on your part and you will notice a remarkable shift in the business relationships you create with others.

Repairable items—components taken out of service, rebuilt, and returned through the inventory control system—can create major problems. There are as many ways of handling these problems as there are plants that have them. Usually, the problem is the cost accounting of repaired components. To capture the cost of the repair on the correct work order some companies make the mistake of letting maintenance manage the repair cycle. Of course, maintenance staff get to it when they can—usually too late. Thus, the repairable items do not get repaired in time and the work order remains opened for a long time, driving up the cost of managing many inactive but open work orders. When an emergency arises and the item is needed, a rush-order to a happy supplier is usually the unhappy result and inventory values grow. Free or no-value issue, with a charge-back of the actual repair cost to the last user, is often the easiest way to handle this problem. Another approach is to close the work order, accrue the repair costs in an inventory account, and charge them as a cost of the item to the next user of the item. This can all be complicated even more if accounting decides to track the costs as a capital expenditure (after all, you are extending the useful life of the asset). Although today's integrated enterprise management systems make this situation easier to control than it was in the past, the basic process must be right—fixing the system or part of the system does not solve the underlying problem. The process is determined and defined before the system is set up.

Use

One of the biggest wastes of tradespersons' time is the time spent waiting for tools, parts, and materials. (A time study performed on North American plants revealed that this ranged from 17 to 22 percent of tradespersons' time.) This is a highly unproductive use of time, and it is not a labor problem but a management problem. Some work-order management systems, in fact, have a stage in the work-order cycle for work orders that are "awaiting materials." In translation, this sometimes means that your scarce tradespeople are doing the waiting.

Good planning integrated with an effective supply chain process is the key to minimizing this unproductive time wasted by tradespeople who are waiting for materials. The time expended while a part is looked up, requisitioned, spotted, issued, and brought to the workplace can be considerable. If the part is not in stock, lead times can be long. (Remember that suppliers are also trying to keep their inventory values under control; they prefer not to stock more than they think they will sell based on historical usage rates and the delivery time promises of their suppliers.) Once the parts arrive, installation is usually speedy, but the time expended cannot be recaptured.

One excellent solution to this problem is the "kitting" of parts by work order. This is especially effective for repetitive work like preventive maintenance and other planned repair jobs that make up most of your labor budget. Parts delivery to the site may sound expensive, but compared to lost tradespersons' productivity and extended equipment downtime, it can be very cost-effective. (Remember that tradesperson productivity is becoming a critical strategic issue due to the difficulties that many companies are having in finding skilled trades labor.) One unskilled delivery person can service many skilled tradespeople at many jobs. If you do this for 80 percent of your total workload (not a bad initial target for planned workload) and you save 10 percent of the total tradespersons' time for additional work, you will increase your labor productivity and save yourself higher overall repair costs.

It is not rare for materials and parts to be left over when work is completed. The repairable or reusable parts are returned to inventory, the appropriate credits made to the work-order charges and the inventory entries adjusted. It is pointless to return parts like bearings that have been opened and subjected to contamination that will render them prone to premature failure and unusable. To avoid scrapping these parts, it is best to leave them fully wrapped and unopened until they are used.

Analyze the Data

One of the simplest ways to judge the effectiveness of your maintenance planning is to review the number of urgent or emergency requisitions received by your buyers. If your work is planned properly, then these will be relatively few. Another is to check the number of stockouts in the stores, to see if inventory control is working. Again, you are looking to find only a few at most. Remember, too, that by counting stockouts you are looking at historical performance only. How many stockouts have not yet happened? Measuring inventory accuracy, managing stock levels, order points, and order sizes are proactive ways to obtain and maintain high service levels. How many direct purchase items are being ordered repetitively by your planners? Consider adding those items to inventory to reduce ordering costs and to save the planners valuable time. Similarly, look at purchases made by maintainers using purchasing cards (P-cards), emergency purchase orders, or purchase orders issued after the parts have been used. These are all indicators of opportunities to improve the service that MRO inventory provides to maintenance. The objective of MRO materials management is to balance the investment with value. Look for ways to continuously improve this ratio.

There is a great deal more to managing inventory that goes beyond the scope of this book, however, be aware that determination of the numbers of each part to hold in stores, the reorder points, the minimum and maximum stock levels, the usage rates, variance from job plans, etc., are all a part of the big picture. Managing inventory is an important process, second only to work management, in keeping maintenance costs under control. An excellent source of additional information on this subject is *Maintenance Excellence: Optimizing Equipment Life-Cycle Decisions.*[1]

E-BUSINESS

E-business is a term that refers to business transactions conducted over the Internet. It is the most cost-effective medium for many business transactions and e-commerce has become a principal means of doing business. Today, many people and companies consider e-business to be business as usual; yet many companies, often in older facilities, fail to take full advantage of it. Other companies, even those with small pockets of automation, are slowly making the shift as the benefits of e-business become more evident.

In 2000, retail e-commerce in the United States was estimated at $28 billion (not including food).[2] By 2004, that rose to $69 billion. E-commerce is growing by an average of more than 20 percent per year, and it is showing no sign of slowing. For business to business transactions, the volumes are 14 times higher for manufacturers and 19 times higher for merchant wholesalers. Given these statistics, it is safe to say that e-business is here to stay.

The Internet has become an information highway and our desktop computers provide us with the on-ramp. Today we also benefit from other new wave technology that enables change. There are cheap and ubiquitous computing devices, from PCs to cell phones to tiny systems in everyday appliances, coupled with low-cost bandwidth and open standards. Computing is just about everywhere now and it offers near limitless access to information, services, and entertainment. Top-performing companies today are making use of the available technology to generate savings, speed up business transactions, enhance the accuracy of those transactions, and manage their mobile workforces.

---

1. Edited by John D. Campbell and Andrew K. S. Jardine (New York: Marcel Dekker, 2001).
2. U.S. Department of Commerce, Census Bureau, Feb 24, 2005.

In some ways, technology is well ahead of our ability use it, but enterprising companies are making optimal use of it in many ways. The days of paper purchase orders and requisitions are nearing an end. Only auditors, those obsessed with micromanaging, and companies unwilling or unable to invest in today's software packages seem to require paper any more.

Today's successful management systems automate most of the day-to-day business transactions associated with maintenance and materials management. Within the inventory management system, a requisition for an inventory item by a maintenance planner can trigger a reservation in an inventory management system (very likely an inventory module within a larger enterprise system). When all materials and other resources have been confirmed as available, a job will be scheduled and a work order issued for execution. That triggers a stock issue for all materials linked to the work order. A picklist is generated (on a hand-held device or more likely on paper) and those parts, etc., are then kitted into a package, identified by work-order number, for delivery to the maintainer at the job site. That same stock issue from stores may drop inventory holdings below the reorder point. Because the item is an inventory item, this triggers an e-business transaction. An automated order for the part is sent electronically to your supplier. The order is filled and shipped. On receipt, the packing slip (possibly on an electronic tablet or another piece of paper) will be signed off as received and the order receipt will be entered into the materials management system, which will update the inventory records. The only paper documents required in the entire process were the picklist and the packing slip; both are used by relatively unskilled labor as checklists and both can be replaced by electronic devices. E-business allows the customer to identify, order, specify shipping, and pay for items online on the supplier's website. Efficient systems working in tandem with e-business substantially reduce the transaction costs associated with these purchases.

The availability of the Internet and e-business has caused companies to rethink the way they manage their business models. Purchasing clerks no longer handle paperwork; they spend their time doing more valuable work, such as negotiating and managing fewer large contracts for many goods and services. As companies merge, the value of flexibility in these systems is highlighted. Information exchange is enhanced, transaction processing is sped up, and costs are dramatically reduced. Most purchasing can even be fully automated since inventory items are preapproved for purchase with specific set order points and economic order quantities. When e-business emerged and caught hold, various e-business portals were set up to manage transactions for whole industries. These still exist today, but in some cases their capabilities have not met expectations. One reason for this is that many companies who rely on e-business have made the transition in a somewhat generic fashion. To get the most out of e-business, you can never forget that the best e-business begins and ends by recognizing and utilizing the unique characteristics of your business and the people who are at the heart of it.

Setting up for e-business can be a lot of work and the larger your company is the more challenging this will be. However, the potential for reward is tremendous and this should provide the incentive needed for the undertaking. When you engage in e-business, not only do you rely on your own management systems, but you also rely on their ability to interface with the Internet and the systems set up by your suppliers and customers. E-business providers are middlemen managing the information technology that is involved, but you still manage your suppliers and negotiate the contracts. One huge advantage of e-business is that it gives your company the flexibility to manage all its procurement through one organization. Of course, many companies still prefer to keep things divided up by region or country, but even these choices are facilitated by the capabilities of today's advanced systems.

MRO IMPROVEMENTS

There is a lot that can be done to improve the performance of MRO stores in support of maintenance. Figure 5-2 describes 12 activities that can contribute to enhanced stores performance, lowering of inventory costs and improved performance by maintenance. Companies that achieve high service levels to maintenance along with low inventory purchasing and carrying costs have done this work. This achievement requires the efforts of stores, maintenance, and procurement to varying degrees and may additionally require upgrades to systems capabilities. These activities are presented in a logical but not necessarily fixed sequence, amenable to implementation.

Activity	Requirements	Benefits	Costs	Comments
Physical Spares Management: Implement basic principles.	• Accurate listing of stores • Standard part descriptions • Warehouse organization—aisle-shelf-bin numbering • Parts identification and tagging • Receiving and issuing data collection • Regular cycle counts • Material requirements on work order • Pick list preparation from work order	• Planners and technicians have parts when and where they need them • Reduced job delays through no parts and wrong parts • Reduced repeat parts collection trips to and from warehouse • Faster picking • Reduced parts duplication • Reduced stockouts	• Initial data clean-up and recording costs • Physical set-up costs • Training costs • Possible additional stores staffing costs	• Extra stores staffing will be offset by reduced maintenance hours • Not all warehouses need to be staffed
Physical Inventory Management: Kit-ups prepared by Stores	• Pick-list printing in stores • Earlier pick-list printing • Planners identify parts by work order	• Faster picking by staff who know the layout • Picking by stores keepers not maintenance technicians • Reduced pick and wait time by maintenance technicians	• Requires stores staffing	• Extra stores staffing will be offset by reduced maintenance hours

Figure 5-2. Stores Upgrade Activities

continued on next page

Activity	Requirements	Benefits	Costs	Comments
Physical Spares Management: Stores clean-up and obsoletes	• Parts "where used" listing • Definition of obsoletes • Knowledge of "what it is" • Disposal of obsoletes • Help from maintenance to identify "where used"	• "Get rid of the junk", and "cleaned up warehouse" are big morale boosts—shows company is serious • Cash for junk • Frees up space • Reduces store management time	• Time consuming • Cost of physical removal	• Revenue from the obsoletes clean-up can pay for additional activities
Physical Spares Management: Job-Site delivery and staging	• Earlier pick-list preparation • Earlier work-order planning • Regular stores delivery routines • Emergency back-up procedure	• One-stop store responsibility • Less travel & time for maintenance technicians (large potential savings) • Substitutes costly maintenance technicians' time for less costly stores deliveryman's time	• Delivery staff	• Stores "delivery route" reduces overall travel • Requires change in operating philosophy and improved planning • Will not eliminate emergency spares collection • Security at parts staging area can be a problem

Figure 5-2. *continued*

Activity	Requirements	Benefits	Costs	Comments
Inventory Optimization: Establish inventory levels, min-max EOQ, lead times, stock counting, P-cards	• Consumption records • Vendor records • Requirements forecasts • ABC analysis • Regular stock counts and reconciliations	• Reduced inventory levels • Reduced spending on spares	• Analysis cost • Disposal costs (may be offset by scrap value)	• Levels generally set too high in the early stages. Need to review periodically. • Regular stock counts plus introduction of P-cards raises confidence • Use of P-cards can reduce accuracy of maintenance cost reporting by work order parts standardization
Inventory Optimization: Parts standardization	• Policy and procedure on materials specification in Maintenance, Design and Engineering	• Faster parts lookups • Time saved by planners • Fewer duplicate parts • Better parts pricing	• Analysis cost • Adds to design time	• Design engineers love to invent new things • Vendors have little influence over manufacturers and their designs
Physical Inventory Management: Warehouse rationalization	• Records visibility • Inter-warehouse policy and procedure • Inter-warehouse delivery process	• Reduced inventory levels overall • Reduced spending on spares overall	• Analysis cost • Inter-warehouse delivery costs	• Does not mean staffed warehouses everywhere • "Warehouse" may equal a field maintenance truck

continued on next page

Figure 5-2. continued

Activity	Requirements	Benefits	Costs	Comments
Procurement: Vendor Optimization	• Negotiations with vendors	• Fewer vendors • Higher spend per vendor • Better parts pricing overall • Better vendor service	• Analysis cost	• Buyers' resistance to strike off vendors • Some part prices may rise but overall costs go down
Procurement: Automatic requisitioning by Maintenance	• Procurement approves contracts	• Streamlined buying process reduces administrative cost	• MRO inventory & procurement systems must have capability	• Perceived loss of control offset by approval procedures
Procurement: E-procurement by Maintenance	• Procurement approval of replenishment practices	• Streamlined buying process reduces administrative cost	• Systems capabilities upgrades may be needed	• Perceived loss of control offset by approval procedures
Physical Inventory Management: JIT supply by vendor	• Requirements forecasts • Performance targets for vendors	• Vendor owns inventory until shipped and can optimize supply • Vendor part of materials planning process	• Possible higher prices	• Perceived loss of control by Procurement • Higher prices may be offset by longer and more secure supply contracts, plus performance targets
Physical Inventory Management: Vendor consigned inventory	• Requirements forecasts • Performance targets for vendors	• Vendor owns inventory until consumed • Lower spares investment • Lower carrying costs	• Possible higher prices	• Perceived loss of control by Procurement • Higher prices may be offset by longer and more secure supply contracts, plus performance targets

Figure 5-2. *continued*

UPTIME SUMMARY

Without parts many jobs cannot be done. There is no point planning and scheduling work if you cannot rely on materials management to provide the parts when you need them. If you want excellence in maintenance you need excellence in materials management.

Top performers do not delay or halt work because of unavailable parts, which are largely a failure of the planning and work management processes but can also reflect on materials management. Maintenance, repair, and overhaul (MRO) materials usually make up a small portion of most companies' material inventories but are the bulk of the inventory transactions. These parts and materials usually represent a small portion of your inventory investment, but they can be critical to running your plant. Individual parts can be of any value; they are purchased and used in small quantities; they are often slow moving but hard to source; they are essential to getting planned work done as planned and on schedule; and there are a lot of them. Managing MRO materials is a big and very important job. If it is done poorly, the value of improving maintenance performance will be seriously limited.

Integrating materials management processes such as stores issues and returns, receiving notifications, and purchasing with the maintenance planning and scheduling parts of the work management process are critical to success. There is no point ordering materials for a rush job if the parts arrive only to sit on a shelf because maintenance doesn't know they are there. This becomes even worse if the job is urgent and maintenance works outside the normal procurement processes and double-orders to meet production demands.

Information sharing and data management is important to having the right numbers of the right parts on hand, to ordering in economic quantities, and to providing a high level of service to meet demand for needed maintenance parts. The Internet has become a valuable tool in enabling e-business transactions that speed information flow and purchasing transactions, minimizing the wait for some parts.

Of course, the maintenance parts storeroom is the focal point for your maintainers. There is much that can be done to make it efficient and cost-effective. The key to success here is to have maintenance, inventory, and supply chain management working together.

6

Performance Management

What gets measured, gets done.
TOM PETERS[1]

Tom Peters, co-author of *In Search of Excellence* and *A Passion for Excellence*, emphasized the quantitative aspects of running a business. He observed that organizations, including his own, that focus on a set of goals (sometimes lofty goals) and measurement schemes to watch progress generally do well at meeting or even exceeding those goals. Measurement influences behavior, and people whose performance is being measured generally respond by performing better. The objective of performance measurement is to influence behavior in a way that helps achieve organizational goals.

Customer satisfaction was Tom Peters' best indicator of future health of a company—more so than market share or profitability. He encouraged companies to use customer satisfaction as the primary basis for bonuses or other variable pay components and for annual performance reviews and to do so at every level in the organization. He also encouraged monthly monitoring of key quality measures, posting progress in highly visible locations in every workspace, and making it topic #1 at every staff meeting. His teachings can be applied to any part of an organization, but work best when applied companywide.

---

1. Quoted in "Tom Peters Revisited: What gets measured gets done," *Office Solutions*, April 28, 1986. See also, Tom Peters and Robert H. Waterman, Jr., *In Search of Excellence* (New York: Warner Books, 1982) and Tom Peters and Nancy Austin, *A Passion for Excellence* (New York: Warner Books, 1985).

In the 1990s, Kaplan and Norton conducted extensive research on benchmarking and published their findings in the *Harvard Business Review*. They introduced a scheme for managing performance measures that would extract the greatest performance from an organization and drive strategy decisions through the use of measures in a balanced score card. The concept was simple enough—the right measures in four dimensions (Financial, Customer, Learning & Growth, and Internal Processes) would be optimized. Of course, instituting these measures requires considerable thought and coordination. It is quite possible to maximize performance in one area while suboptimizing it in another. An example of suboptimizing from the world of maintenance is minimizing MRO inventory holdings, which then results in poor service levels for maintainers who cannot get the parts they need in a timely manner.

For businesses that run on large, sophisticated equipment and facilities, maintenance performance has a dramatic impact on overall capacity and cost. Measuring that performance, however, is often based solely on the cost of tradespeople and materials or wading through a muddle of terms like *mechanical availability* and ratios like *maintenance costs over plant replacement value*. Maintenance costs are often seen by cost accountants[2] as some sort of necessary evil that should be minimized. Beware of that perception! While there is truth to it from a purely cost accounting perspective, shortsighted cost cutting in maintenance has led to many production, safety, and environmental problems in many companies worldwide. Recognize that those costs are directly linked to the generation of revenue—without maintenance your plant won't run and you'll produce nothing.

If you want productive maintenance, measure maintenance productivity and do it from the perspective of the customer. If you want to achieve your maintenance strategy, constantly review your strategic objectives and master plan. If you want to be competitive, compare what you are doing to what others in the field are doing. Learn from your most successful competitors.

---

2. Fortunately many management accountants see maintenance costs as an investment, but correctly recognize that maintainers who are often focused exclusively on technical details don't generally manage that investment very well.

MEASURING MAINTENANCE

Productivity

Productivity is simply what you get compared to what you put in. With maintenance, what you get is better equipment performance, usually measured in production output terms. What you put in is money. A simple ratio of output to input, or its inverse, is an easily understood measure that quickly shows if you are getting more or less bang for your buck. Looking at costs per unit of output instead of using absolute or total costs gives you an excellent basis to trend. A trend line showing maintenance cost per ton of production tells you quickly whether or not the maintenance function is improving, getting worse, or stable. When you add physical assets to your plants and fleets in form of additional automation, computerized control systems, larger and higher capacity production equipment, etc., you can expect maintenance costs to go up. If you look only at costs, you will see a negative trend; however, if you look at the ratio of output to input, you should see that output is climbing relative to costs, indicating that productivity is actually rising.

Equipment performance is a key to delivering productive output, but it is not the goal that maintenance is striving to achieve. Many maintainers believe that they have done their job if they deliver working equipment. In one sense, this is true. In a broader sense, however, these maintainers are missing the real purpose of their work: to sustain productive capacity so the company can earn revenue at a reasonable cost. Their real job is to sustain the *function* of the equipment, not the equipment itself. A great deal of maintenance money is often spent in "emergency" situations, on restoring equipment to working order even though its function has already been restored by backup or standby equipment. While this reduces the risk of loss of functionality if the backup fails, the risk reduction may not be worth the cost. Most companies make no attempt to quantify this and go with old habits that may not be their best option. Bear in mind that there are many ways to contain costs well beyond their measurement.

Equipment Performance

How do we measure equipment performance? The most obvious parameter is whether equipment is running or not, but the answers to the follow-up questions tell much more. Is it available for use? If it does run, how long do you expect it to keep chugging along before the next failure? What is the average time it would be down for repair and maintenance? How fast can it operate compared to what it was designed for? How precisely does it run? Does it always produce the quality required? Is its performance improving or deteriorating? There are commonly accepted terms and definitions to answer each of these performance questions:

- *Availability*[3]—a measure of uptime, as well as the duration of downtime. It is calculated as:

$$\frac{Scheduled\ time - All\ downtime\,[4]}{Scheduled\ time}$$

- *Reliability*[5]—a measure of the frequency of downtime, or mean time between failures (MTBF). It is determined by:

$$\frac{Total\ operating\ time}{Number\ of\ failures}$$

or

---

3. There are commonly used measures of availability: mechanical availability and production availability. Mechanical availability accounts for downtime due to maintenance action (repairs, etc.) whereas production availability accounts for all of the downtime including time to shutdown, cool down, isolate, recommission, and ramp up to full production. Mechanical availability is usually greater than production availability, but its use can lead to arguments with production people who are more interested in how much utility they get from their assets.

4. Some prefer to consider only unplanned downtime and ignore downtime that is planned. The underlying assumption is that planned downtime is needed. However, planned downtime is only needed if it can be shown as necessary or if there is no need for the additional production (e.g., you need only 2 out of 3 possible shifts). Also, the duration of the planned downtime can usually be improved through planning, work management practices, and benchmarking. When speaking of downtime, be sure to specify what you are including in your definition.

5. In a strictly mathematical sense, reliability is a probability that the asset will perform its mission over a fixed interval of time under given operating conditions. We commonly use MTBF (or its inverse—the failure rate) as a more intuitive measure of reliability.

$$\frac{Total\ operating\ cycles\ (km,\ tons)}{Number\ of\ failures}$$

- *Maintainability*—a measure of the ability to make equipment available after it has failed, or mean time to repair (MTTR). It is determined by:

$$\frac{Total\ downtime\ from\ failures}{Number\ of\ failures}$$

- *Process rate*—a measure of the ability to operate at a standard speed, cycle or rate. This is calculated by:

$$\frac{Ideal\ cycle\ time^6}{Actual\ cycle\ time}$$

- *Quality rate*—a measure of the ability to produce to a standard product quality, or

$$\frac{Quality\ product\ produced^7}{Total\ product\ produced}$$

- *Overall equipment effectiveness*[8] (OEE)—an overall measure that considers uptime, speed, and precision. It is measured as a product of

$$Availability \times Process\ rate \times Quality\ rate$$

The value of any of these measures has a lot to do with how the equipment was designed and built. Thus, the best test of equipment performance is often its performance trend over time. This will provide you with feedback about changes in operating and maintenance practices.

---

6. Cycle time is the time required to produce a product or service. Ideal cycle time can be determined through benchmarking or by using historical measures of the best production performance in the organization. Cycle times can also be replaced by production rates or rate of delivery of a service.
7. Often this is simply the total product produced minus the quantity of rejected output.
8. OEE is widely used in applications of Total Productive Maintenance (TPM). "World-class" levels of OEE are on the order of 85 percent, but beware of making comparisons, particularly between different manufacturing processes and product lines.

One cautionary note about equipment performance and benchmarking is that comparisons of equipment performance in one organization or even in one operating environment with another environment can be misleading. Even identical equipment that is operated under different conditions, at different rates, or under different loads can provide dramatically different performance results. For example, a pump used to pump lubricating oil will perform differently if it is used to pump water, fuels, caustic soda, or acids.

Cost Performance

In many companies, it is extremely difficult to obtain accurate and relevant maintenance cost information. Labor is often charged through cost centers, and only significant materials expenditures are charged to the equipment. Overhead costs are often allocated on the basis of direct labor, whether those overheads are related to maintenance or not. Most organizations track costs in a way that is conducive to accurate accounting but do not track them to specific pieces of equipment in the asset register. This makes determining the value of reliability improvement efforts very challenging. By aggregating costs so that they are convenient for accounting but not for maintenance, companies can severely hinder their ability to make meaningful equipment-specific decisions.

Accurate maintenance information is useful for two reasons: 1) maintenance productivity can be measured and, therefore, managed, and 2) it promotes rational equipment decisions, such as whether to repair or replace. Maintenance costs are usually segregated into the following categories:

- *Labor*—all the wages and benefits of the tradespeople and temporary helpers.
- *Materials*—all the supplies, parts, components, repairable items, consumables, and other items used by maintenance.
- *Services*—all shops, utilities, facilities, and stores warehousing.
- *Outside services*—all contracted services for HVAC or other specialty services, training, and consultants.
- *Technical support*—engineering, supervision, planning, materials coordination, clerical, and data entry.
- *Overhead*—other support functions, such as accounting and MIS personnel, general utilities, facilities, taxes, rent, and other general expenses.

These categories are broad and rather generalized. A more useful way to consider maintenance costs is to break them down in the following way:

- Specific areas, such as labor, materials, services, and technical support—all of which are influenced by area management and staff.
- Job or work order for labor, materials and services, so the costs can be designated to a particular piece of equipment.
- Expense type for labor and for material and all services to monitor trends in key parts, consumables, and services.

As with equipment performance, tracking cost trends is more sensible than looking at individual numbers or single averages.

Many companies want to know if their overall maintenance costs are in line with those of other companies in their industry. One of the best measures is cost per unit of production but that is a difficult measure to obtain from competitors and everyone seems to measure costs a bit differently. A commonly accepted measure is the overall cost as a percentage of replacement asset value. Here, too, the same problem exists with ensuring costs are measured consistently. Replacement asset value, particularly for fixed plants, is often no more than an educated guess, sometimes based on insured value of the plant.

Process Performance

Maintenance management is a business process with inputs and outputs. The inputs are costs; the output is equipment performance and productivity. Between the two comes the complex job of making sure the equipment works at top performance. That job can vary dramatically from industry to industry and from product line to product line, so there is no single set of measures that is ideal for every situation. Many books on this subject suggest measures for maintenance under different circumstances. Additional suggestions are provided below, along with some performance benchmarks:[9]

---

9. Many of the performance benchmarks shown are taken from "Best-in-Class Maintenance Benchmarks" by James B. Humphries, published in *Iron and Steel Engineer*, October 1998. The numbers used here are a compilation of top quartile figures for companies that were all considered top quartile in their industries. The numbers are not industry specific unless stated.

- *Maintenance spending as percentage of capital replacement cost.* This gives an indication if the maintenance spending is in line with your industry sector. Coopers and Lybrand performed a study in the early 1990s, which revealed maintenance spending in manufacturing companies ranged from 3 to 8 percent of capital replacement cost, with the majority falling into the 4 to 7 percent range. They also found a correlation between this value and how satisfied people were with their overall maintenance performance. Companies spending less than 4 percent or more than 7 percent were least satisfied, a clear indication that underdelivery is possible with either underspending or overspending. It is very difficult to get an accurate figure for capital replacement value, so comparisons made using these percentages can provide only a rough idea of how you are doing, particularly in industries with unique variables. (For example, the oil and gas industry fell in the range of 1.5 to 2 percent due to the capital investment tied up in static assets like pipelines that require very little maintenance.)
- *Emergencies.* If something immediately and negatively affects safety, environment, profitability, or customer service and automatically necessitates overtime to restore service and eliminate the consequences of the failure, then it is a true emergency. Both the amount and impact of emergency maintenance can be measured. Anything over 2 percent of your maintenance workload (labor hours) strongly suggests there is room to improve.
- *Planned versus unplanned.* Ideally you will have very little unplanned work. With a well-designed maintenance program, you will know what to expect so it can be planned in advance, particularly for critical equipment. Having 95 percent of total maintenance labor hours planned is considered top quartile performance.
- *Schedule compliance.* This is a good indicator that your plant and organizational discipline are in a firefighting mode. Schedule compliance is measured by dividing the total labor hours for all work completed as scheduled by the total number of labor hours for all work scheduled in the same time period. For example if you have scheduled 1,600 hours of work for next week and completed 1,000 of those during that

week, compliance is 62.5 percent. If compliance is high, then you are operating under control. If it is low, then you are likely to experience excessive amounts of emergency work and higher costs than necessary. Seventy percent is considered top quartile performance but you can do far better than that. The keys to obtaining high performance and avoiding firefighting are excellent planning, accurate scheduling, disciplined work assignment and execution, and a maintenance work program that is mostly proactive.

- *PM schedule compliance.* Doing the right proactive[10] maintenance activities when they are scheduled is probably the easiest and most effective way to improve equipment performance. This is measured as above but using only PM work for the measure. PM compliance should be 100 percent.

- *Work orders generated from PM.* This can tell you a lot about the thoroughness and effectiveness of the PM program. When an inspection is carried out, you can expect some work to be identified some of the time. If not, then the inspection was either unnecessary or not done correctly. If your inspections are always turning up work, then you are very likely inspecting too infrequently and incurring more breakdowns than you want. If your inspections are too frequent, you simply spend too much. There is no benchmark for this measure. It will vary depending on your PM program effectiveness, which can be monitored by observing a drop in emergency work and increases in planned work and schedule compliance.

- *Urgent versus normal purchase requisitions.* This is another test of maintenance planning, MRO inventory management, and the appropriateness of equipment maintenance tactics. If the planning process is working, maintenance knows ahead of time what parts are required and urgent requests are minimized. If inventory management is not working well, then no amount of maintenance planning will help. If your maintenance tactics are inappropriate, they will be ineffective and you will experience a greater number of breakdowns requiring emergency response.

---

10. "Proactive" refers to preventive, predictive, and failure-finding work. See Chapter 8 for further explanation.

- *Stores inventory turnover.* Dividing the value of annual issues by the on-hand value of stores provides an indicator of the activity in your inventory. Specifically, this is measured by dividing the total value of stores issued to maintenance over a year by the value of the stores held in inventory at the end of that year. Anything over 2.0 is good. If turnover is low, you are carrying too much inventory and tying up working capital.
- *Stores stockouts.* The percentage of inventory requests filled on request indicates what you are stocking and the service level provided for the investment. Ninety-nine percent is often considered top quartile performance but may also indicate overstocking. A more practical target for stockouts is 5 percent. It is important to remember that many stocked items[11] have little impact on safety, environmental, or operational performance, and it does not matter much if they are unavailable. Aim to achieve the highest levels for the most critical spares.

For the greatest value, tailor your process performance measurements and evaluate your results based on the unique circumstances of your situation. For example, if cost overruns and poor equipment performance are the effects, what are their root causes? The answer could be excessive overtime, but the reasons for this can vary. It could be anything from emergencies that resulted from poor PM compliance to quality problems arising from a lack of trade skills training.

Customers can also provide valuable insight into your maintenance performance. In a large Toronto hospital, nursing staff (the customer) were generally happy with the work that maintenance was doing but very unhappy because they never got feedback about when their requests would see action. It was important for them to know when things would be done. Once the hospital maintenance department centralized its dispatching system and started communicating estimated dates for the work to be completed, the concerns all but disappeared.

Response time can also be an issue for your "customers" who typically want to know that you are taking care of their needs. This

---

11. One estimate puts the figure at 60 percent.

affects maintainability and may result from the organizational structure (centrally dispatched versus area-based crews, for example). A big stumbling block for maintenance departments that are highly reactive to customer demands is the difficulty of getting the right parts from the warehouse. The lack of planning in these environments makes it very difficult to provide an inventory that matches demand.

BENCHMARKING MAINTENANCE

Benchmarking is a tool with which an organization compares its internal performance to external standards and then acts to close whatever gaps exist. The objective is to achieve and sustain best-in-class performance through continuous improvements.

Contrary to popular belief, benchmarking is not just appraising how your performance compares to that of direct competitors or others. Rather, it is looking behind those measures to the practices that produce them. It is especially about understanding which measures and practices are critical to your success and finding out who performs best, regardless of industry sector.

Consider the case of one mining company that wanted to benchmark its truck engine overhaul practice. It first looked at critical success factors and concluded that the most important of these were reliability (having long periods between failures) and shop cycle time (reducing the size of the queue and therefore the capital cost).

Then maintenance documented its own procedures, measured reliability and cycle time, and set about looking for benchmarks. The company's sister mines had similar practices and poorer results. The direct competitors were not much better. Some of the other mining operations in different commodities were improving reliability but this was being done through expensive, contracted overhauls by the original equipment manufacturer.

Finally, the mining company discovered an engine rebuild shop with a flawless reputation for reliability. Using just-in-time manufacturing techniques, the shop ran with remarkable cycle times and short queues. Although it was an airline's jet engine rebuild shop, its planning, scheduling, execution, and control procedures were directly applicable to those at the mine.

High reliability and short downtime produced higher mechanical availability that translated directly into higher fleet production availability. That meant that fewer trucks could provide the same level of production support. Some trucks could be parked and their maintenance costs reduced. When it became time to replace the fleet, the company was able to replace it with fewer trucks and saved millions in capital costs.

As the mining company discovered, looking beyond your own limitations can provide substantial benefits. It is not enough to improve just incrementally from your past performance or that of other company divisions. To compete globally, look everywhere you can to find and learn new methods. Becoming a student of the best, particularly of the best in unrelated business sectors, can be valuable. The basic approach to benchmarking is:

- Know your own operation, both its strengths and its weaknesses. This may require some form of assessment to identify the areas you want to improve.
- Understand the key factors that drive you to high performance. These are usually beyond your control but may require your response. The better you respond, the higher your performance. For example, customer demand for rapid response and problem solving on the first visit drives your efforts to achieve excellent work management practices and high skill levels in your maintenance service delivery staff.
- Know those industries and companies that excel at the maintenance processes used in your operation, including competitors, industry sector leaders, and others.
- Compare your measured performance with theirs and learn how they are performing better than you. Pay attention not only to what they are doing, but also to how they got there.
- Set realistic but challenging targets. Incorporate the best practices with the appropriate consideration for the changes you are imposing on your organization.
- Measure results and strive continually for superior performance.

A European microelectronics company manufacturing computer chips for calculators set for itself what seemed an unattainable goal—improving a production line's reliability (MTBF) from 24 hours to 48 hours within one year. The process could tolerate a few extended production shutdowns but not frequent interruptions, as there were quality losses both at shutdown and at start-up. Availability, or the duration of shutdowns, was less significant than how often they occurred, or the reliability factor.

The company thought it faced a tall order—its equipment capability was to be doubled. But when it benchmarked similar process lines in Japan, it found that reliability there (MTBF) was at 200 hours! The original goal of 48 hours suddenly became irrelevant. Even if the goal were achieved, the company would not attain parity, let alone competitive advantage!

Benchmark what is critically important to customers: the value chain that affects the organization's success. In all cases, remember that the benchmarking process is exhaustive and that the improvement plan at the end of it will cost significant time, effort, and resources. Benchmarking maintenance makes sense only if it will bring real gains to the company. Moreover, don't make the mistake of thinking that benchmark performance data are readily available in the public domain—they are not. Benchmarking data are usually acquired at great expense through commissioned studies, benchmarking projects, extensive visits, and interviews. Those who have gone through the pain of gathering benchmarking data seldom want to give it away to others. Above all, do not benchmark with the expectation that simply measuring performance will cause it to improve—it won't. Having realistic targets will help drive performance, but achievement requires training, guidance, new equipment, and a host of other things. None but the simplest of changes is free. The following are examples of productive benchmark activities and processes for maintenance:

Strategic
- Creating and fostering a service attitude towards production
- Creating and implementing strategic improvement plans
- Maintenance partnering with production
- Contractor service level monitoring and performance management
- Measuring and managing performance of the maintenance function

Management
- Training needs analysis and program development for maintenance
- Organizational structures and management techniques

- Incentive programs
- Individual and team performance management
- Encouraging participation in continuous improvement activities

Systems
- CMMS selection and implementation
- Encouraging use of the CMMS at all levels
- Elimination of duplicate and ad hoc management systems
- Keeping users abreast of system upgrades and changes
- Reviewing new technology and deciding which to choose

Choose the businesses you want to benchmark with, keeping several factors in mind. The required information must be available and the benchmarking partners you choose must be willing to share it. Bear in mind that benchmarking for information that is already available in published annual reports or on websites will not be especially valuable. Determine whether you can glean enough from others' innovations to help your competitive position and whether or not they will even let you look. A great deal of up-front research is helpful to ensure you get the greatest value from your benchmarking efforts. Internal divisions and sister companies are easy benchmarking partners because accessing their data is simple, but it is unlikely that you will find many new, innovative processes unless the sister company or division you choose also happens to be a world leader.

Information from direct competitors will be difficult to come by—legally. Most countries have antitrust and competition avoidance laws to prevent the sharing of information that could impact its markets, but industry sector leaders and businesses in other industries who have mastered specific processes can make excellent models. Across-the-board comparisons with these companies may not be relevant, but they can inspire you to quantum leaps in selected processes. (Remember the mining company that reached new heights following an airline's model of reliability.)

As interesting as the quantitative comparisons will be, the most important part of the benchmarking process is putting the information to use. It can become a driving force behind your plan to improve maintenance continuously. You can use it to help your firm achieve a shared vision of excellence based on the proven successes of others. Several companies and associations have accomplished just that. E. I. du Pont de Nemours & Co. (Du Pont), for example, has been benchmarking maintenance performance since 1987. The company investigates maintenance practices of competing companies in the petrochemical field as well as in industries in other sectors. Du Pont believes that benchmarking sharpens its focus for improvement and quantifies its goals. Maintenance management in the company has been elevated to the importance it deserves. Recently, its benchmarking effort has found:

- Japan and Europe use substantially more contractors than the United States.
- Japan spends less to maintain its investment and its productivity is higher.
- Japanese companies have less stores investment with higher turnover than European and U.S. companies.

General Motors Advanced Engineering group is another example of a company committed to benchmarking and has conducted a maintenance benchmarking study in several industries, including assembly, distribution, manufacturing, processing, and consulting/academic. The objective was to determine both the average as well as the world-class measures for key parameters. Some of the more interesting findings of this study were:

- More than half of all maintenance performed by those surveyed was reactive. Eighteen percent was considered an acceptable reactive maintenance level for world class organizations.
- Preventive maintenance averaged about one-third of the effort, with world-class levels at just under 50 percent of all activities.
- Predictive maintenance—using machine condition data to warn of impending failure and identify defective parts—averaged only 13 percent of the total. Perceived world class was 35 percent predictive activities, representing another major gap in actual performance to a vision of the world's best.

The International Iron and Steel Institute (IISI) produced another interesting benchmark study involving 17 of its members. It concluded that maintenance in steel industries is the third highest cost item after raw materials and labor, representing between

8 percent and 15 percent of steelworks sales and between 13 percent and 25 percent of liquid steel costs. Key recommendations to reduce these costs and improve effectiveness, based on best practices found in the study, were:

- Apply computerized maintenance management systems to control and analyze all aspects of performance.
- Ensure full and active participation of maintenance people in the design, selection, and installation of new equipment.
- Set higher maintenance standards for all work.
- Institute comprehensive condition-based monitoring and analysis.
- Employ a well-trained, multiskilled workforce, following systematic planning and control of work.

An early Coopers and Lybrand study of the hydroelectric generating industry in North America provided benchmark statistics based on thirty utilities. Like the IISI study, it averaged results and subtracted one standard deviation for the benchmark. Among the top five utilities, the average for each parameter shows:

- Maintenance costs $1,500 per megawatt installed capacity each year.
- Generation availability of 95 percent, with forced outage at 2 percent and planned outage at 3 percent.
- Emergency work at less than 3 percent, with preventive work at over 60 percent.

A leading eastern Canadian forest products company participated in a maintenance benchmark study that was commissioned by a smaller pulp and paper company (not a direct competitor) and discovered that among the various participants, overall productivity was the best at one of its own mills. Previous internal comparisons contradicted this finding and the company commissioned an internal benchmarking study to determine what practices were driving its top performers and then disseminate this information to all its mills and improve overall company performance. In the process, the company discovered several key characteristics that were driving success, and the findings were shared with each company mill. Nearly 10 years later, the company consistently leads the forest products industry in productivity.

Fluor Daniel,[12] a large maintenance outsource service provider to hundreds of plants, carried out its own study of maintenance performance among 148 top quartile companies. Published in 1998, the study examined various measures and provided a range of benchmark performance for each of them. Although the study does not explain how the top performers got where they are, it is very helpful in providing realistic targets for performance among a variety of industries. Figure 6-1 shows some of those measures along with changes based on the authors' experience. Refer to the original article for definitions of the terminology used to avoid misinterpreting the various measures.

In 2005, Reliabilityweb.com and Genesis Solutions completed a year-long, online benchmarking survey of over 800 companies. Based on Terry Wireman's book, *Benchmarking Best Practices in Maintenance Management*,[13] it shows strengths and weaknesses in maintenance practices in 16 different areas. While the survey does not elaborate on what to do or how to do it, it is an excellent place to start to see just where you are in comparison with hundreds of other companies.

What all of these examples illustrate is that benchmarking produces impressive results. Apply it and you can achieve performance breakthroughs.

Balanced Score Cards

Kaplan and Norton's balanced score card,[14] introduced earlier in this chapter, was compiled from a study of 12 companies at the leading edge of performance measurement. The "balanced score card" contained a set of measures to give top managers a quick but comprehensive view of their respective businesses. The measures are in the areas of financial performance (how do we look to the shareholders?), customer satisfaction (how do our customers see us?), internal process performance (what do we choose to excel at?), and innovation and improvement (can we continue to

---

12. James B. Humphries, VP Manufacturing Technology and Operations Support, Fluor Daniel, Greenville, SC, "Best-in-Class Maintenance Benchmarks," *Iron and Steel Engineer*, October 1998.
13. Terry Wireman, *Benchmarking Best Practices in Maintenance Management* (New York: Industrial Press, 2004).
14. Robert S. Kaplan and David P. Norton, "The Balanced Score Card: Measures That Drive Performance," *Harvard Business Review*, 1992.

BENCHMARK	QUARTILE			
	BOTTOM	THIRD	SECOND	TOP
RESULTS METRICS				
OSHA Injuries per 200,000 Hours	>5.5	5.5–3.1	3.0–1.0	<1.0
Stores/Replacement Value Percentage	>1.3	1.3–0.8	0.7–0.3	<0.3
Maintenance Percentage of Operating Cost	Shown in Figure 1 on page xviii.			
Maintenance Cost/Replacement Percentage				
Discrete	>5.0	5.0–3.2	3.2–2.0	<2.0
Batch Process	>3.5	3.5–3.2	3.2–2.4	<2.4
Chemical, Refining, Power (continuous)	>4.8	4.8–3.0	3.0–2.5	<2.5
Availability				
Discrete	<78	78–84	85–91	>91
Batch Process	<72	72–80	81–90	>90
Chemical, Refining, Power (continuous)	<85	85–90	91–95	>95
Overall Equipment Effectiveness	Not Measurable	<48	48–78	>78
PROCESS METRICS				
Mechanic Wrench Time	<31	31–41	42–52	>52
Percentage Planned Work	<65	66–78	79–94	>95
Request Compliance Percentage	<68	68–77	78–90	>90
Schedule Compliance Percentage	<15	16–35	36–70	>70
Work Order Discipline Percentage	<54	55–83	84–95	>95
PM Percentage by Operations	0	0.9	10–24	>25
Replacement Value ($M) per Mechanic	<3.2	3.2–5.0	5.0–7.5	>7.5
Suggestions per Mechanic Per Year	Not Measurable	~0.5	0.5–4	>4
Stores Turnover	<0.5	0.5–0.7	0.7–1.2	>1.2
Stores Service Level	<93	93–96	97–99	>99
Contractor Cost Percentage	<8	8–19	20–40	>40
Stores Issues/Total Material Percentage	>82	82–68	67–20	<19
TRAINING AND STAFF RATIOS				
Span of Control	<9	9–17	18–40	>40
Mechanics per Effective Planner	<25	25–59	60–80	>80
Replacement Value ($M) per Maintenance and Reliability Engineer	<50	50–200	200–250	>250
Mechanics per Plant Worker Percentage	>32	32–21	20–10	<10
Total Craft Designations	>7	7–6	5–3	2
Training Hours per Mechanic	>80	80–70	69–40	<40
Training Cost per Mechanic	>3000	3000–1800	1800–500	<500

Figure 6-1. Selected Performance Benchmarks

improve and create value?). The score card prevents information overload for the managers by providing only a few truly meaningful key measures.

The advantages of the score card are that it brings together measures from seemingly disparate aspects of a company into one coherent picture. Balancing the measures against each other safeguards against suboptimization in any one area.

The original balanced score card was devised for use by an entire company, not just a single department, and that is how it works best. Each department, however, has its own score card that feeds the numbers at the higher levels all the way up the corporate ladder. Ideally the entire company is using the technique, but even individual departments, including maintenance, can use it to their advantage.

For maintenance, the score card is applied to the four dimensions identified earlier in this chapter: financial, customer satisfaction, internal processes, and human development. The financial dimension focuses on productivity and costs. Customer satisfaction focuses on the concerns of customers: reliability, availability, response time, and resolution time. Internal processes look at your work and MRO materials management process measures (how efficient you are). The human development (improvement) dimension looks at measured efforts to improve equipment reliability and availability and proactive maintenance coverage. Figure 6-2 shows an example of a balanced score card for maintenance.

Targets for the performance measures are set using benchmarks or realistic internal goals. Those targets are set so that achieving any one of them does not result in a drop in performance elsewhere. For example, MRO inventory cannot be allowed to drop to zero or there will be no parts available for emergency work, so there is a balance between inventory turns (a financial measure) and stores service level (a performance measure). The percentage of proactive maintenance is also unlikely to reach 100 percent due to its high incremental cost beyond some point of diminishing returns that pushes the maintenance cost per unit of output up. The key to success with balanced score cards is to maintain balance.

Tom Peters said, "What gets measured gets done." Take this premise a step further and you will recognize that what gets benchmarked, measured, and optimized, gets done best.

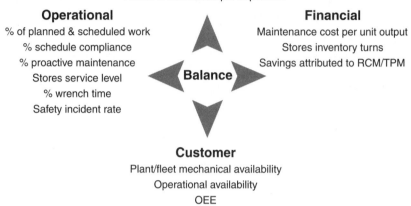

People Development
Number of multiskilling tradespeople
Annual hours of training per mechanic
Number of trade designations
Ration of mechanics per supervisor

Operational
% of planned & scheduled work
% schedule compliance
% proactive maintenance
Stores service level
% wrench time
Safety incident rate

Balance

Financial
Maintenance cost per unit output
Stores inventory turns
Savings attributed to RCM/TPM

Customer
Plant/fleet mechanical availability
Operational availability
OEE

Figure 6-2. Maintenance Score Card

UPTIME SUMMARY

The work management process is essential to keeping costs under control in maintenance, but you will not know if you are doing well if you don't measure what you are doing and the results you get. Performance management is another critical element for maintenance management. Costs are important, results are important, and so are the processes you use to turn costs into results. Performance management is central to managing those processes so you get the most output for the least input: the greatest cost-effectiveness.

Being effective in managing maintenance performance entails management of a number of measures that tell you about the work management process, materials management, training tradespeople, reliability improvement efforts, and so on. What you measure, how you measure, and how often you measure are all important.

Benchmarking has its place in helping you set realistic and achievable performance targets. More importantly, it can help you see what other companies have done to achieve higher levels of performance. A number of widely used benchmark standards are available for use if all you want is hard targets. Benchmarking visits and real learning will help you see ways to improve so you can meet those targets.

Balanced score cards provide an approach to tracking performance measures so that you achieve a balance between (or among) competing priorities. Trade-offs are inevitable and a classic example of this is the trade-off between inventory cost reduction and maintenance service levels. Watching a balanced set of measures that also considers the uptime outputs empowers you to make informed decisions that optimize performance in all areas to achieve the desired business output.

7

Management and Support Systems for Maintenance

Information and communications technology unlocks the value of time, allowing and enabling multi-tasking, multi-channels, multi-this and multi-that.

LI KA-SHING
Hong Kong, East Asia's Richest Man and
Founder of Hutchison Whampoa

For Li Ka Shing, information and communication technology systems are valuable tools that handle time-consuming tasks so we can use the time for other activities that add greater value for our companies. Among other things, information technology helps businesses keep track of transactions, historical records, and documentation. It automates parts of some business processes and many calculations. Some systems also "learn" from us and even take over some (usually simple) decision-making tasks. These "expert systems" are based on both logical sequences and on "fuzzy logic" that closely mimics the way fickle humans process information.

There are many automated systems that are useful in maintenance—perhaps even too many for some of us. The dizzying array of available choices makes it difficult to determine which of them will provide the most benefit to our businesses. The first part of this chapter describes various support systems that have the greatest potential to produce a substantial return on investment quickly. These tools and systems can help make managing the maintenance function much easier and more efficient, freeing up valuable time and revealing developing failures that can be handled before they result in complete loss of function. The last part of the chapter is about Computerized Maintenance Management

Systems[1] in their various guises. These are packaged software tools designed specifically to support the maintenance business process. Some of these systems are quite simple and others are very complex and prices vary accordingly. If they are implemented and used as intended, they help you manage more efficiently and deliver results. Whether simple or complex, these management systems are enablers. They are not complete solutions to management problems, nor are they a substitute for people or processes. Their greatest value is that they provide complementary support.

HARDWARE AND SOFTWARE TOOLS: AN OVERVIEW

There are many information technology and electronic communication tools that support the maintenance and materials functions. This is a technological arena that is constantly changing and evolving as computer and processing chip capabilities grow. A wealth of information is available on this topic on the Internet. Search for maintenance and reliability sites, and you will find more than you could possibly digest.

Along with desktop and laptop computers, there are now portable digital assistants that track work orders and their status in the field and data-logging devices that collect condition monitoring readings. Radio-frequency wireless devices are used in storerooms to label parts and to read bar codes and transmit stock transaction data while wireless Bluetooth technology transmits continuous streams of condition-monitoring data to centralized collection points, and electronic paper records data like an electronic clipboard. There are tablet PCs for field diagnostic work and various mobile computing and communicating devices for mobile workforce applications. Similar powerful tools are being developed all the time, as hardware is put together in a variety of configurations to help people with a variety of tasks.

---

1. The term Computerized Maintenance Management Systems (CMMS) as used in this book generally refers to a broad range of products from those that are truly specialized for maintenance to those that are much broader in scope including maintenance. The latter are also known as Enterprise Resource Planning (ERP) or Enterprise Asset Management (EAM) systems.

Condition Monitoring

Condition-based monitoring makes up the lion's share of successful proactive maintenance programs. In equipment, most failure modes give some warning that they have begun and that they are progressing towards a fully failed state. Equipment, systems, or process parameters are monitored periodically to detect telltale signs that failure is imminent. The particular warning sign will vary from asset to asset, depending on the failure mode. For example, deterioration of lubricant properties will warn of impending bearing and sliding contact failures, and increased temperatures reveal that insulation is breaking down. Watching those lube properties and temperature trends, maintenance can see emerging problems and take timely and appropriate action. Many conditions can be monitored with human senses—touch, smell, sight, and sound, but these are not the most consistent of monitoring devices. What you consider abnormal may sound quite normal to someone else. To get around this weakness, maintenance relies on a vast array of condition-monitoring tools.

There are various parameters to watch for in the physical (particle, dynamic and visual), chemical, electrical, and thermal realms. Appendix 4 of John Moubray's book, *Reliability-centered Maintenance II*, contains a comprehensive listing of the various techniques that can be monitored. Most of these have corresponding monitoring devices, such as:

- Vibration analyzers monitoring displacement, velocity and/or acceleration to produce overall (broadband) readings, whole vibration spectra, etc.
- Spike energy and shock pulse monitors for very high frequency vibrations.
- Ultrasonic and acoustic monitors to detect high frequency sound waves in air or metals.
- Ferrography to detect metal wear particles.
- Pore-blockage monitors to detect wear particles.
- Light extinction and light-scattering particle counters.
- Ferromagnetic sensors (chip detectors) for large particles in oil.
- Spectroscopes to detect wear in metals.
- X-rays to observe cracks and other physical defects.
- Gas chromatographs to detect gases released from deterioration of insulating oils.

- Electron microscopes to detect microfractures or cracks.
- Exhaust emission analyzers for engine performance and fuel economy.
- Chemical titration to look for deterioration of lubricants and fluids.
- Dye penetrants to detect surface cracks.
- Magnetic particle crack detectors for surface and subsurface cracks.
- Borescopes for visual inspection inside equipment.
- Strain gauges to monitor creep and strain under load.
- Viscosity monitors to determine lubricant properties.
- Infrared scanners to detect temperature gradients.
- Meggers to monitor resistance in electrical circuits and insulation.
- And many, many more.

Many of these devices come with software for recording and analyzing the signals. They help the user interpret what is being observed so that diagnosis of problems is more accurate. The data they collect can be used in fault diagnosis and in decision making about what maintenance intervention is appropriate and when. Data for future use can be stored either within the software provided (e.g., vibration data stored in software provided for its analysis) or separately. Sometimes it is stored in the CMMS and sometimes in a data warehouse. Regardless of where it is stored, the data should be readily available to planners and reliability engineers for later use. Understanding the ways that the data can and will be used is very important and helps determine what data to store as well as how and where to store it. In many instances data are collected and stored without regard to future use or usefulness. If you don't know what you want to do with it then why collect it? Adding technology for the sake of technology adds little value and can create a technology management nightmare for your engineers and IT professionals. For data to be a valuable corporate asset, it must be used.

Condition-monitoring devices and the systems that work with them have become big business because of their huge potential to prevent or reduce unexpected downtime and its costs. Understand what is available and how it will benefit your company before you jump into acquiring more and more technology. Make sure your investment in technology fits your strategic goals as well as your immediate technical requirements.

Portable Computers and Hand-held Devices

The hardware and software tools that work with the various condition-monitoring devices are often portable so that they can be used in the field for immediate diagnosis of problems. Portable computers as well as dedicated field devices are now commonplace in most large companies. These tools can be used in place of paper work orders and to record condition-monitoring data. Some of them are wireless, for instance, cell phones and PDAs that help you keep up with CMMS changes. Others contain memory chips for uploading and downloading data at the beginning and end of a shift. All of these eliminate paperwork and minimize errors because data is only entered once. Bar code scanners for work order and parts data and data-logging devices that take condition readings also improve accuracy.

Decision Support Tools

In addition to the software used with condition-monitoring devices, there is an array of software that manages data storage, analyzes the data, and performs reliability analyses that facilitate decisions about equipment or component replacement and inspections. Reliability analysis makes extensive use of statistical modeling techniques, many of which are impractical to perform without a computer. For example, maintenance planners can use software tools like Reliasoft's Weibull++, Dr. Nick Hastings' RELCODE, Dr. Jardine's OREST, and others to conduct Weibull[2] analysis quite easily on a computer. Dr. Jardine's PERDEC and AGE/CON, Omdec's EXAKT, Fulton Findings SuperSMITH and others offer other useful reliability and economic models.

One excellent decision support tool, EXAKT, takes failure history data, condition-monitoring data, cost data, and various economic criteria into account before giving a "go" or "no go"

---

2. Weibull Analysis: A commonly used statistical technique to analyze failure data for characteristics such as its Mean Time Between Failures, whether or not the failures are random, premature, or age related, and to observe the consistency of the data.

response about continued operation of equipment that is being monitored. By correlating past functional and potential failures with condition-monitoring data, it can determine which signals give the best indications of impending failure and observe when those signals are indicating problems. This tool has helped companies to extend the mean time between equipment removals by quantifying, managing, and reducing uncertainty so that the best[3] decisions may be made over the long run. It improves on human judgment and helps maintainers predict more accurately the remaining useful life of the asset before it fails.

Equipment and component replacement decisions require an analysis of historical failure data and economic data. These analyses determine the age at which life-cycle costs are minimized by considering variable usage rates, depreciation and resale values and how they decline with age, inflation and discount rates, and asset replacement costs. Excellent software tools can facilitate this investigative process.

Various mathematical models support spare parts analysis to determine initial spare inventory levels and parts distribution. These models take either item or system-based approaches, the latter being more complicated but far more valuable for planners attempting to squeeze high availability of spares to support critical maintenance work from limited budgets.

Other expert systems help operators and maintainers make decisions that would normally require the input of experts or consultants. These systems try to replicate a human expert and include intelligent reasoning engines. A good example is Solvatio, an automated fault diagnostic tool used to detect and diagnose problems in running equipment. Customized for each application, this tool guides the user during the search for the problem and its cause, takes corrective measures, and then updates the knowledge database. This updating function is the way the system "learns" from its expert human operators. It is an indication of the future direction of related software industry.

Another leading software package, Ivara's EXP, was designed to be integrated with a proprietary CMMS using preprogrammed

---

3. "Best" in this case refers to an optimized decision considering cost, probabilities, and organizational objectives for the asset in its operating context.

warning, alarm, and shutdown levels to trigger messages and work orders when condition monitoring readings exceed predetermined levels. This is an "expert system" in the simplest sense. Maintenance planners receiving these notices know almost as quickly as the process operators when something is going wrong and can respond quickly to help keep equipment running.

Integrating condition-based monitoring data with fault diagnostic and prognostic tools are areas of current research and significant development effort. These systems are not yet widespread, but in ten years' time you can expect to see them used as commonly as the CMMS is today. As is often the case, the most successful companies will adapt and deploy these new technologies as soon as possible to gain competitive advantage.

The Importance of Data

All of these software tools rely heavily on accurate input of the right[4] data. Needless to say, if the data going into your systems are inaccurate or incomplete, then the result will confirm the familiar "garbage in—garbage out" adage.

The state of many companies' maintenance data, even those using excellent CMMS's, is often not all that good. One of the biggest obstacles to the effective use of most CMMS's is the lack of accurate data, particularly data about failure history. Many hours of effort can go into "cleansing" the available data, and even then there is some uncertainty about its accuracy. This situation is so prevalent that you might want to give serious consideration to converting only basic equipment and parts information to a new electronic database— leave the historical records in the old system and save yourself millions in data-conversion costs. Moreover, while condition-monitoring data are readily available, especially with automated collection, the sheer volume of the data can pose storage problems, and data that come from work orders are notoriously inaccurate and incomplete.

One company is already tackling this data problem head on. OMDEC has created a software tool that is provided with its

---

4. The right data include a description of the as-found state of the asset at the time of a repair or preventive renewal. OMDEC provides a simple-to-use template for documenting a work order in a way that will support subsequent reliability analysis.

EXAKT program mentioned above. It is used to gather data from CMMS generated reports to generate an "events table" for use in the software algorithms. The company has done an excellent job of considering numerous and varied data problems currently encountered. While some of the input was still manual at the time this book was being written, the overall technology looks promising.

A great deal of work is currently being done by mathematicians and computer programmers in the field of machine learning, such as that done by Solvatio. The approaches they are using include neural networks and support vector machine methods that simulate the human thought and learning processes. Neural networks are computing systems with simple processing elements, a high degree of interconnection among them (just as in the human brain), simple scalar messages (yes/no), and adaptive interaction among the elements. These systems learn by adapting as signals propagate through the network based on anticipated results and observed results. Support vector machine methods are mathematical supervised learning methods. A detailed discussion of these is beyond the scope of this book; they are mentioned here to illustrate that this is a very active field of technological advancement in maintenance management.

Advanced decision support tools of this nature require a shift in thinking and in what your people do with them. For example, both EXP and EXAKT use RCM-like data models. Technicians using the software must be familiar with the structure and language of RCM in order to translate field observations from work orders and CMMS reports into the tool for the analysis. This again underscores the fact that while computer systems make many jobs easier, it is qualified and motivated people that operate computers properly. The key to data problems and solutions is your people.

CMMS, EAM, AND ERP[5]

The number and complexity of equipment systems managed by a typical maintenance engineer is awesome. When you consider the number of assets in a typical plant and the resources used to main-

---

5. CMMS—computerized maintenance management system; EAM— enterprise asset management system; ERP—enterprise resource planning system.

tain it (its parts and supplies, the various specialist skills, and the effort required to predict, prevent and repair problems), it is incredible that anyone can keep it all straight. But to make the most efficient use of all these resources, that is precisely what you must do. You must know, for example, what is in use and what is not; what and who is available for work; which spares, tools, test equipment, and consumable items are available (or not); what skill sets are available; what work has an established work plan; the schedule for PM and other required work, and many other things. You must also be able to coordinate and integrate this knowledge and this requires some sort of information management system.

The sheer volume of maintenance information can be staggering. An international airport facility in the Far East, for example, with 7,000 equipment systems and 20,000 SKUs (stock-keeping units) in maintenance stores, generates 100,000 work orders each year. At an electrical appliance manufacturing plant with 2,000 pieces of equipment and 30,000 stores SKUs, 150,000 work orders (110,000 of them "urgent") are filed annually. A Canadian public transit fleet generates 250,000 work orders or service requests for 950 vehicles. It controls 25,000 stores SKUs and has 415 tradespeople and a direct maintenance cost of over $100,000,000 per year. A large integrated mining and metals operation in Asia that has over 800 maintenance employees, another 800 contractors at any given time, 9,000 pieces of equipment, 5,000 planned component changeouts annually, and a budget of over $80,000,000 per year for maintenance, does nearly 50 percent of its work on an urgent basis. The number of data transactions for these businesses easily exceeds 1 million per month. It would be impossible to handle this volume manually, and this is the primary reason that computerized maintenance management systems (CMMS) have been almost universally adopted.

In addition to managing prodigious amounts of data, these systems also categorize the data and analyze. The statistical techniques used by CMMS facilitate decisions about reordering stock, which orders go to which vendor, who is available at what times for work to be done, what equipment is available for work, which work order to do first, which equipment is falling below its reliability targets, which equipment is still under warranty, which standard job plan to use, and when to write a work order for condition triggered corrective maintenance work (i.e., condition-based maintenance).

Most businesses today have some sort of CMMS and the trend, especially in medium size to large enterprises, is to use the maintenance modules that come with the corporate Enterprise Resource Planning (ERP) or Enterprise Asset Management (EAM) system. Some companies have developed their own systems in-house, but most have chosen one of the hundreds of commercially available packages. Unless you have a passion for computer programming and your knowledge of maintenance management can rival that of the leaders in the CMMS industry, developing your own system is not something that is likely to pay for itself. Interfacing home-grown software with any vendor-supported software (e.g., purchasing or inventory management) will lead to an unending stream of modifications to your software just to keep up with vendor-supplied upgrades and revision changes. Some companies have opted for homegrown collections of spreadsheets and databases to serve their maintenance needs, but they rarely interface with each other. Those collections of systems do not make information retrieval and data mining easy.

Integrated computer systems and information technology are very much a part of our lives today. Today's workforce grew up in the age of information technology. The Internet is virtually everywhere and computers are common in homes and even via wireless devices that can be used anywhere today. Navigation through most software packages is highly intuitive, making it easy for casual users to find their way around.

Information technology grows rapidly. In 1965, Gordon Moore observed the exponential growth in the number of transistors per integrated circuit. He predicted that this trend would continue, and his prediction of capacity doubling every 18 months became known as "Moore's Law." It is an observation that is still in force today. Intel, the world's largest maker of computer chips predicts that the trend will continue at least to the end of this decade. The growth and evolution in IT is phenomenal. It has led to dramatic changes in the capabilities and availability of software tools to support maintenance.

If your CMMS is more than three years old, it might benefit your company to take a look at what is currently available. The market for CMMS has changed dramatically over the past 10 years, and the number of vendors supplying these specialized systems is still in the hundreds. The capabilities of these systems can range from little more than work-order tracking for a small job shop to multisite enterprise management of the entire maintenance and inventory process spread across continents. The more capable maintenance systems are now referred to as Enterprise Asset Management (EAM) systems. The growing popularity of these important business systems was not missed by the makers of Enterprise Resource Planning (ERP) software. Originally the ERP systems looked after materials requirements mostly for production purposes. Later ERP systems included a much greater array of functionality, including maintenance. Some ERP companies bought out the smaller EAM companies and integrated the two products. Financial management systems were often the backbone of these ERP and EAM systems: some were transformed into wholly integrated suites of software and some became a patchwork of different systems "integrated" together and working in a more or less seamless fashion. Today, ERP vendors often target the chief financial officer (CFO) of their customers' companies in making their sales. Their products quite logically serve financial data collection and reporting needs first. The addition of any sort of maintenance capability is usually done to make the package more broadly applicable and to enhance its appeal in the marketplace. Some of these systems evolved to meet the needs of specific industries like mining or pulp and paper. Their built-in processes continue to serve those industries well and have been adapted to meet the needs of other industries. Over time, some financial systems companies gobbled up ERP and EAM companies, integrating their products.

Over the past 10 to 15 years, many software companies were spun-off, acquired, or merged. There was a great deal of fear associated with the reliability of IT systems as we approached the year 2000. That fear foreshadowed what was to come. The IT markets crashed, the "dot com" bubble burst, and what remained was the "dot com bomb." The dust has more or less settled. Many of the players of ten years ago have not survived. Many new players have appeared. The IT markets remain no place for the faint of heart, and the evolution continues with only a few dominant players left in the ERP market and the number of serious EAM and CMMS players much depleted. This state of affairs, while it has somewhat narrowed the number of choices, has not made system selection much easier. Moreover, system implementation is just as challenging as ever.

It has been well documented that up to 70 percent of ERP systems implementations fail to achieve their stated goals, and the use of only 20 to 30 percent system functionality is quite common. In all fairness, today's systems are designed for clients in many varied industries so there is a lot of functionality that is specific to each industry built-in and not intended for use by all. In larger companies, a common refrain is that maintenance demands are not being met by the systems that are installed. These companies usually have one of the larger, fully integrated ERP systems. Complaints that the systems are "user hostile," too complicated, or programmed with unfamiliar terminology are common. With few exceptions, those systems began life as either financial or materials requirements planning systems and grew to include maintenance almost as an afterthought. The maintenance modules are often designed around that functionality, system architecture, and data structure rather than around the need to manage the maintenance process.

Smaller companies are more likely to be using an array of specialized systems rather than the larger (and more expensive) integrated packages. They are the companies that make up the bulk of the still vibrant CMMS market. In these smaller companies, there is often a high degree of satisfaction with the CMMS—they use most of the system capabilities and are generally pleased with the results. The two most important CMMS features commonly found in companies that have had success with these systems are ease of adapting to maintenance processes and user-friendly navigation. With these two features, the systems get used.

The larger and more "functionally rich" systems tend to compromise in the area of user friendliness. They are usually more challenging to implement and to learn. For both reasons, they are often underutilized. Companies that have invested in these systems often alienate the maintenance employees these systems are intended to help. Even younger maintainers, children of the computer era, find these systems cumbersome and frustrating. The companies that manufacture and sell these systems are aware of this (even if they deny it) and are working hard to correct the deficiencies. In some cases, the damage has already been done; in others, technology meant to make work easier has made it more chaotic. The author and his colleagues have visited several facilities that have purchased and are using a CMMS, unaware that their global ERP systems have the same capability. Fortunately, there are many specialty software companies that develop tools for integrating user-friendly applications with corporate ERP systems and for extending their functionality in ways the ERP cannot support on its own. Looking into these products requires some time and effort, but the payoff is well worth it when your users come onboard and begin to use your systems as intended.

What appears to be happening in the major ERP and EAM systems is a trend toward exercising ever tighter control over transactions and, by extension, over the actions of those who make the transactions. This trend was reflected in a quotation used in an advertisement for American Express that appeared in *Chief Executive* magazine in June 2005: "I control the path of every dollar at my company. I control spending differently for each employee. I control all the Cards, and I can do it online. Control is a power thing." There is an inherent problem with this kind of thinking. People do not like to be controlled and they do not like feeling that others have "power" over them. Attempting to control people and their behavior actually stifles creativity and initiative. This control syndrome is a legacy of the industrial age that has persistently refused to disappear. Chapter 2 discusses "self-organizing teams" and the benefits they can bring to a business. If the management systems available to these teams do not work compatibly with people, potential benefits are minimal and difficult to achieve.

The smaller CMMS' have limited functionality, so they don't attempt to control everything. They usually offer a great deal of user-friendly flexibility. That gives more control to the users and because of that they are more empowering—it is small wonder they are very popular. Smaller organizations do things less formally, usually more simply, and with a greater degree of human interaction than is typical in larger organizations. They can do this because smaller is also more human and therefore more natural. Moving away from this toward bigger, more integrated, and more electronic is going against the grain.

Companies that have bought into bigger, better, and more integrated with the underlying motive of gaining tighter control over things risk discovering that this may be detrimental in the long run. Instead of using guiding principles, these companies are imposing a system of rules, and the rules are being broken. Control can become a game, and people will find myriad ways to circumvent controlling rules that do not work or are unduly restrictive.

Computer systems rules are often very tight and unbending. If they do not serve an immediate purpose, however, people find a way around them. Those companies that appear to have well thought out business processes supported by an array of IT systems, often compound the problem with work-arounds.[6] When the workers who put the work-arounds in place leave, the processes grind to a halt. Maintainers just want to do their job and to do it well. They do not want to spend a lot of time navigating their way through a complex, user-hostile computer environment in their greasy overalls. When they are looking for parts or materials, the last thing they want to do is wade through endless screens of information and fill-in-the-blanks.

So what do these systems really do for us? The complete list of functionality of these systems is too extensive to include here, and this is especially true of the many "nice to have" features that do not always serve a needed practical purpose. It is important, however, to provide a list of basic functions a good system should provide and what it should do:

- Keep track of physical assets using the asset register, parts, are materials master files, and keep track of vendors and manufacturers and their contact information.
- Automate parts of the work and materials management processes to save time, improve the productivity of planners and schedulers, help coordinate maintenance activities, and integrate parts ordering with supply chain management systems. This often eliminates a great deal of paper documentation.
- Collect and manage large volumes of transaction data, such as work orders, purchase orders, repairs, parts usage, equipment condition monitoring results, and reliability statistics.
- Carry out calculations such as currency conversion; determine total pricing on materials orders, labor, parts, and contract cost allocations to various accounts; convert failure history record data into reliability statistics, and define work schedules.

---

6. A "work-around" is an alternative and usually simpler way of achieving a result. It is used to bypass an approved or formal approach because it is too cumbersome or simply does not work.

- Manage the movement of data among corporate information systems like finance, accounting, purchasing, human resources, time tracking, and asset tracking.
- Manage large volumes of supporting information, such as drawings, technical manuals, standard job plans, parts specifications, machinery specifications, and tradespersons' skills. This capability is becoming more and more important.
- Generate reports on work done, work outstanding, backlogs, parts usage, repair costs, labor utilization, equipment condition, and reliability statistics.
- Extract data for special purposes, including reliability analysis and improvement efforts.

There are many more capabilities but most of them will fall within these few broad categories. All of these capabilities are intended to help companies save time and effort overall. In large, integrated systems the degree of interconnectivity among business functions, business units, and processes is high. Often that means that seemingly simple transactions appear more complex at the point of data entry. Less capable systems do not exhibit that front-end complexity because they do not support it as well at the back end. They appear to be user-friendly and are often helpful to those working at the point of entry, including maintainers and stores people.

Large, complex systems are based around financial integrity whereas the CMMS is focused on equipment and work management. Unless the financial systems and CMMS are integrated, the cost data collected in the CMMS will usually vary from that contained in the financial systems and that can lead to confusion. However, the CMMS uses terminology that is familiar to maintainers while the financially based systems tend to use unfamiliar financial terminology. Although CMMS are weak in back-end number crunching capability, the trade-off is that they are actually used by front-end staff.

CMMS Overview

At the heart of maintenance execution is the management of work and the management of materials. Chapters 3, 4, and 5 addressed various ways to enhance maintenance and materials management. Figure 7-1 shows an overview of what a CMMS could cover in

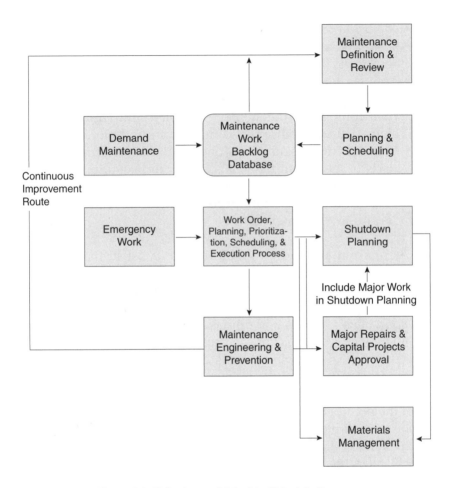

Figure 7-1. Maintenance Linked to Materials Process

maintenance with a link to materials, and Figure 7-2 shows materials processes linked to maintenance. Maintenance software manages a series of transactions all tied to work orders. Those transactions are linked to MRO materials transactions through those same work orders. There are numerous detailed links between the various subprocesses that are not shown in these two figures, for example, the links between planning a job and ordering stores material for issue against its work order. Maintenance and materials management processes must be designed with these links in mind before a computer system is configured. Once configured, the computer program lays out the entire cycle, beginning with the requirements and ending with an analysis or purchasing and inventory control. The complete maintenance plan is addressed, from identifying what work is to be done to analyzing the completed work.

Maintenance and materials processes converge in the plant and equipment configuration and bill of materials, and in the common requirement to provide reports. In its simplest form, the CMMS automates the various subprocesses and the flows of information in these linked processes.

The CMMS of today may run on a computer network that uses mainframe computers or networks of desktop machines interconnected on an intranet or via the Internet, using either hard wiring

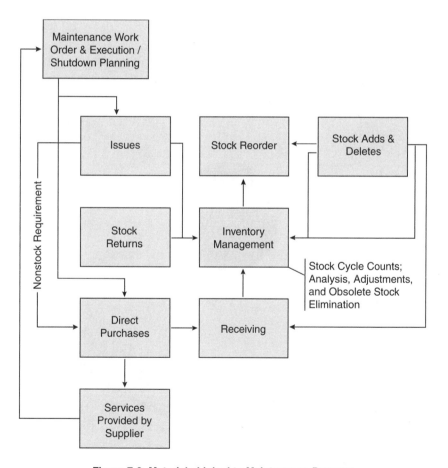

Figure 7-2. Materials Linked to Maintenance Process

or wireless network connections. Many of these systems can now be accessed from anywhere at any time over any secure Internet connection via hand-held devices. The busy maintenance manager can now check up on things at work even while away from the office.

The CMMS is usually divided into modules of related functions, which operate the various data management and analysis activities. Following is a brief description of eight of the more common modules and what they do (see Figure 7-3). These modules are used to manage various maintenance and materials processes (like those shown in Figures 7-1 and 7-2), but the modules do not

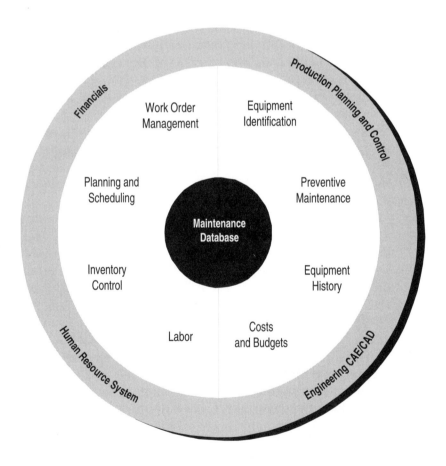

Figure 7-3. Key CMMS Modules

necessarily match the process headings because they usually have more than one process function.

- *Equipment identification.* This is usually one of the first modules to be set up and used. All the equipment covered by the CMMS is logged in with "nameplate" data. Then, the assemblies, components, and parts that make up the equipment are identified and linked according to hierarchy or relationship.
- *Preventive maintenance (PM).* This is a critical module that helps establish the schedule for all proactive and regularly scheduled work. It describes required tasks and materials, allocates costs, and helps maintain schedules, often automatically generating work orders for execution.
- *Equipment history.* Key functions of this module are to keep histories of overhauls, repairs, costs, labor, downtime, and utilization, and to track failure causes and special events in the equipment life cycle.
- *Costs and budgets.* Most packages are able to accumulate projected and actual costs in multiple cost centers for labor, materials, services, and allocated overheads.
- *Labor.* This module keeps an inventory of individuals, their skills, vacation schedules, training history, availability, and utilization to enable accurate work order and project scheduling as well as backlog control.
- *Inventory control.* Available with most packages, this manages the stores inventory. Many businesses use their accounting or production control software to do this job, often on a separate computer. Today's integrated software packages usually manage inventory for maintenance as well as production and office supplies together. The function of this software is to track inventory on hand as well as use, costs, and allocation of inventory items used. It usually integrates with the company purchasing software, although some systems contain a purchasing module as well.
- *Planning and scheduling.* This develops task times, resources required to do the work, and schedules for all types of maintenance work, whether preventive or corrective.
- *Work-order management.* This manages the process of opening a new order, estimating its cost, tracking its status, and ranking it according to priority.

Depending on how sophisticated your package is, many more functions are possible, especially if it is part of a suite of other business system applications.

CMMS Implementation

Like any sophisticated business computer system, the CMMS cannot be simply installed and turned on. Plug-and-play systems are rare and their capabilities are limited. CMMS suppliers are constantly working to develop industry specific templates, a measure that reduces implementation time and costs, but a great deal of dedicated effort is still required to bring the systems online successfully.

It is this area of implementation that leads to many of the failures noted earlier. Rarely are failures of these systems related to inappropriate matching of computer software requirements to supporting hardware infrastructure. The software vendors and your own IT professionals work hard to ensure that does not happen. More often than not the failures occur in the implementation process.

A key to success in implementing a CMMS is to consider maintenance, inventory, and supply chain processes together. Even if inventory management and supply chain have been worked on already, they will need to be integrated as seamlessly as possible with maintenance planning and scheduling processes to ensure the efficient management of maintenance resources. Considering only one or two of these critical processes is almost certain to result in messy results and unhappy users.

Implementation refers to the process of configuring the barebones system that you buy from a vendor to meet your specific requirements. It is a setup and tailoring process and the outcome is a custom product that, if properly configured, is right for your business. However, you are probably not an expert in setting up these systems; after all, if you are in a capital-intensive industry, software is not your business. Get expert help from an implementation consultant, someone who does this for a living. This individual can guide you through the configuration process and help you make the configuration choices best suited to your specific needs.

The implementation process has remained relatively constant despite the dramatic changes in information technology and in the systems themselves. It always begins with the desire to have a system to support your business processes. Because most companies already have a system in place, the real issue is looking at the benefits to be derived from changing what you have to some newer version or to an entirely different system. If you are considering a system that is geared only to maintenance and materials, Figure 7-4 provides some practical guidelines.

Overall Objective	Goal	Business Requirement	System Requirement
Increase Capacity	Improve availability, reliability and maintainability	• Reduce failures • Reduce stoppages • Increase speed	• Support analysis of equipment history and reliability • Manage equipment data • Keep skill profiles • Keep bills of material • Support creation and scheduling of PM routines
		• Reduce variance • Reduce rework	• Monitor machine variance from desired performance • Monitor work-order status and identify rework
		• Performance monitoring	• Track cost and performance data on equipment • Track cost and performance data on work management process
Reduce Costs	Reduce overall maintenance costs	• Reduce labor	• Enable work and control • Enable planning of labor and materials
		• Reduce inventory holding	• Analyze inventory usage • Analyze inventory investment
		• Reduce emergency work	• Support PM scheduling • Support reliability data analysis
		• Reduce paperwork	• Automate work orders • Automate purchase orders
		• Performance monitoring	• Track costs by area, job, type of expense, labor

Figure 7-4. CMMS Objectives

Once you know your objectives, you can begin to find a system that will help you meet them. Be aware that no system can meet all of your objectives on its own. It must be supported by sound business processes and be operated by motivated people using those processes. If you are implementing a CMMS for the first time, it is especially important to understand that you are not just buying "a tool"—this particular tool can support and streamline your business processes and serve as an excellent catalyst for implementing a wide range of changes in the way you do maintenance management. You are well advised to think beyond the tool itself and fully appreciate its power to enable many other functions and operations. Consider redesigning your business processes as the most important part of the system implementation project, otherwise you may find that you are only making your old and possibly ineffective processes faster.

Replacement of an existing system is often driven by obsolescence. Occasionally, a system is replaced because a vendor has gone out of business or no longer supports older version. Software companies do not support their old products forever. The rapid pace of technology growth in that industry prohibits this; to remain competitive in the business, these companies choose to stay abreast of technology changes. The tide never stops, and if you do not want to be simply swept along, you must keep focused on your objective and needs—maintenance and materials. If not, you may become part of a much larger project, a corporate move to an enterprise-wide ERP system. If this occurs, your objectives will become part of a larger picture and some of the features you want may be compromised in the name of corporate data integrity and the integration of all business functions.

Regardless of the scale and scope of the changes and the nature of the software you acquire, the implementation process is basically the same. It will follow a methodology like that shown in Figure 7-5. The time frame associated with implementation may vary, but the figure shows a typical project for a single site. If you have multiple sites to implement, then a roll-out task begins following initial "go live" and debugging. Duration will depend on the approach you take (big-bang vs. phased) and the complexity and extent of changes at the additional sites.

Following this kind of methodology ensures that the system will be implemented and will match your business requirements.

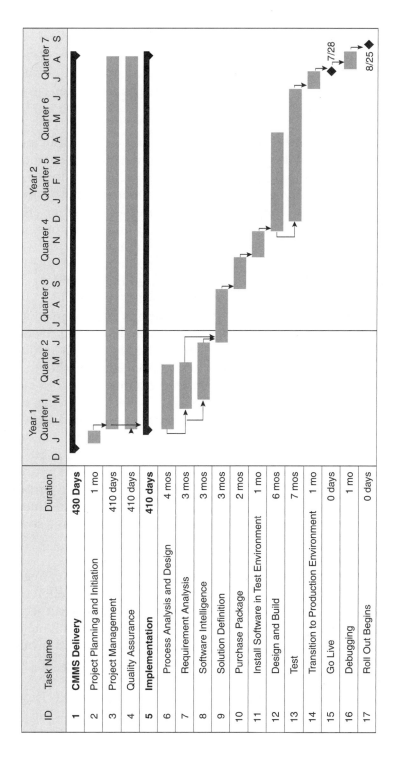

Figure 7-5. CMMS System Delivery Methodology

Success also hinges on the underlying business processes and how well you manage the transition to the new system. The benefits will not derive from the system itself; they will come from the business process changes you implement and follow. The major steps in the methodology are as follows:

Process analysis and design. Process design is discussed in more detail in Chapter 11. It is included here as a first step in any major system implementation project. Your processes should be reviewed, analyzed in detail, and redesigned to meet your business needs. This involves mapping all the processes, whether auto-mated or manual. In detail, define what you do in each business process, what information flows are involved, and how you want them handled. For example, part of the maintenance work identifi-cation process may come from condition-based monitoring. At this point you do not need to worry about how it gets there, just iden-tify that it is needed. It is often argued that process design should be done later, once the system has been selected, to avoid rework-ing process maps to fit system functionality. Not so. The system should support your processes or some other system should be selected. Of course, it is unlikely that you will find an exact match, so you will search for the best fit. Always remember, however, that your choice should be predicated on what is best suited to your processes—do not attempt to fit your processes into what a system can do. It is also advantageous to learn what system capabilities exist and whether these capabilities can facilitate your process design work. Figure 7-5 shows a lot of overlap between process analysis and design, requirements analysis, and software intelli-gence. Depending on your choice, these three steps become some-what iterative.

Requirements analysis. This step ensures that your requirements are identified and documented. Ask yourself if this information is to be input directly into the CMMS up front or whether you will accept manual monitoring and analysis. In this step, you are identifying the major capabilities that the system "must have" to meet your busi-ness requirements at a high level. There is no point in getting too detailed here. Do not be so specific that you tie the vendor's hands. On the other hand, it is important to make informed decisions. Benchmarking, along with other research into what is available, will help you appreciate what is possible. The next step is to scout your system, both software (application) and hardware (technology), from among the many products and vendors on the market. If your hardware environment is fixed, then your software choices will be more limited, but not as severely as you might expect.

Solution definition. This phase expands on the process mapping started earlier and takes you into a more detailed definition of what the system will do and how. It moves you from the required modules identified earlier to the specific functions that the software package supports. In the earlier days of CMMS, these functional specifications resembled laundry lists and were very long and detailed. They listed very specific technical requirements for each module but omitted information about the module's functions. Today, most available systems have virtually all the same features—they just execute them in different ways. If you give a vendor a long list that describes system features that you want, that list will almost certainly be returned to you with all the boxes ticked "yes"—we have that feature. Why waste your time on that very predictable outcome? Specifications that you send to vendors can be brief. Simply let the vendor know what you want the system to do. You can evaluate vendor submissions on how well it does what you want it to do later.

Select vendor solution. At this point, interfaces with other company systems are defined. Many maintenance CMMS and EAM packages may have already been integrated or at least interfaced with the major financial systems of your business, but it is best to ask whether this has been done and to query users whether the systems work well. Again, there is little value in being overly detailed at this time.

You are now ready to contact suppliers and ask them to submit solutions. Do your own research first and eliminate those systems that do not meet your basic requirements. This reduces the number of vendors bidding for the contract and also reduces your workload in evaluating vendor submissions, which are usually bulky and very detailed and require a thorough review.

Vendor pricing can be confusing, so be cautious in your comparisons and make certain you are looking at all the costs. The cost of the licensed "seats" is just the beginning; when you add it all up, the total bill can be two to five times the value of the licenses. Do not forget to factor in costs associated with implementation, user training, future maintenance and upgrades, user help desks, and 24-hour technical support.

Keep in mind that the CMMS sales market is highly competitive (like any software product market). Most vendors are reputable and reliable, but some vendors have been known to do just about anything to get your business. Not all vendors do this, but there are a few vendor "stunts" you should watch out for:

- Not "flowing" all of the terms and conditions from your contract down to subcontractors. In one case an implementation subcontractor used credentials that violated another vendor's confidentiality in a sales situation while in partnership with a different prime contractor.
- Proposing to use staff who are (at the time of proposal) neither part of the supplier's company nor even under contract.
- Subcontracting the consultant who helped you in the requirements definition and specifications phase as the project manager for implementation services.
- Buying their way into the requirements definition and specification process as advisors.
- Presenting a single unified team in the proposal but using team members from various companies that do not all agree on strategy.

In some cases the vendors even sabotage themselves. One software vendor, for example, had a team working on requirements definition for a client. The vendor was not excluded from the bidding and was invited to bid on supplying the software. The RFP had been reworked before it was sent out to bidders. Normally, the previous work would have given the vendor a tremendous advantage over its competitors, but this vendor failed to bid on several required sections of the modified RFP. When asked why, the vendor responded, "Because they were not in scope when we worked on the project." The vendor simply assumed that the customer had accepted the earlier work without question and added or deleted nothing. That was a fatal assumption, and another supplier was awarded the contract.

In another case, a client had over a dozen operating sites worldwide, most of them using a particular vendor's software. As part of a global transformation project, the entire company was switching to a single, globally integrated software platform. The vendor the client had worked with previously was one of the few contenders capable of delivering a desired solution and was asked to submit a proposal. The vendor's proposal was appalling. It failed to respond to major RFP issues and did a rather poor job responding to other concerns. That vendor had just been taken over by another software company (something that happens frequently in the software industry) and the client, who was hoping to integrate the new software with software already deployed, gave the vendor a second chance. The second proposal was no better than the first and, once again, another supplier's proposal was accepted. The vendor had incorrectly assumed that that the client, who was already using the company's software, would make a choice based on prior association. The company failed to appreciate that although its software was installed in most of the client company's global sites, the versions installed at these sites were not conducive to integration, a major objective for the client.

A final note on vendor solutions is to separate the contract for external support from any contract for implementation support services. Some companies prohibit the consultants who help them select their systems from even bidding on the implementation services. This helps to keep the playing field more even in a competitive landscape.

Design and build. Once you have selected your system, you can begin the implementation process by customizing the package to fit your operation. There is no point customizing a new system to suit old processes that fail to take advantage of the new system's full capability. The first step, then, is to review, analyze, and redesign your processes. The process review should consider using successful new practices and changing or eliminating inefficient or ineffective practices. Integrate your maintenance, inventory, and supply chain management processes. Failure to do this can create a great deal of angst if new systems do not deliver on their promised results. This phase of the project provides a wonderful opportunity to get your business processes right, efficient, and fully integrated with each other. (See Chapter 11 for more on process design.) Redesign and customization can take anywhere from three months to two years, depending on system complexity and how much it is integrated with other functions like HR and finance. Do not be surprised by version upgrade during the course of your implementation. New versions of many of these packages appear in 24-month cycles or even more frequently. You will need operation procedures for data conversion, installation, and daily use. Do not neglect or scrimp on training. This is probably the single most common cause for implementation failure. When you have all your requirements tailored into an acceptable solution, you can turn the system on for general use, but it is best not to "go live" without testing whether it works.

Test. Make sure that the users (the maintenance and possibly production people), not the systems department or supplier, test the CMMS in the workplace. You want the system to operate under conditions as near to real life as possible. During the testing phase, you will find many of the little bugs and mistakes that filtered into the complex tailoring process. You may also find bugs in the software itself. It is preferable to find these bugs now, in a controlled test environment, than to find them when you have hundreds or thousands of users trying to do their jobs on a system that is supposed to be right but is not. Your operators and maintainers are best able to judge whether the system is covering the ground in maintenance management, user and technical procedures, backup and recovery, security, volume, and performance. Let them "play" with it and follow the new processes and procedures with it. They will find most of the bugs for you, and you can correct them before turning the system loose on the entire company.

Transition. This final phase is important to get your new system up and running without any major kinks. It involves converting data, fully installing the new CMMS and manual procedures, and, most importantly, handing over responsibility to user management. When your system is ready to "go live," your first task will be to transfer into it "dynamic" information that users will need. This includes any open work orders from the old system, information on open purchase orders and material requisitions and inventory stock levels, and other similar information. All information is transferred into the new system at the last moment before you switch it on so that people do not lose the work they have already done.

If you are doing this across multiple sites you will probably want to do some tailoring to accommodate minor differences in the way those sites work, test again, and go through the "go live" transition at each site. Your first site implementation will be the template that can facilitate the process at other sites, but do not assume that each site will be the same. These sites are staffed by people, and this means variables.

Whichever package solutions you eventually purchase, it is a good idea to buy the maintenance contract as well. First, it ensures that your software will remain current with the periodic updates issued. Second, if you become an active participant in the software company's user conferences, you can influence the direction these updates take. If your industry is strongly represented in the customer installed base, updates will likely be geared to your business. The cost of the maintenance option is usually about 10 percent to 15 percent of the software cost. The key to success in any project, including CMMS implementation, is your people. They must accept and use the new system, and it is best to involve them in the process from the start. Involve them in developing the business case for a new system. Involve them in defining system requirements and selection. Involve them in implementation. The system will be successful if it truly helps them to do their jobs better, makes their jobs a bit easier, and helps the company excel. Your people may accept and use an enterprise-wide integrated system that is not user friendly if it enables them to achieve their personal goals. If it makes their job harder they will not be supportive; if they use the system at all, they will not use it well.

The "people factor" is an important consideration for evaluating whether a CMMS is a worthwhile investment. But because these systems take a long time to specify, select, implement, other factors must also be considered when weighing the cost-benefit ratio. These are discussed below.

Justifying Your CMMS

Total costs for a CMMS can easily run from tens of thousands into the tens of millions of dollars for enterprise systems. If you are buying maintenance as part of a corporate ERP, for example, the cost may be hundreds of millions. Software costs are typically less than half of the total cost at the lower end of the range and less than

20 percent of the cost at the higher end. If you consider the entire cost—customizing, interfacing with other systems, training, implementation effort, communications, the incremental hardware capacity (such as add-on printers, scanners, radio frequency, and portable devices), the costs add up. And this does not include the cost of your own staff and the related costs of changes in processes and practices that will be required to make the system work. In the long run, the CMMS can save you money and it enables data collection in support of efforts to improve asset availability. Nevertheless, a convincing case for improved maintenance productivity and increased asset availability is needed in order to justify this expense.

Maintenance productivity can be defined as output divided by input. Output is measured as equipment availability, operating speed, precision, and reliability. Input is money spent on labor, materials, services, and overhead. In and of itself, CMMS will do little to improve your productivity. CMMS, EAM, and ERP vendors do not like to admit this because it makes their job of selling systems considerably tougher. What systems do, however, is to help you "lock in" process improvements or trigger process improvement initiatives so that you become more productive. If a system does not do either of these, there is no need for it.

Failure rate and duration, as well as other performance standards, depend greatly on a maintenance program that is properly developed, scheduled, and executed. That, in turn, relies on equipment failure histories, records of repairs and overhauls completed, and lists of the correct materials and resources used. Even with the best systems available, collecting and analyzing the available data is a challenge. Minimizing downtime for inspection, repair, and overhaul requires scheduling and coordination of labor and parts. It is not data management that makes this happen; it is people. These people need training; often, they need to change long-established behavior patterns. Both training and behavior modification come at a price.

Despite the cost, effective data management clearly has an impact on maintenance output. Many companies have found that using information management effectively can produce significant results:

- Equipment effectiveness (the product of availability, speed, and precision) can jump from 50 percent to 85 percent.

- Reliability (mean time between failures) can rise 20 percent.
- Workforce productivity can increase 20 to 30 percent.
- Usage of materials can be reduced 20 to 50 percent.

More efficient use of labor, materials, and outside contractors often means savings of 5 percent to 15 percent of total maintenance costs. It is always difficult, however, to attribute the savings to any one activity or change. The CMMS is only a tool. It acts as an information framework around which to manage maintenance. Did the savings actually come from inputting data, manipulating information, and generating reports? Of course not! Did they arise from developing and implementing a solid PM program that is supported by a module that is now there to be used? Possibly, but this is a moot point. What really matters is that you will not get the savings if all of the work is not done.

Surveys by various software vendors, maintenance periodicals, and consultants working in the field show that real benefits are achieved in both increased productivity and direct maintenance costs, but they come from how you use the system not from the system itself. One intangible benefit is often improved communication between and among operations, materials management, and among your tradespeople. Some companies have found it difficult to achieve these benefits without outside help. The example below illustrates what can occur.

A wood products plant was getting nothing from its brand-new, state-of-the-art CMMS, which was purchased from one of the most reputable vendors. The company was spending a great deal of effort on implementing the system with no outside help. A top maintenance supervisor was leading the implementation, a job he had never done before. The system was not working right and bills for dial-up technical support were high. There was a root cause for all of these problems—no one at the plant had reviewed the underlying business processes and the new system was merely automating the old ones. The added complexity of the system actually increased the time it was taking to issue work orders and order materials. Retained to improve the situation, the author and his team first shut the system down and started doing everything manually. The underlying premise to this was to discover whether the problems were being caused by the way the work was being done. If it was not being done correctly manually, it would never be done correctly with a computer. This, in fact, proved to be the case. Once flaws in the work process were revealed, the business processes were quickly streamlined and became efficient. An experienced implementation consultant cleaned up the errors that had been made in the earlier tailoring efforts and matched the system tailoring to the new processes. Several weeks were spent on training users who then tested the system. Two months after the system was turned off, it went live and this time, it worked. Users were happy; work orders and material orders were faster; and records were finally being kept—automatically and efficiently. The informal interpersonal networks that were built up during the period of manual operation created positive working relationships; when glitches turned up, there was always a way to fix them quickly. The company in question got the help it needed, but it paid a price for the long delay in getting things to work smoothly while its people muddled around in unfamiliar territory.

A Case Study in CMMS Implementation: Molson Canada

An interesting case study for CMMS application is Molson's Brewery in Canada. This case study appeared in the original edition of *Uptime* published in 1995 and is updated in this edition to show the development and use of a system based on what is now considered "old" technology. It is an excellent example of how the implementation process works and is still relevant today. It demonstrates that a CMMS can be a long-term investment regardless of technological advances in information technology. It also shows the importance of key people in championing and sustaining these investments. Regardless of the technologies being used, the situation described here can be found in many companies today.

The brewing industry in Canada consists of many medium-size and small plants in each province because provincial laws stipulate that beer be made in the province where it is sold. Molson has plants in every region, coast to coast, across Canada.

In the early 1980s, each of Molson's plants had its own local maintenance approach. The plants had time-based preventive maintenance programs, corrective maintenance for breakdowns, and overhauls during scheduled shutdowns. Systems were ad hoc, both manual and automated. In the mid-1980s, the engineering group recognized the potential cost savings and capacity improvement of making three changes in the way in which maintenance was managed. First, fix the process; second, automate it; and third, get leverage by doing it the same way in all Molson plants. Molson developed a systematic approach to work-order management, PM development, and maintenance store management. The brewery then purchased IBM S36 minicomputers and the ShawWare (MAR-CAM) maintenance and materials management package. After a blitz of implementation, improvements were achieved in the planning and control of maintenance. With the usual promotions and engineering staff turnover, implementation slowed down before the full integration of the process and systems was completed. Furthermore, Molson's underwent a merger with Carling O'Keefe, the third largest brewery in Canada. The restructuring was comprehensive, with complete integration of operations.

In the early 1990s, it was difficult to get vendor support of the S36s and their application programs, but there was a need for upgrading. IBM AS400s replaced the less capable S36s, and the manufacturing, financial, and CMMS systems were upgraded as well. A network was established, linking the largest of the eight regional plants. The CMMS configuration in these plants included five AS400 minis, 120 PC/terminals, and 30 laser printers, networked across all functions and all locations.

The capital cost for the project totaled over $3.5 million. This included software, hardware, networking, outside help, and in-house information technology staff. In addition, three user representatives were assigned full time—a champion from maintenance engineering, a storage inventory specialist, and a systems application specialist. With this investment, Molson's senior management was looking for quantifiable returns. After the first two years (1993–1994) of implementation, improvements in plant performance and cost reductions were excellent, approaching the $3.5 million capital cost. Equipment effectiveness was up, and overtime was down. Maintenance productivity is up at the three largest plants, and stores inventory savings were substantial. Other savings were being realized in purchasing efficiency, reduced overhauls, and staff effectiveness.

At the time, the project champion was confident that these savings would grow as the remaining plants took full advantage of the system capabilities. Maintenance costs represent about 16 percent of operating costs across Molson plants. The overarching vision was to reduce this to 12 percent over three years—the number achieved by their best plant. That was achieved. The project manager believed that the main reasons for this success were supportive management, accountability for results, and a true vendor partnership with the software company.

Now, some 13 years later, the system known internally as MARS is still in operation. Since initial implementation, several of the brewery's plants have been shut down to consolidate production capacity and gain scale efficiency. The system is being used at all five of the remaining plants in Canada. However, because of differences in the degree of implementation at the various locations, only Montreal and Toronto (the largest plants) are really using it for maintenance management. (In late 1995, the system administrator function was eliminated. Then, in early 1996, the engineer who had been most responsible for introducing the software at Molson left to pursue other career opportunities. Without a real champion, the software was not as rigorously implemented in the other plants.)

The system's original vendor underwent several management and ownership changes over the years and continues to evolve. The company now boasts a form of "reliability centered" processing, a graphic user interface (GUI) front-end, and other enhancements. In mid-1998, the engineer overseeing Molson's MARS at the time decided that Molson should no longer upgrade the application to keep it current with the vendor's ongoing offerings. The company would, however, continue to improve the MARS system in-house. Since that time, numerous minor improvements suggested by users have been implement. Several of the more significant upgrades were to

- Interface the system with the corporate e-Procurement application,
- Implement hand-held RF devices in Montreal for stores issues and physical inventory functions,
- Develop many ancillary reports and data extracts to assist users' specific requirements,
- Implement a capability for importing vendor pricing updates, and
- Interface with the payroll application to import Montreal maintenance labor costs.

One veteran user of Molson's MARS recently reported that the company is using four fully implemented MARS modules to their fullest. The four modules in use are for MRO procurement, inventory control, accounts payable, and maintenance management. For reporting and scheduling functions not provided by the software, Molson uses current stand-alone products.

Although MARS is an old CMMS technology, Molson plants are currently using the work-order management component at 100 percent for equipment care. The planning function is used for work-order generation from PMs, customer requests, condition-monitoring[7] alarm acknowledgement, and generation of condition-based maintenance work orders, routine repairs, and modifications. They track labor, stock and nonstock parts and materials, as well as contracted services by entity in their asset register, through a cost-centered link between general ledger accounts and equipment numbers. Scheduling is performed using a feed from the MARS generated backlog of work orders exported to a separate spreadsheet or project planning software tools to assist in tracking execution. The automated PM capability is utilized for inspections and minor repairs as well as for tracking inspection history. Approximately 50 percent of the PMs have a linked material list to stores and equipment nameplate data that is entered manually to keep this information accessible. Tradespersons' names and work execution dates are manually entered onto their PM work-order records to track both "as found" and "as left" conditions—keys to later reliability analysis.

In addition to implementing the MARS system, Molson set out to improve maintenance work management practices. The company has succeeded in moving away from firefighting (i.e., reactive work) to performing more proactive work. The old method of waiting for something to break and then throwing resources at it has almost completely disappeared at Molson. The use of more accurate terminology has helped to change behavior. The tradespeople, for example, are now called "line support" and are delegated to proactive work from a line support resource pool. This has paid large dividends in terms of increasing "uptime" for the lines. The

---

7. Condition-monitoring signals are gathered by a separate system and relayed to the MARS software.

company has also introduced a progressive overhaul approach as described in Chapter 3.

Stores inventory is managed using a combination of Max and Min settings, contract vendor supplied items for high turnover consumables, and low-cost and high-volume vendor managed items. Stores inventory management in MARS is described by its users as running "like a Swiss watch."

Labor costs are tracked in MARS, although not as accurately as in the separate payroll software system. In the Toronto plant, the link between MARS and payroll is not as complete as that in Montreal.

Accounts payable was centralized across Canada and became a corporate accounting function. The A/P module now has an e-commerce link to assist in hands-free invoice payment. As long as there is a work order in the system linked to a purchase order, which is a system generated electronic purchase requisition, parts and materials receiving records are balanced and A/P runs very smoothly.

WHERE ARE WE HEADED WITH SYSTEMS?

There is a real need in the market that is only now being addressed by the software community. The trade-off between user-friendliness (and hence user acceptance) and the need for a high degree of visibility and control of costs often lead to compromises that satisfy no one completely.

Large integrated systems (ERP systems) offer very high degrees of control and provide for single data entry for multiple uses at just about any scale. They have also evolved to provide a vast scope of functionality serving data-processing needs across entire companies. These enterprise systems are truly remarkable in both scope and scale, but they are also very expensive and hard for many to use, even with training. Despite the high cost and the unresolved issues related to using these systems, software companies that sell them and financial people who like the high degree of control they offer view them as the "Holy Grail" of computing.

Small single function or single process systems (for example, dedicated CMMS) do not provide the scale or scope of ERP systems, and integrating them with other single process systems can be quite expensive. Maintaining those integration points can be a challenge—every time either system changes, the custom integration software must be updated too. Just ask anyone who has integrated a major CMMS with a major financial or procurement package. These systems, however, are usually easy to use and are often preferred by shopfloor and operations people, the end users. They are less popular with corporate financial people who prefer greater cross-enterprise cost visibility.

Recently it appears that the financial concerns have won out, particularly in the wake of the financial debacles that have spawned ever-tighter regulations and reporting requirements for publicly traded companies. In the late 1990s and early 2000s, the smaller systems appeared to be losing ground in the market, particularly in the larger companies where the siren song of data integration sung by the ERP vendors is still well received. There are fewer and fewer of these smaller systems in the market. At the same time, it is becoming increasingly clear that the large integrated systems are not serving user needs very well. As a result, some functions of the large systems are not being used at all; single modules are ignored while users work around them by using another system or a combination of systems, even if these are not officially mandated by the company's IT people. Compounding this situation is the growing array of purpose-built and highly specialized decision support tools, monitoring tools, and engineering systems discussed earlier in the chapter. They rarely integrate with either the large systems or the smaller ones, yet they depend in part on some of the data that these systems contain. This has led to the development of various "middle-ware" packages, which gather data useful for these tools.

For the moment, neither the large nor the small software companies seem to be inclined to offer a simpler solution to the problems encountered by their customers as they are more or less locked into their perceptions and ideas of what is best for their chosen market. For most vendors of large systems, moving away from those positions is untenable because it threatens their "unique" and expensive solutions and exposes them to greater competition. Companies that produce smaller systems simply do not have the market clout to do anything but go along with this. With only two major choices available, customers are compelled to pick the lesser of two evils. Going the large, integrated route invariably means adding a number of specialized stand-alone or bolt-on packages; going with a patchwork of smaller functional systems also means additional stand-alone packages. This guarantees a lot of work for

IT people worldwide but does not serve the needs of the user very well. Fortunately, there is a solution on the horizon that has the potential to work for both users and software companies alike.

A standard for data exchange that covers all business processes and functional areas could define the data elements needed to feed these various systems. Already there is one standard, MIMOSA,[8] that enables the free exchange of machinery and operations information. Based on Internet protocols, MIMOSA moves the software packages away from older client-server technologies to fully web-architected systems.

As this book was being written, many (but not all) of the CMMS, EAM, and ERP solutions were attempting a similar Internet interface, and, on some levels, they even appeared to be based on Internet technology. However, most still relied on client-server technology and unique or nonstandardized databases. Fully web-architected systems use a common web-services standard for full interoperability. Unless they follow an Internet-based standard, the systems will not work on the Internet.

If they can comply with the demands of this Internet-based standard, information software companies will eventually be able to exchange information between and among their systems much more easily. Data warehouses already work on this concept to a certain extent. Because there is no Internet-based standard for data warehouses, they have all created their own. Integration among various client-server systems still requires that each be interfaced to the data warehouse and often requires data conversion from one to the other. There have already been mergers of different data warehouse standards, but, to date, there appears to be no industry-wide collaboration.

With access to fully web-architected systems, a user company will be able to pick whatever software solution it prefers and easily interface with other web-architected systems. Through simple interface, for example, data collected by maintenance will be easily accessed by purchasing, accounting, human resources, and others, without expensive and complex data conversions. Similarly,

---

8. MIMOSA stands for Machinery Information Management Open Systems Alliance. It is a nonprofit trade association that develops and encourages adoption of open information standards for operations and maintenance.

the maintenance system will be able to optimize its various data tables by adding important data extracted from those other systems. The maintenance system will use employee trade skills information from the HR system. Parts usage for any given maintenance work order will be available via the data warehouse and used by the inventory management system. Data required for reliability analysis will be extracted from condition-monitoring systems, work orders, operational control and monitoring systems, and accounting.

The large integrated system vendors (ERPs) probably have the most to lose from this Internet-based interface standard because it all but eliminates their strongest suit—their respective unique versions of client-server technology. The web-architected model opens each of their modules up to competition from smaller system suppliers that might have more user-friendly products. The smaller system vendors are likely to benefit from increased connectivity to other systems, but the nature of the competition among them for specific customers will probably change. Data warehouse suppliers will probably see the need for their products disappear. In the end, the user will have the most to gain.

UPTIME SUMMARY

Computerized systems are important and now seemingly indispensable tools for business. Just remember the last power failure you experienced and you will understand that there is very little that is not computerized these days. Technology and its business applications continue to grow and proliferate. The world of maintenance is no exception. Most maintenance work is not computerized, but it is complex and managing it requires sophisticated tools. Using those tools effectively will improve the efficiency with which you deliver maintenance services. Use them poorly and you only add cost.

There are two broad categories of technology with which maintainers work: support systems and management information systems. The first category includes the various specialized support systems for data gathering, processing, analysis, and decision-making support. These tools are meant to help today's knowledge workers, your maintenance technicians and engineers, do their jobs efficiently and effectively. They are used to monitor equipment condition, analyze equipment performance trends, analyze failure history data, perform complex reliability calculations, provide support for equipment replacement decisions, and forecast probabilities. They are often designed as stand-alone systems to be used by trained specialists, and they seldom integrate seamlessly with management information systems. These tools, in the right hands, can produce remarkable results and quickly earn a return on your investment.

The second category includes the various management information systems: computerized maintenance management systems, enterprise asset management systems, and enterprise resource planning systems. These systems automate business processes and information flows associated with a variety of business transactions. In maintenance, these systems use the work order as their primary transaction document. They can produce management reports, schedules, and plans from which it is possible to see trends in performance measures and then make management decisions. Their main function is to support management processes. They are expensive to acquire, install, implement, and operate. They can take months or even years to get going. However, when coupled with business process redesign, the implementation of effective maintenance, inventory, and supply chain processes, they can add a great deal of value.

All of these systems are undergoing constant development and expansion of capability. The single purpose systems and simpler forms of management systems tend to be easier to use. The broader the capability and the greater the functionality of a system, the more difficult it is to use. Suppliers of these systems are working hard to change that. One development is the emergence of standards for data interchange using Internet architectures that would permit multiple systems, each having different purposes, to share data. This opens up the possibility for specialized decision support systems to gather needed data from management systems and vice versa.

The world of maintenance support and management systems is complex and crowded with competing products. Explore what you really need to achieve, define how systems can help, and keep the choices as simple as you can. It will all change again tomorrow.

PART III

Choosing Excellence

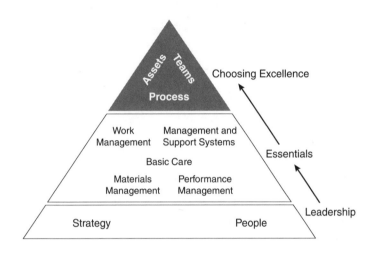

This part of the book describes several methods used by successful companies to take their performance from merely good to great. There are three possible approaches—asset, team (people), and process centric—and they are best used in combination. Asset-centric methods focus on improving reliability of physical assets to obtain more uptime. There are both proactive and continuous improvement (reactive) approaches to doing this (described in the first two chapters of this part of the book). High-performing companies with strong engineering and technical "cultures" tend to favor these methods. Team-based methods, such as Total Productive Maintenance, are based on getting the most from your people who will, in turn, get the most out of your assets. These methods frequently incorporate reliability-based approaches, using them as tools in a more holistic approach. Process-centric methods are used by almost all companies to varying degrees. Even poor performers have processes, albeit these are often informal and disorderly. High performers have both efficient and effective processes that serve the needs of their people in delivering uptime.

Chapters 8 and 9 cover asset-centric approaches, methods that focus directly on the assets you maintain and operate. Chapter 8 focuses on Reliability-Centered Maintenance (RCM) as the predominant proactive method to get the greatest return on your investment in reliability methods. Chapter 9 addresses several continuous improvement methods that can enhance any maintenance program.

8

Asset-Centric Approaches 1: Being Proactive

There is little point in doing maintenance the right way
if you are doing the wrong maintenance.

JOHN MOUBRAY[1]

Doing the right maintenance work the right way is not all that difficult, but there is no one "right way" to make the transition from where you are to achieving your vision. In fact, there are as many ways to approach it as there are companies that want to make the shift. You can start virtually anywhere. Although it is not essential to think about overall maintenance strategy first, this is strongly recommended because it provides the overall direction that you will follow. You may, however, choose to start with work management because this helps eliminate some of the chaos. You may also decide to focus on performance measures, which help inject some discipline into the process, or even begin by installing a new computerized management system. All of these are steps that go in the same general direction so you cannot go wrong with any of them, but you will ultimately find that it is easier to stay on track if you follow some sort of strategic approach. In this part of the book, you will learn about approaches or methods that work at the site or

---

1. John Moubray was a recognized leader in the field of reliability management. He authored *Reliability-Centered Maintenance II*, which was first published in 1991 by Butterworth-Heinemann, Oxford, UK, and founded Aladon LLC to develop and deliver RCM services globally. Moubray created a global network of professional RCM practitioners (including the author) who have collectively helped well over a thousand companies in nearly every industry and country of the world.

business unit level and embrace doing the right things in maintenance the right way.

John Moubray's excellent point about making sure you are doing the right maintenance lies at the heart of the process. If you are on the wrong path, you will not get where you are trying to go, at least not directly. For this reason, you must make choices that are consistent with your stated goals and lead to high reliability of your physical assets. One path is proactive, another is reactive, and both are supported by a variety of techniques that can make implementation more precise.

Maintainers often use condition monitoring and overhaul tactics in proactive programs. Some opt for a traditional approach to developing maintenance programs, basing choices on historical precedence ("we've always done it this way"), on experience (hard-learned lessons), and on technical manuals from vendors. Others choose to use rigorous methods like Reliability-Centered Maintenance to determine the most appropriate failure management strategies. Where a maintenance program is already in place, PM optimization is sometimes used to align existing programs with RCM concepts. Using the traditional approach alone will not produce optimum results, and despite its name, neither will PM optimization. Even RCM is not perfect. It is, however, the most thorough method you can use.

Wherever companies put maintenance tactics in place using traditional approaches without RCM, they fall short, often far short, of choosing excellence. In some cases, these companies are not familiar with RCM and other optimization methods, but more often than not, they are trying to avoid investing in these RCM methods because they are not totally sold on their potential value. They generally opt for a short-term approach that gets them short-term results. In companies with this mindset, it has always been easy to spot failure modes that were not addressed or tactics that addressed failure modes the wrong way. Very often, the overt symptom of this is also easy to see: far more maintenance work than is really necessary. These well-intentioned but short-sighted efforts at quickly creating "PM" programs often fail to improve reliability performance substantially, they rarely reduce costs, and they often damage the credibility of the maintenance department because they fail to deliver on promised business improvements. The quick and dirty approach, the silver bullet, simply does not work and basic care (Chapter 4) is not enough on its own. The most effective maintenance programs are developed using RCM at the design stage to determine which tactics are the most appropriate in each circumstance. RCM works extremely well at both the design stage and after an asset has entered service. It is the most thorough method available to determine maintenance program requirements and it is highly recommended, especially if the consequences of failure include safety, environmental, and severe business loss risks.

Reliability management is all about maximizing uptime and minimizing the frequency of downtime incidents. The primary benefit of reliability management is that it increases asset reliability by increasing Mean Time Between Failures (MTBF). This, in turn, leads to increased availability, greater production potential, and revenue generation. Increased reliability also reduces costs because it reduces the need for expensive repairs and downtime with production losses. Chapter 6 discussed overall performance measures, including reliability-related measures that are a key output of maintenance efforts. A few technical measures and their definitions[2] are a useful way to introduce RCM:

- **Availability**[3] (A) is the proportion of time that an asset is available for use.

  $A = (Scheduled\ Uptime - All\ Downtime) \div Scheduled\ Time$

  Or, more simply, $A = Uptime \div Total\ Time$.

- To improve "A" we want to increase uptime and decrease downtime. In some definitions total time excludes downtime for planned maintenance activities. Be aware that in this case, there is an underlying assumption that some planned maintenance is necessary—that is not always the case. Planned maintenance downtime, like downtime for any other cause, serves to limit availability. Sometimes it is needed and sometimes it is not.[4]

---

2. There are many textbooks on reliability that present precise mathematical definitions. The reader is encouraged to review these. One particularly good reference is *Maintenance, Replacement and Reliability Theory and Applicatons* by A.K.S. Jardine and Albert H.C. Tsang, originally published in 1979 and revised in 2006 by CRC Press, Taylor and Frances Group.
3. See the definition and discussion in Chapter 6.
4. RCM is a very useful methodology that helps us determine where PM is and is not appropriate as a failure management policy.

- **Mean Time Between Failures** (MTBF) is the statistical mean of the failure distribution curve associated with any specific plant, vehicle, equipment, or component failure history. Most failures tend to be random in nature so MTBF is often approximated by dividing the "life" of the asset, or the combined life of a fleet of identical assets, by the number of failures experienced in that lifetime. "Life" in this case is the length of time the asset survived from the time it was put into service until the time it failed. A common error that is made in calculating MTBF is to include all downtime events as failures. Many are not actually failures and should not be factored into this statistic.

- **Mean Down Time** (MDT) is the average length of time taken to restore an asset to service. MDT is calculated by dividing the total downtime (shutdown time + time taken preparing the equipment for work + repair time + warm up + start-up time, etc.) by the total number of reliability-driven downtime incidents for any reason including repairs and preventive actions. Downtime for purely process or production-related purposes is usually not included although it can have a substantial impact on availability.

- **Mean Time to Repair** (MTTR) is the average length of time taken to repair an asset when it has failed. MTTR is calculated by dividing the total repair time for a number of failures by the number of failures. To increase availability (A) you want to minimize the time to repair.

- **Reliability**[5] (R) is the probability that any asset will survive for a specified duration of time (or mission). As a probability it has no dimension. If the failures are random in nature (and most are), then reliability is a function of the asset's MTBF. Consequently, MTBF is often used to express reliability. The greater the value of MTBF, the more reliable the asset.

RELIABILITY-CENTERED MAINTENANCE

RCM is a method for determining the most appropriate maintenance policy for any given asset in its present operating context. RCM is not a way of doing maintenance and it is not the same thing

---

5. See definition and discussion in Chapter 6.

as condition-based maintenance. It is an analysis and decision-making method. RCM can be used on its own or in combination with other methods. For example, it is sometimes used within the context of Total Productive Maintenance (see the chapter on People-centric Approaches) to define failure management policies for dealing with specific failure modes that arise in an asset's specific operating situation or context. It is an entirely proactive approach that anticipates which failures are likely to occur, what will happen when they do occur, and what can be done to minimize or eliminate their consequences. RCM is about eliminating or reducing consequences, not just about improving asset reliability. Sometimes (in fact often) RCM reveals running assets to failure as the best alternative. RCM output is correlated to specific operating environments and circumstances and is therefore "right" for any given context or situation. It can be used in an existing asset environment or it can be used at the design stage for a new asset. For greatest benefit, it should be used early in the asset life cycle (preferably at the design stage) where its findings can influence the design itself and save considerable capital cost outlay and optimize operating and maintenance costs for the entire operational life of the asset. In the 1980s, the author used an early version of RCM extensively in a naval ship design project, where it resulted in substantial improvements in fleet availability to the extent that fewer vessels were needed to replace a larger fleet. That alone saved nearly $2 billion in capital costs. In the mining industry, it has helped mines devise a plan to park excess vehicles and reduce both operating and maintenance costs.

Some Background on RCM

RCM was launched in the U.S. commercial airline industry during the early 1960s. It developed in response to rapidly increasing maintenance costs, poor availability of assets, and concerns about the effectiveness of traditional time-based preventive maintenance. The problems were obvious, so was the need—more reliable maintenance programs.

Studies of existing engineering techniques and preventive maintenance practices were conducted. The results revealed two surprising facts about the traditional, time-based, preventive maintenance approach:

1. Scheduled overhaul has little positive effect on the overall reliability of a complex item and can even worsen its reliability.
2. There are many items for which fixed-interval maintenance is ineffective because assets do not fail as a result of age or usage.

This research also revealed the six patterns of conditional probability of failure described in Chapter 4. Knowing which failure pattern you are dealing with is a big help in determining what maintenance or other failure management approach is technically most feasible. The results of these initial studies have extended far beyond the airline industry that prompted them. They were used to develop the basis of RCM, a logical approach to creating a preventive maintenance program that can be applied to any industry.

RCM was first applied on a large scale to develop the maintenance program of the Boeing 747. Later, it was used for the L-1011 and DC-10. The results have been impressive. These aircraft achieved significant reductions in scheduled or time-based maintenance, with no decrease in reliability. For example, only 66,000 labor hours of structural inspections were required before first heavy inspection at 20,000 flying hours on the Boeing 747, as compared to 4,000,000 labor hours over the same period on the smaller DC-8.

RCM (or MSG-3 as it is known in the aerospace industry) is now used to develop the maintenance programs for all major types of aircraft. Other applications include the Navy, utilities, the offshore oil industry, and manufacturing processes. RCM is particularly suitable in private-sector or military facilities with large, complex equipment where equipment failure poses significant economic, safety, or environmental risks. Today, there are many variations (industrial and military) on the original RCM concept developed in the airline industry by Stan Nowlan and Howard Heap.[6] In 1999, SAE published a standard, JA-1011, "Evaluation Criteria for Reliability-Centered Maintenance Processes." According to the standard, RCM is suitable "for use by any organization that has or makes use of physical assets or systems that it wishes to manage responsibly." In 2002, SAE published another standard,

---

6. F. S. Nowlan and H. Heap, *Reliability-centered Maintenance* (Springfield, Virginia: National Technical Information Service, U.S. Department of Commerce, 1978).

JA-1012, "A Guide to the Reliability-Centered Maintenance Standard," that amplified and clarified key criteria listed in JA-1011 and summarized issues to be addressed before successful application of RCM. Since that time, various so-called "RCM methods" have emerged; some of these, unfortunately, do not fully comply with the SAE standards and should not be confused with true RCM. Many of these "RCM" methodologies are based on purely engineering hardware and component approaches. Even when supported with databases of failure modes, the approach advocated by some of these RCM spin-offs can mean a great deal more work to arrive at essentially the same results. Streamlined versions that attempt to shortcut the method also exist. Although these methods have been somewhat successful, they invariably leave something out and complete only part of a full job. The purpose of this chapter is to address RCM's functional approach, which develops failure management policies based on maintaining functions of assets as opposed to maintaining the assets themselves. The description of the RCM process that follows is based on the author's knowledge[7] of RCM II.

The RCM Process

The first step is to decide which assets you will examine using RCM. At the design stage, you might choose to analyze all systems. In an existing operation[8] you might pick the assets that are causing the greatest financial pain, those that are most unreliable, or those that are known to create safety or environmental problems when they fail. Prioritize your assets and deal with the highest priority items first. You may eventually want to analyze other assets with lower priority, a practice that some companies follow. Once you have decided what to analyze, you are ready to begin the RCM process. The best way to do this is through a seven-step approach that answers specific questions in the following order:[9]

---

7. The author was formally trained in RCM II by the late John Moubray and is certified by Aladon as an RCM II Practitioner.
8. An alternative albeit less-thorough approach for existing operations, known as "PM Optimization" is discussed in the next chapter.
9. SAE, JA 1011, "Evaluation Criteria for Reliability-Centered Maintenance (RCM) Processes," August 1999.

1. What are the functions and associated desired standards of performance of the asset in its present operating context? (What do we want the asset to do?)
2. What are its functional failures? (What are its failed states?)
3. What causes each functional failure and what are the failure modes that lead to those functional failures? (How does it get in those failed states?)
4. What are the effects of those failure modes on their own? (Exactly what happens when each failure mode occurs?)
5. How do those failure modes matter? (Do we have any safety, environmental, operational, or other consequences that we want to minimize or eliminate?)
6. What proactive steps can we take to minimize or eliminate those consequences and are they worth our while to do them? (Are there any condition-based or fixed-interval maintenance actions that we can use, and do they reduce our financial and other risks to acceptable levels?)
7. If we cannot do anything proactively, then what else can we do? (Can we accept the failure consequences, or can we redesign the asset or do something else that will make the failure disappear or at least become tolerable?)

When systems are being designed, they often include some level of built-in redundancy. Redundancy is needed only in very critical circumstances, but it has often crept into overall design processes. If RCM is applied at the design stage of the asset life cycle, it can identify where equipment redundancy can be eliminated and reduce the associated costs.

RCM favors condition-based or predictive maintenance tactics over traditional time-based methods; run-to-failure is acceptable, where warranted. Condition-based maintenance works well for most failure modes because most failures give some advanced warning of condition deterioration and these methods are often unintrusive—you can perform the checks while the asset is still operating. Time- or usage-based methods (fixed-interval maintenance) is also appropriate but only where the failures are not random in nature. (As equipment and systems become more complex, they also tend to exhibit more random failure characteristics so you can expect more of your maintenance program to comprise condition-based rather than fixed-interval replacements

or restoration/overhaul work.) Of course every proposed maintenance task is checked to see if it reduces risk to tolerable levels (for
safety and environmental consequences) or that it is indeed the
least costly approach. In some cases, running the asset to failure is
the most beneficial solution, a result that often surprises many old-
school maintainers.

A summary of the main steps required to run a successful
RCM program is presented below. The steps follow the familiar
Plan–Do–Check–Act sequence. Each is discussed in the following
sections:

1. Select plant areas that matter,
2. Prepare for the RCM project,
3. Apply the RCM process,
4. Implement selected tactics, and
5. Optimize tactics and program.

Steps 1, 2, and 3 constitute the planning activity. If you stop
there, as many companies do, you will achieve nothing with RCM.
Step 4 entails doing, a step that many miss. Step 5 entails checking
and acting to improve on the results, again something that is often
missed.

Step 1: Select plant areas that matter

Businesses typically have thousands of pieces of machinery and
equipment. These can range from pumps and valves to process systems and plants, rolling mills, presses, fleets of load-haul-dump
(LHD) trucks, buses, ships, other vehicles, or buildings. They may
be fixed or mobile. Each asset will benefit from RCM in varying
degrees. Before beginning the RCM process,[10] it is often useful to
identify and prioritize the physical resources owned or operated by
the enterprise. This initial stage involves:

- Establishing a structured, comprehensive list of all physical
  assets owned or used by the organization that require some
  form of maintenance or engineering attention. This list is

---

10. The most successful companies also opt for formal training in RCM
    before taking any action so that they fully understand what it is they
    are getting into from the outset.

referred to as the plant register, plant inventory, or equipment family tree. It is usually contained in the company's computerized asset management system.

- Assessing the impact of the physical resources on the key business performance areas. These include impacts on plant availability, process capability, quality, cost, safety, or environmental risk. Although there are various methods that can be used to perform this assessment, the precise method is not critical. Of more importance is selecting a method, documenting it and its results, and then proceeding with the review. Usually, the highest and lowest priority systems will be obvious, and in some cases a detailed assessment is not even required. Managers can usually tell you what it is that keeps them awake at night! It is not always worth the effort to figure out the exact order of importance as long as you eventually deal with the critical areas. Be cautious about what you decide not to analyze, however. Seemingly insignificant items can have surprisingly significant business impacts that are uncovered during the analysis. At the start, it may be enough to recognize the "bad actors" or the "high-cost assets" or those that create process bottlenecks to select your first candidates for analysis. Once you have established your top priority analysis candidates, quantify and summarize the benefits you intend to gain from RCM.
- Establishing the boundaries between equipment systems. Boundaries include everything necessary for a physical resource to do its job. This helps define the scope of the review and organizes it into manageable pieces. In doing this, you may find that the boundaries you set do not match the listings in your asset register. This is quite normal—the very practical functional approach taken in RCM does not always match up with the hierarchical physical breakdown of your plant and equipment.

Step 2: Prepare for the RCM project

RCM requires a modest investment of time for the training and for the analysis work itself. It often provides paybacks of several times the initial costs within the first year, an excellent investment for most companies. For an asset in its design stages, you will need to assign engineers and technicians, preferably those with maintenance and operations experience, to the team. In an existing operation, RCM will utilize some of your best maintainers and operators; their time is scheduled for their RCM work and replacements may be identified to backfill for their time away from their usual jobs. The times for training and the analysis are planned into your schedules. Do not use teams of untrained analysts or untrained facilitators if you want quick, efficient, and effective analyses. Project management is required and, as discussed in the chapter on Work Management, planning pays off—failing to plan is planning to fail.

RCM analysis in an existing operation is usually carried out by small teams of operators and maintainers working with a facilitator and trained to perform the analysis. Ideally, the team members and facilitator are your own employees. If they perform the analysis and make the decisions, you are empowering them, and they will take greater ownership of the results. For a new asset in the design stage, the outputs of RCM are easily assimilated by the new crews that will be maintaining and operating it. Indeed, if they are experienced in new start-ups, they will appreciate having a maintenance program at the outset.

Training is needed for all project participants and preferably for all of your maintenance people and most of your operators.[11] They will eventually be called upon to execute the results of the analysis work and it helps a great deal if they understand the changes they will see in their old practices. The training of facilitators is much more extensive than that for analysts and end users because these facilitators will become your in-house RCM experts.

Initially, you might be unsure about your commitment to a full-blown RCM project that deals with many assets—you may want to prove to yourself that it will work at your site. A pilot project is an excellent way to do this and you can use a contract facilitator for the pilot project to minimize your up-front investment in training. Except in the case of a Greenfield application, it is ill advised to use contract analysis teams because you want your own people to take ownership of the results.

---

11. Although this seems excessive to many readers, it is the most effective way to gain buy-in from the workforce so that the results of the analysis are implemented effectively and with minimal resistance.

If you take the pilot project approach, carry out the analysis and implement the results. Compare your projected savings and reliability improvements with those you anticipated and see if the results justify a more extensive application of RCM. In most cases it will.

Step 3: Apply the RCM process

In this step, you carry out the analysis. Led by a facilitator, your trained RCM analysis team carries it out by asking and answering the seven questions listed above.

1. Determine the functions of your asset. The purpose of any failure management policy is to make sure the equipment is working properly and producing on schedule. That is its function. Every physical asset has a function—usually several. These can be categorized as primary, secondary, or protective:

- *Primary Function*: This is why the equipment exists at all. It is usually evident from its name, as well as from the interfaces that are supported between physical assets. An example of a conveyer's primary function, for instance, is to transfer rock from hopper to crusher at a minimum rate of 10 tons per hour.
- *Secondary Function*: In addition to its primary purpose, a physical asset usually has a number of secondary functions. These are sometimes less obvious, but the consequences of failure may be no less severe. Examples of secondary functions include maintaining a pressure boundary, relaying local or control room indications, supplying structural support, or providing isolation. Sometimes there are superfluous functions—things the asset can do that you don't really need or even want. In one tissue mill, for example, the permanent removal of a guard that was installed to protect equipment from a dripping air-conditioning system (that had long ago been removed) resulted in a substantial decrease in repair time for machine roll changes.
- *Protective Function*: As processes and equipment increase in complexity, so do the ways in which they can fail and the consequences of those failures. To mitigate potentially dire results, protective devices are often used. Typical protective

functions include warning operators of abnormal conditions, automatically shutting down a piece of equipment, and taking over a function that has failed.

In addition to defining the asset functions, this process highlights the desired level of performance. These can include capacity, reliability, availability, product quality, safety, and environmental standards. Although this may sound relatively straightforward, technical and maintenance performance are typically judged differently. This performance can be defined as:

- *Built-in or inherent* (what it can do or was designed to do)
- *Required* (what we want it to do)
- *Actual* (what it is doing right now)

In many instances, the equipment can deliver what is required of it with proper maintenance. Situations can arise, however, where what is required exceeds the capabilities of the physical resource. In these cases, no amount of maintenance will bring the asset performance to the desired level.

If there is a bit of a gap between the performance needed and the built-in ability or the performance currently being achieved, the equipment must be modified. Options include replacing it with a more capable item or changing or reducing operating expectations.

Again, the purpose of the RCM review is to define the maintenance requirements for a physical asset that are necessary to meet the business objectives in its operating environment. It is important to remember that identical assets in different operating environments or modes may have different failure modes and different functional expectations. The level of performance reflects what is required or wanted from an asset.

2. Determine plausible functional failures. Once you have defined what you want the asset to do, you can define the failed states or ways that it can fail to achieve those functions. Partial and total shortcomings are considered.

Often, we tend to think of an item failing when it stops working—a "go" or "no go" situation. Examples of this are a car that does not start or a compressor that does not start up to provide high-pressure air. Although this situation is typical for some equipment (notably electronics and electrical equipment), what constitutes a failure in other equipment is not as clear. Your car may start and run, but its acceleration is poor and it uses too much gas. The compressor may run, but it does not provide enough air pressure or volume. Both of these are functional failures.

The performance standards defined when we outline the functions of the asset provide clear guidance. If performance drops below a desired standard, it is considered a failure, even if the equipment is still performing at some reduced level. Any functional failure is the inability of a physical asset to deliver its expected level of performance. Any function can therefore fail in several ways, each with its own (usually different) failure modes and effects.

- Total loss of function means an item stops working altogether. For example, a pump in a pumping system fails to provide any flow at all.
- Partial loss of function means that the item works but fails to achieve the expected level of performance. For example, a pump in a pumping system fails to provide an adequate flow but it is still running.
- Multiple levels of performance are expected from an individual function and only one fails. One function may have failed or partially failed while another is fine. For example, a pump in a pumping system fails to contain all of the pumped liquid (it is leaking) but the pump is still providing the desired flow rate and pressure.

The expected level of performance defines not only what is considered a failure, but also the degree of specific maintenance needed to avoid that failure. As illustrated in Figure 8-1, this frequently creates intradepartmental conflicts. It is essential, then, that all concerned (the technical, operations, and maintenance departments) play a part in drafting the performance levels. Agreement is essential.

3. Determine likely failure modes and their effects. The next task is to list the likely failure modes and describe their effects. A failure mode describes in simple terms what caused an asset's functional failure. For example, if a pump's functional failure is "fails to contain the pumped liquid," the failure mode is likely to be "mechanical seal leaking," "casing ruptured," "casing gasket deteriorated," "vent valve leaking," or "drain plug corroded."

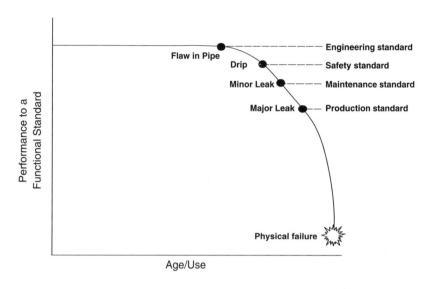

Figure 8-1. Performance Standards and Function Failure

Failure modes are spelled out because the process of anticipating, preventing, detecting, and correcting failures is applied to each failure mode independently of the others. While many potential failure modes can be listed, only those that are fairly likely need be considered. These include:

- Failure modes that you know have occurred on the same or similar equipment. This is determined through a review of maintenance work order history and experience.
- Failure modes that you know are already the subject of preventive maintenance tasks. You may already be preventing some of them.
- Failure modes that you know have not yet happened but are considered possible because of experience and/or vendor/manufacturer recommendations. The extent to which these less-than-likely failure modes are included will depend on their consequences. The greater the potential consequences, the more of these rare failure modes you include. For example, failure of a nuclear containment structure to contain radioactive materials leaking from a reactor would have severe consequences so it would be included.

Possible causes of the particular failure should also be identified because they have a direct bearing on the maintenance tactics used. The ruptured pump casing, for example, might be caused by corrosion, which you can deal with preventively. On the other hand, the pump case might be hit and damaged by mobile equipment, an unpredictable and unlikely event that requires a different kind of prevention. Some failure modes may have many different causes, and the nature of those causes makes a difference in how maintenance will address it. For example, a seized bearing might be caused by a lack of lubrication, wear, corrosion, fatigue, dirt, incorrect operation, or faulty assembly.

When stating the effects, describe as precisely and as completely as possible what actually happens when each failure mode occurs:

- Evidence (if any) of the failure to the operating crew under normal conditions.
- Specific hazards the failure may pose to worker safety, public safety, process stability, or the environment.
- Specific effects on production output and the maintenance required to correct the failure once it has occurred.

4. Select technically effective and feasible maintenance tactics. The results of failures can range from trivial to catastrophic. The severity of failure impact influences the way a company views the failure and the steps deemed necessary to mitigate its consequences. Depending on the gravity of the situation, the action taken may be predictive or preventive maintenance or adding backup systems. In some cases, labor intensive activity may not be worth the effort and expense. To manage any failure successfully, a proactive maintenance task must be:

- *Technically feasible.* The task deals with the technical characteristics of the failure. Fixed-interval maintenance works for most age or usage-related failures whereas condition-based maintenance works best for random failures.
- *Risk-effective.* In the case of failures having safety or environmental consequences, it reduces the risk to an agreed-upon tolerable level.
- *Cost-effective.* In the case of failures having other business impacts, it reduces or eliminates the cost consequences.

Whether a particular approach is technically appropriate to solve the failure depends not only on the kind of help but also on the nature of the problem. Technically feasible tactics for condition-based and time-based maintenance must satisfy the following criteria:

Condition-based

- It is possible to detect a physical resource's degraded condition or performance.
- The failure is predictable as it progresses from first instance to complete breakdown.
- It is practical to monitor the physical resource in less time than it takes for the problem to develop completely.
- The time between incipient and functional failure is long enough to be of some use—that is, actions can be taken to avoid the consequences of the failure.

Time-based

- There is an identifiable point at which the physical asset shows a rapid increase in failure rate. It has a definite useful "life."
- Most assets survive to that age. For failures with significant safety or environmental risks, look for evidence that there are no failures before this point.
- The task restores the asset's condition. (This might mean partial restoration if the asset is overhauled, for example, or complete restoration if the item is discarded and replaced.)

To be cost-effective, proactive maintenance will reduce the likelihood and/or consequences of failure to acceptable levels, be readily implemented, and stay within budget. Within these limits, a maintenance tactic is considered cost-effective if:

- For hidden problems, it cuts the chance of a multiple failure to an acceptable level.
- For failures with safety and environmental effects, the risks are kept to a comfortable minimum.
- For failures with production setbacks, the cost of the tactic is, over time, less than the cost of production losses.
- For failures with maintenance consequences, the cost of prevention measures is, over time, lower than repairing the failure that would otherwise result.

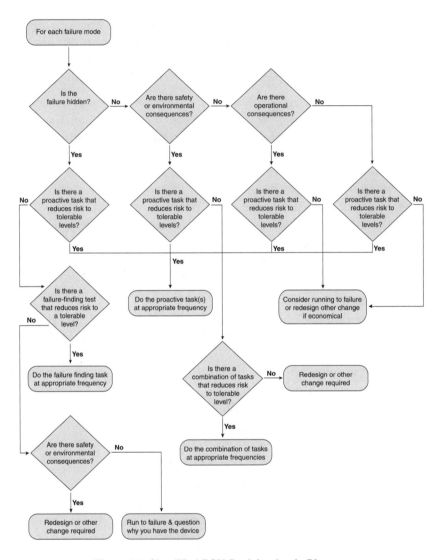

Figure 8-2. Simplified RCM Decision Logic Diagram

If maintenance measures are neither technically feasible nor cost-effective, then, depending on the risk of failure, one of the following default actions is selected:

- For hidden failures, a failure-finding tactic to reduce the likelihood of multiple failures. An example is testing the readiness of standby equipment.

- For failures with unacceptable safety or environmental risks, redesign or modification.
- For failures with production of maintenance consequences, run-to-failure or corrective maintenance.

A logic tree diagram can be used to integrate the consequences of failure with technically feasible and cost-effective maintenance tactics. A simplified version of this diagram is illustrated is Figure 8-2.

The tactics used to deal with failures should be selected in the following order:

- *Condition-based monitoring (CBM) tasks.* These are inspections or other checks of conditions at regular intervals to look for signs of deterioration. They usually have the least impact on production, help focus corrective actions, and get the most out of the economic life of the equipment. Once the maintenance task has been chosen, the frequency is determined. For condition-based tactics, the frequency is linked to the technical characteristics of the failure and the specific monitoring technique. Depending on these factors, the time can vary from weeks to months. As a general rule, the monitoring task is performed no less frequently than half the time it takes for the failure to progress from its first signs of deterioration to the failed state. Deterioration from the point in time at which a potential failure can be detected to the failed state is known as the P-F interval as shown in Figure 8-3.

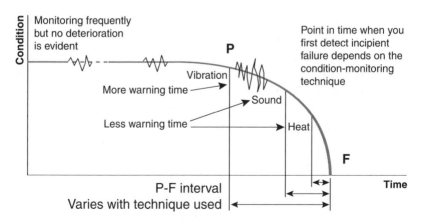

Figure 8-3. Deterioration of Functional Capability

- *Time-based repair/restoration tactics.* These tasks are for failures that result from aging or usage of the asset. The restoration is performed at a fixed interval regardless of the condition the equipment appears to be in at the time. This approach is less preferable than CBM for a number of reasons. It usually affects production or operations, the age limit can mean premature removals, and the additional shop work required increases the cost of maintenance. Fixed-interval task frequencies are applied according to the expected useful life of the physical asset. That is determined by the age at which wear-out, fatigue, erosion, and corrosion have progressed beyond a tolerable point. At that point, the probability of failure increases to unacceptable levels.
- *Time-based discard tactics.* These are generally the least cost-effective preventive maintenance measures. They tend to be used where repair or restoration is impossible or ineffective, such as for components like filter elements, o-rings, and, in some cases, integrated circuit boards. Frequency is determined as it is for time-based repair/restoration tasks.
  - *Combinations.* In some cases, a combination of tactics may be necessary to reduce safety and environmental risks to an acceptable level. In general, this involves a condition-based maintenance method along with some form of time-based maintenance. An example would be the in-place inspection of an aircraft engine by borescope every 50 flying hours, combined with time-based inspection and overhaul in a shop every 200 hours. Each task serves to reduce risk to a degree; when combined, they reduce overall risk to tolerable levels.
  - *Failure-finding tactics.* This applies only to hidden failures (failures that are not evident to operators during normal operation). Hidden failures often occur in back-up or safety systems where the protective device is normally dormant. There is no way to detect a hidden failure but to check for it before a failure makes it visible. How often the failure-finding tactic is needed depends on the required availability of the backup or protective device and the level of risk of multiple failure that can be tolerated.
  - *Run-to-failure tactics.* This applies when nothing else will work and the consequences of failure can be tolerated.

Run-to-failure is not a viable choice for safety or environmental consequences because it can lead to physical and legal consequence that no business wants to risk. If you cannot take any proactive steps to predict or prevent failures or cannot detect a hidden failure, some other course of action is indicated if safety or environmental issues are a concern.

– *Redesign tactics.* Depending on the failure mode, you may opt to redesign the system to eliminate the failure mode or its consequences. An alternative is to provide training to operators or maintainers, install warning signs, or some other appropriate "one time only" corrective action. For failures having operational or nonoperational consequences (cost of doing business), run-to-failure may prove to be a cost-effective option.

After deciding on the appropriate tactical choice, determine the task frequency and decide who should execute the task. Those choices mark the end of the formal RCM analysis process. By this point you will have completed and documented your analysis and you have a number of failure management choices (preventive tasks, predictive tasks, failure finding tasks, redesign recommendations, training changes, or run-to-failure). It takes a fair amount of work to get to this point, but if you implement the results of your analyses, the payback is usually substantial.

Step 4: Implement selected tasks

It often requires a great deal of effort and coordination to put the results of the RCM in motion. In an existing operation, the failure management choices you have made now replace the old "PM Program" that you have probably been using for some time. For a new asset, this step will help maintainers and operators get the program off to an excellent start. When inputting tasks for your maintenance management system, do so in conjunction with input about planning efforts and any other requirements for task execution. Tasks are triggered at the frequencies specified in the RCM analysis. In the case of condition-based maintenance (CBM), the required actions to take if specified conditions are exceeded are precisely noted (for example, what to do when a vibration level goes above a specified limit). Some new tasks are the same as old PM tasks; others are minor variations on the old tasks and some are entirely new. Regardless of which you are dealing with, it's the task as defined through RCM that must be implemented. Specific actions taken to implement the RCM program include:

- Tweak existing maintenance schedules so they match recommended RCM choices.
- Develop or revise maintenance task instructions.
- Specify spare parts and adjust inventory levels to support them.
- Acquire needed diagnostic or test equipment.
- Revise or write new operation and maintenance procedures. Sometimes this entails developing checklists and other aids.
- Specify the repair or restoration procedures for the fixed-interval tasks.
- Develop (or start using) tracking systems for CBM readings and for initiating corrective work orders when condition limits are exceeded.
- Conduct any needed training in the new or revised procedures.

Step 5: Optimize tactics and program

RCM is not perfect. Although it excels as a tool for identifying individual and even multiple failure modes, one of its weaknesses is that it cannot systematically identify combinations of failure modes that can cause serious consequences if those combinations are not hidden. Only Fault Tree Analysis and Root Cause Failure Analysis methods will do this. Despite this and other minor weaknesses, however, RCM has numerous advantages and benefits if it is implemented properly.

RCM analyses always depend on the quality of the effort invested. Once the RCM review is complete and the maintenance work identified, periodic adjustments to improve the program should be made. The process is responsive to changes in plant design, operating conditions, maintenance history, and discovered conditions (i.e., conditions that were not anticipated during the analysis). In particular, the frequency of the tactics is adjusted to reflect the operating and maintenance history of the physical resource. The objectives of this ongoing activity are to reduce equipment failure, improve preventive maintenance effectiveness and the use of resources, identify the need to expand the review, and react to changing industry or economic conditions. To achieve these goals, three complementary activities are integrated into a living program:

1. *The periodic reassessment and revision of the RCM review results.* The frequency of reassessment depends to some degree on equipment age but is usually conducted every two to five years. This ensures that undocumented design changes, changes to operating context, and new failure information are taken into account.

2. *A continuous process of monitoring, feedback, and adaptation based on RCM outputs.* This process analyzes and assesses the data produced by production and maintenance activities for failure rates, causes, and trends. Many of the parameters to be measured are identified during the initial RCM analysis. The process of continuously improving on RCM includes observation of the variances between actual and target performance. Corrective actions can then be taken. These may include changing the task type, scope, or frequency; revising procedures; providing additional training; or changing the design. Continually reviewing and improving the initial maintenance program is akin to a quality management process that continuously improves product quality.

3. *Monitoring of the functions of the assets that were analyzed and their performance parameters.* This is monitoring RCM inputs—the functions of the assets. Failure to perform to the stated functional parameters will be identified as results are monitored, but the need for additional analysis due to a change in operating context or environment will be revealed by monitoring the functions that were defined. Are they still the desired functions? Do you still want reliability or availability or both? Are the performance standards still applicable or have they changed? By watching these you can continuously adapt RCM analysis results to ensure that your systems continue to perform as needed by the business. Reliability modeling and simulation modeling[12] can help answer these questions and keep the RCM program alive.

---

12. See the next chapter on Reliability and simulation-modeling techniques.

The Benefits of RCM: Creating Value for Customers

As desirable as it may be to have a comprehensive, logically based maintenance program, it is of little use unless it helps maintenance, and the company as a whole, create value for its customers and shareholders. Recall from the Introduction that value is delivered by increasing service and quality while reducing cost, time, and risk.

$$Value = \frac{Quality \times Service}{Cost \times Time \times Risk}$$

RCM delivers value in these five areas:

- *Quality*: The maintenance program that results is tailored precisely to the failure modes you are likely to experience and it does it proactively, before you suffer the consequences. Maintenance tasks are defined precisely, leaving little room for error when they are converted to work orders for execution. All decisions are made using a consistent and logical approach and are fully documented. Any failures that are allowed to occur are only for failure modes that you can truly "live with"—there is no need to react to failures because you can now respond in an orderly fashion every time. Hidden failures that are often missed are caught because the maintenance program is more comprehensive than programs developed by traditional or other methods. Customer perceptions of maintenance improve. You are doing a better job because fewer failures mean more uptime and delivering what the customer wants.
- *Service*: Maintenance resources can be used much more efficiently doing only what needs to be done. Higher asset availability delivers more uptime to operations, and higher reliability means fewer disruptions to production or customer service. Customer requirements are met. RCM focuses on defining, up front, what functions the customer requires of the assets and then sets out to achieve them. The team-based approach to performing RCM results in greater cooperation between and among maintenance, production, and operations and enhances future communications and teamwork. Both maintenance and operations tend to take more ownership of their roles in asset reliability.
- *Cost*: Doing only the maintenance required to deal with failure modes affecting functions desired by the customers

means lower costs of the overall maintenance program. Unnecessary or overmaintenance of assets is eliminated. Repair costs are reduced since many failures will be caught before they reach catastrophic levels and before they result in secondary damage. The emphasis on condition monitoring reduces the need for invasive preventive tasks that are often more expensive to execute and require additional downtime. Improved asset care results in longer asset life and/or increased resale value at end of useful life of the asset.

- *Time*: Fewer failures are allowed to occur so downtime and repair times are reduced. Elimination of many inappropriate overhauls reduces planned downtime and increases availability. Frequencies of maintenance and other tasks are more precisely determined so tasks are not performed too frequently or infrequently.
- *Risk*: Safety and environmental integrity are a priority and dealt with quantitatively. Unacceptable failure consequences are dealt with. Hidden failures are dealt with so the likelihood of multiple failures is reduced. Invasive work is minimized wherever possible, reducing the risk that maintenance activities will induce failures.

SIMPLIFIED RCM METHODS

In addition to its reputation as the best method for developing proactive approaches, RCM is also thought to be both challenging and expensive to implement. Admittedly, it does require effort and time and of course there is a price to be paid—there is no free lunch, but the negative reputation was earned as a result of failures to implement it correctly, not the method itself. Various competing "brands" of RCM have arisen to capitalize on its perceived weaknesses. These simplified methods invariably leave something out of the process or attempt to automate something that is still well beyond the capability of computers to do—thinking. Beware when using these methods that you are taking risks that could impact negatively on safety, the environment, or your operations. However, where you are confident that those risks are negligible or nonexistent, simplified methods can be helpful.

One such method, "Maintenance Task Analysis" eliminates the first steps in RCM (defining the operating context, functions and

functional failures) and leaps directly to listing failure modes. This
is a shortcut to the RCM method that produces quick results that
are certainly better than doing nothing but short of those produced
using RCM. It is useful for noncritical[13] equipment and where there
is an urgent need to put a program in place but insufficient time
for RCM.

IMPLEMENTING RCM SUCCESSFULLY

To achieve success and manage change in an existing operation,
there are a few key success factors to observe in addition to those
discussed earlier in the book:

- Have clear and quantifiable improvement goals and monitor
  your progress towards them as the analyses are completed.
- Involve your unions or employee associations in the process.
- Provide widespread training in RCM. The process will initi-
  ate a significant shift in corporate culture and training is an
  excellent way to get that off to a good start. Go well beyond
  those who will participate directly in the process.
- Prepare yourself to manage substantial shifts in the way your
  maintainers and operators work to accommodate the results
  of your analyses. There may, for example, be concerns about
  job loss if workloads seem to be dropping.
- Integrate the RCM effort with other PM improvement programs.

RCM complements other improvement initiatives, such as just-
in-time (JIT), total quality management (TQM) and total productive maintenance (TPM). The basic building block of this strategy is
the cross-functional RCM review team of company employees. To
answer the RCM process questions, input is required not only from

---

13. "Noncritical" means that there are no safety or environmental
consequences likely to arise from equipment failures and that
operational consequences can be tolerated. This presupposes
knowledge of the consequences and hence the failure modes that
lead to them, yet that knowledge is not always there. Defining
equipment as noncritical without thorough analysis is inherently
risky. The analysis to define criticality can be as time consuming as
the parts of the RCM analysis being avoided so the author questions
the value of this approach on its own. Where this method is applied
RCM should follow as soon as there is sufficient time to perform it.

maintenance but also from production, materials, and other technical departments. As a result, the RCM review is best conducted by small teams (three to five members), with at least one member from each of the above functions who is knowledgeable about the physical resource under consideration. In a Greenfield application of RCM, you are less likely to have maintainers and operators available so you may find yourself relying on engineers and technicians who have only some maintenance and operations experience, or on contractors. The other key member of the review team is the facilitator who provides expertise in RCM methodology and guides the review process.

Few organizations can spare their best operators and maintainers on a full-time basis, so RCM review teams usually meet at scheduled intervals. Typically, this involves one or two meetings per week, each lasting approximately three hours. The RCM review process for most systems takes about 10 to 15 meetings to complete. The physical resource chosen for analysis is broken down into sections for study by subgroups. For the Greenfield scenario, the teams are often dedicated full-time to the process so that maximum output can be achieved in the relatively short design time frames.

The RCM review team also coordinates how the recommendations are carried out. Team meetings during this phase are of similar duration but less frequent. In addition, a phased-in approach is used to manage change successfully. By applying RCM gradually across an entire site or fleet of assets, you can avoid the culture shock of immediate and universal change. This gradual application also makes the process of analyzing many assets easier and keeps the costs of doing the analysis in check.

The following is an example of the use of RCM in manufacturing. A mining company with a fleet of 240-ton trucks in continuous operation wanted to reduce unplanned downtime. Maintenance analyzed the data in the truck dispatch system to determine the highest delay causes and selected an assembly that was both significant and reasonably straightforward—the hydraulic box dump assembly.

A team of in-pit and shop maintainers led by a facilitator with RCM expertise met for two to three hours every week over thirteen weeks. During the course of these meetings, the primary function of the hydraulic box dump assembly was defined: "Provide hydraulic power to smoothly and symmetrically raise and lower a loaded (240-ton) dump tray. The maximum overall cycle is 47 seconds for an empty tray at the regulated pressure of 2400 psi ±50 psi with the prime mover at 1910 rpm." This function is stated crisply, with several standards of performance that make the definition of a function failure clear:

- Fails to raise the dump tray at all with a regulated pressure of 2400 ±50 psi.
- Tray is raised too slowly (overall cycle time > 47 sec empty) at a pressure of less than 2350 psi.
- Tray is raised too slowly (overall cycle time > 47 sec empty) at a pressure of less than 2400 psi but with the engine less than 1910 rpm.
- Tray is raised erratically.
- Tray cannot be raised to full height.
- Tray is lowered too slowly.

About 150 modes of failure were determined using cause-effect diagrams and then transcribed to worksheets using terse phrases such as "Hoist control valve spool jammed by foreign material or wear and tear." The effect corresponding to the jammed spool above is "Sufficient pilot pressure not available to move dump control valve spool and so tray cannot be lifted. The pilot valve is changed, which requires two labor hours and the truck is down for less than four hours."

The cost-effectiveness of this RCM example is clear. Downtime costs about 500 tons per hour and is worth $20,000 in lost production ($480,000 in a one-day period). The team was able to find the root causes of all critical failures, change both maintenance and operating procedures to reduce the incidence of some causes, and make some simple modifications in hydraulic system design to eliminate others.

Today's challenging maintenance environment demands a thorough and comprehensive approach to determining what work to do. RCM is the best method to do just that. If properly applied, its benefits can be seen in improved safety and environmental performance, better service and throughput, improved quality performance and reduced business risk. Although it clearly involves the help of several functions in the organization, it is very much a proactive asset-centric methodology. The next chapter deals with other, less proactive methods.

UPTIME SUMMARY

Being proactive with your assets is all about managing failures before they occur. You can reduce or eliminate the consequences of failure by forecasting what is likely to happen and deciding in advance about what to do about it. The advantage to doing this is that major business impact due to equipment breakdown can be avoided. High-performing companies manage proactively by foreseeing and avoiding problems.

Reliability-Centered Maintenance (RCM) is the most proven proactive approach for developing maintenance programs from scratch. It is a logical process that can be used during the design stage of an asset's life cycle or later, after the asset has entered service. It uses knowledge of how things fail and prompts logical decisions for individual asset failure management policies. One of the great strengths of RCM is that it does not require failures to have occurred in order to generate data for analysis. It anticipates the most likely failure modes and deals with them and their consequences before the fact. Above all, RCM offers high reliability at optimum cost.

Programs developed using RCM provide for the safe minimum amount of appropriate proactive maintenance. These programs provide a balance of cost vs. reliability that is tailored specifically to your assets in your operating environment. The tendency to over- or undermaintain, often a result of using other methods, is avoided.

RCM was developed and first proven in the aircraft industry and then quickly adopted for use in nuclear power generation. Today RCM is used in all capital-intensive industries where reliability is important. It is the cornerstone of any reliability improvement program.

The keys to success in RCM are careful application of the process itself and follow-up by implementing the results in your maintenance program. Many failures of well-run RCM programs occur because the outputs of the analysis are not put into practice in the operational environment. The follow up is critical. Optimizing the maintenance program after it has been put into place is done on a continuous basis.

9

Asset-Centric Approaches 2: Continuous Improvement

Every day you may make progress. Every step may be fruitful.
Yet there will stretch out before you an ever-lengthening,
ever-ascending, ever-improving path. You know you will never get
to the end of the journey. But this, so far from discouraging,
only adds to the joy and glory of the climb.

SIR WINSTON CHURCHILL

The previous chapter explored RCM, an entirely proactive, asset-centric approach to excellence. RCM is proactive because it anticipates what is likely to go wrong in the future. With this knowledge, you can avoid any undesirable consequences and prepare for the anticipated event appropriately. RCM enables quantum leaps in performance that is driven by continuous improvement methods used after RCM implementation. Using these methods converts failures into learning experiences; because important things have been learned, similar failures can be avoided in the future. In this sense, these methods are reactive to what has already happened. They provide incremental improvements and can be used independently or in conjunction with RCM or Total Productive Maintenance (TPM). They can also be built into process designs. Truly excellent companies use the continuous improvement methods described in this chapter to complement and improve upon what they can achieve with these other, more dramatic methods. Companies that choose to rely solely on the methods in this chapter will experience improvements, sometimes substantial ones, but they will take a long time to do so. As Churchill noted, the path is ever lengthening, ever ascending, and ever improving.

PM OPTIMIZATION

As a proactive approach, RCM was designed to be used at the design stage of any asset's life cycle. However, RCM is often used after an asset has been put into service to develop or more correctly, to redevelop a failure management program. If a plant or fleet of assets is put into operation or service without adequate attention to its maintenance program (as is often the case), then maintainers and operators will quickly develop a combination of maintenance and operator tasks that aim to manage or eliminate the consequences of failures. Manufacturers' recommendations, the past experience of maintenance and operations people, problems already experienced and dealt with, outputs from process safety analyses, and the results of Root Cause Failure Analysis are all used to develop those tasks. Many of these tasks are performed informally and on an ad hoc basis, often without any documentation. Others are formally documented and managed in the operation's maintenance management system. These organically grown programs typically expand as failures continue to occur and new experience is gained.

Eventually, for a variety of reasons well explained by Turner,[1] these programs tend to deteriorate. The vicious cycle usually begins at the design and commissioning stages. Maintenance engineers are often not involved in these stages. If they are, they generally deal with project work that consumes their maintenance budget because the projects are invariably over budgetary limits. At this point, the new asset or plant has yet to receive all its spare parts and is going through its start-up phase, normally characterized by teething problems. Documentation for maintenance is lacking, and maintenance analysis, if any, is incomplete. At commissioning time, the design team leaves and the maintenance engineer is left to second-guess the design intent while supporting operators who are testing the systems, often pushing them beyond their limits. Design and maintainability problems surface, but there is no money to correct them. Maintenance policy is developed in an ad hoc fashion, often using traditional approaches that result in

---

1. Steve Turner, "PM Optimization—Maintenance Analysis of the Future,"http://www.reliabilityweb.com/excerpts/excerpts/pm _optimization.htm.

overmaintaining and generating additional problems in the process. The new maintenance program is put in place, again with little or no documentation. As the plant ramps up to full capacity, maintenance, the number of tasks, and the frequency of taskwork multiply as new problems surface. "More is better" becomes a maintenance standard. The maintenance workload soon exceeds available labor and repair takes precedence over prevention or prediction. Fewer failures are prevented and the workload grows. Rapid and temporary repairs are performed and reliability suffers.

This cycle is all too common. The situation deteriorates to the point where minimal maintenance resources (staff) can barely keep up with the breakdowns that prevent operation. Availability ends up well below benchmark levels and maintenance costs are usually high. The situation is unacceptable to the business; eventually something will be done. The primary focus of that something will usually entail cutting costs and increasing reliability, often in that order. If the situation has not deteriorated to a critical state, the company may even try to improve on its maintenance program by using RCM, either across the board or selectively focusing only on key assets. Another alternative is PM Optimization (PMO).

Whereas RCM begins with a zero-based functional approach, PMO does not. It begins with an existing maintenance program, evaluates its effectiveness, looks for critical omissions, and rebundles the results into a more effective program. Because PMO begins with an existing maintenance program, it is unsuited for use at the design stage of a project. One popular method of PMO[2] has the following steps:

1. Prioritize the assets to be analyzed based on their importance to the business. Priority is given to those assets that can cause safety, environmental, or severe business consequences when they fail.
2. Compile a listing of the existing maintenance tasks being performed by maintenance and operations personnel. Gather the information for this list from existing PM records, your maintenance management system, operating

---

2. PMO2000™—**pm**optimisation, by OMCS International. www.reliabilityassurance.com.

procedures, checklists, and interviews with operators and maintainers.

3. Determine the failure modes that the maintenance tasks address.
4. Determine additional failure modes that may have not already been addressed.
5. Determine what functionality would be lost as each failure mode occurs. Some methods consider this step optional because the consequences are usually apparent.
6. Describe the effects of each failure.
7. Describe the consequences of failure (safety, environment, business loss, etc.).
8. Describe what can be done to predict or prevent the failure.
9. Describe what can be done if you cannot predict or prevent the failure.
10. Review the results and approve implementation.
11. Implement the results in the field.
12. Continuously review the program for improvements.

Once the failure modes have been identified, the remainder of the PMO approach is essentially the same as RCM (except for the sequence of the step that defines functionality). The PMO methods take advantage of the fact that an existing maintenance task may address several failure modes at a time and that examining the failure mode lists generated makes it is easy to spot duplicate tasks. RCM's strength, at the design stage, is that you do not have to experience the failures in order to do something proactive to avert their consequences.

Neither method is entirely perfect. Even the authors of PMO methods acknowledge that RCM is more thorough. Neither method deals well with multiple failures in combinations if such failures are evident to operators. These combination failures are dealt with more effectively using Fault Tree methods or, after the fact, using Root Cause Failure Analysis methods.

There is a great deal of competition among practitioners of RCM and PMO, and these practitioners support their respective positions with excellent arguments for why their particular method is the best. Be aware that both methods work well and that both have strengths and weaknesses. Explore them both thoroughly and carefully consider your operating and regulatory environments before choosing one or the other.

ROOT CAUSE FAILURE ANALYSIS (RCFA)

RCFA is used after the fact to deal with failures that have already happened. It aims to identify the various causal factors that led to the failure to determine which, if any, can be dealt with differently to avoid having the problem arise again. A "root cause" is the most basic reason for the problem occurring that, if eliminated, will eliminate the problem. It is always an event or condition in the chain of events that led to the particular problem you are trying to solve. RCFA is one of several problem-solving[3] approaches widely used in the maintenance world.

A common challenge to companies embarking on root cause failure analysis is the determination of what problem to tackle first. Pareto analysis and log-scatterplots are excellent methods for prioritization. These tools are discussed in the team context in Chapter 10.

Like RCM, RCFA has its variants. One popular method is known as the "Five Whys." Simple and effective, this is similar to the learning process of inquisitive children and is widely used in the analysis phase of the Six-Sigma "Design, Measure, Analyze, Improve, Control" (DMAIC) approach for existing systems. It is also a popular feature of the Toyota Production System of lean manufacturing and has been used extensively on its own. The Five Whys technique does not require the use of analytical tools like data segmentation, hypothesis testing, regression, or other statistical tools. Simply asking "why?" five times penetrates the layers of symptoms that often obscure the root cause of a problem. It is like peeling an onion, but there are usually fewer layers. Five questions is only a rule of thumb. Occasionally, you will get to the root of a problem with fewer questions; sometimes more are needed. The trick is to stop when you have found some condition or event that you can manage and hence manage the entire chain of events.

RCFA using the Five Whys is easy to do without a lot of additional tools and supporting data. It works very well in situations when statistical analysis does not help—for example, when problems involve human factors or human error. The method is very simple:

---

3. See also *Maintenance Excellence: Optimizing Equipment Life-Cycle Decisions* by John D. Campbell and Andrew K. S. Jardine (New York: Marcel Dekker, 2001).

1. Gather a problem-solving team comprising those who know the issue best and are most likely to have a positive contribution to its solution.
2. Write down the problem; be specific. By writing it down you increase your focus on the problem. You can clearly see what it is and what it is not. This helps keep the team on track.
3. Ask the group "why?" the problem has arisen. Brainstorm for an answer. You might get several possible answers. Cluster your answers to eliminate duplicates (some answers may simply be stated in different ways).
4. Explore all answers. Eliminate those least likely to take you to a practical solution. If an answer does not provide you with something that suggests a solution, ask the question again, focusing on that particular answer.

An example problem illustrating this Q and A process comes from an oil-loading facility. The cargo-loading pump that moves crude oil from the onshore storage tanks to the bulk cargo tankers failed while in service.

Q: Why did the cargo loading pump fail in service?
A: Because it ran dry.
Q: Why did the pump run dry?
A: Because after pumping from the storage tank to the ship for several hours the tank was empty and the pump was left running.
Q: Why was the pump left running on an empty tank?
A: The pump was left running on an empty tank because the operator had other work to do and there is no low-level shut-off switch to shut it down automatically.

At this point you have a "root cause"—a problem that can be solved relatively easily, and you got there with only three questions. You can stop here and simply add a low-level shut-off switch and circuitry to eliminate this "cause" of the problem. Or, you could delve further:

Q: Why was there no low-level shut-off switch?
A: Because our design standards don't call for it. The contractor that built the loading facility didn't include it.

You can now move to correct a deficiency in your design standards and avoid any other future occurrences of the same problem. Of course, you will also want to check other pumping facilities to see if they already have the same problem.

The Five-Whys can also be used in conjunction with other forms of cause-and-effect analysis, such as the fishbone diagram or fault trees. Figure 9-1 shows a fishbone diagram for a pump failure incident similar to the one described above.

The diagram shows that there are four things that could have contributed to the failure: people, the asset design, the methods used, and the process itself. In each case, you ask why it could have contributed to failure. Keep asking "why?" until you get a useful answer that suggests a practical solution. In this case, two possible corrective actions emerge: putting more emphasis on operator training or changing design standards for this type of system.

A fishbone diagram helps identify various possible causes of any effect. For any potential cause, the Five-Whys can be used to drill down to root cause. The fishbone diagram is adaptable and can be modified to include additional categories of failure-causing events or conditions. In manufacturing, for example, these might include machines, materials, methods, measurements, environmental, and people factors. For most maintenance problems, the "machine" category is the most important. It is often examined alone, but it is also useful to consider people, processes, methods, materials, environment, application, and applied operating load.

Fault trees are more complex than fishbone diagrams and are usually used in the design of systems that require high reliability (such as nuclear plants or avionics) where it is critical to quantify the probabilities associated with various combinations of events that can potentially lead to undesirable consequences.

The Five-Whys method is simple and versatile and can be used in tandem with a number of analytical tools. It does, however, have a few limitations:

1. It relies on brainstorming for potential answers. Some groups (and this often applies to small groups) lack the creativity to do this effectively and can miss some useful answers. A large group, on the other hand, may produce too many answers. Exploring them all (with more whys) can lead to analysis paralysis.

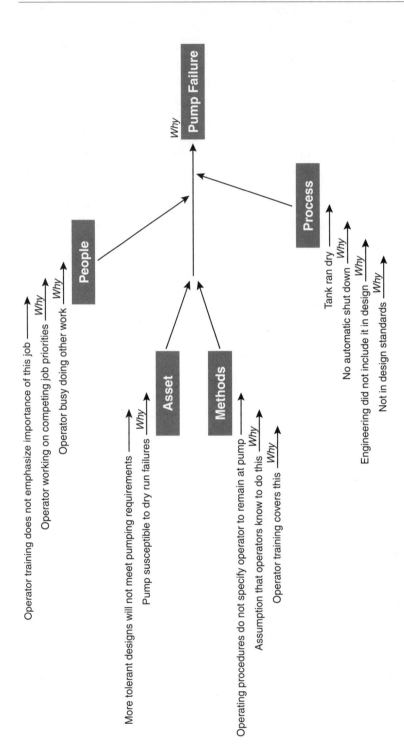

Figure 9-1. Fishbone Diagram

2. It is not always repeatable. Different groups analyzing the same problem can easily come up with different solutions. This is not necessarily a bad thing; there is often more than one perfectly feasible solution to any given problem. It can, however, be counterproductive if too much time and energy must be expended on sifting through too many answers.

3. It may not identify a root cause. There is no way to be sure you have actually hit the root cause that provides the best opportunities to solve the problem. The ability of the group to identify root causes depends on the extent and depth of talent available within the group. Brainstorming is essentially a creative process and it relies on creative minds. The example above illustrates that there were two root causes depending on how far the group was willing to go in its questioning.

There are several commercially available methods that achieve RCFA goals. Root Cause Analysis[4] is another popular and successful method that has been formalized by Robert and Kenneth Latino and marketed under that name. In Europe, TapRoot® is another widely used commercial variant.[5] A successful problem-solving method with far broader applications than maintenance is the Kepner Tregoe[6] Problem-Solving and Decision-Making Method.

DECISION OPTIMIZATION

Decision Optimization refers to the use of any one of several optimization tools. These tools are used to make decisions about asset replacements, repair vs. replace, fleet replacements, inspection

---

4. Robert J. Latino and Kenneth C. Latino, *Root Cause Analysis: Improving Performance for Bottom Line Results* (Boca Raton, Florida: CRC Press, 2002). RCA and software to support it are products of Reliability Centre, Inc., Hopewell, Virginia. www.reliability.com.
5. TapRoot® is a product of System Improvement, Inc., of Knoxville, Tennessee. www.taproot.com.
6. Kepner Tregoe is a consulting and training services company, The business is based on *The Rational Manager: A Systematic Approach to Problem Solving and Decision Making*, a book coauthored by Charles Kepner and Benjamin Tregoe (New York: McGraw Hill, 1965). www.kepner-tregoe.com.

intervals, and repairs. As seen in Chapter 5, similar mathematical modeling methods apply to materials management. You can even apply optimization methods to organizational decision making to determine staff sizes.

Asset optimization tools enhance reliability and reduce costs. They add value to the output of RCM and may lead to modifications in RCM output decisions. They may also be used in conjunction with RCFA or on their own. They are particularly helpful in the area of capital planning to identify the timing of investments that will minimize the life-cycle costs associated with ownership of an asset.

Unlike the Five-Whys' method, decision optimization tools require data. The various mathematical methods that are familiar to reliability engineers are included in this category of technical tools. (Several are mentioned in Chapter 7.) They typically deal with specific technical problems that require solutions based on statistics and economics. Like the root-cause methods, these tools are often used after the data has been collected. Of course, you do not need to wait for a statistically significant number of failures to occur before using them; you can rely on data collected by others and available in databases if it is reasonably likely to be representative of your circumstances. That is what many reliability engineers do when designing new systems that require high reliability. Because they cannot afford to wait for failures on what are very often highly critical systems before making decisions, they rely (at least initially) on databases of relevant failure statistics.

There are many mathematical approaches to solving typical maintenance and equipment replacement problems. Many of these have come from the field of operations research. Some of the problems[7] that can be solved include:

- Optimizing the age at which equipment replacements are made using various usage and operating cost profiles to determine the most cost-effective age for replacement.
- Optimize the decision for the time to swap duty and standby equipment combinations to achieve maximum backup availability and reduce the risk of multiple failures.

---

7. For a comprehensive listing, refer to *Maintenance, Replacement and Reliability* by A.K.S. Jardine (New York: Pitman Publishing, 1973).

- Optimizing the decision about when to replace capital equipment to maximize discounted cash-flow benefits or to minimize total costs.
- Optimizing the intervals between preventive replacements to achieve target availability.
- Optimizing the time for group replacements of large number of identical assets instead of replacement as they fail in order to minimize overall cost.
- Optimizing inspection frequencies to maximize profits, minimize downtime, and maximize availability of emergency equipment.
- Optimizing decision making related to overhaul and repair vs. replacement policies and cost limits.

Jardine[8] has provided excellent coverage of these and many other maintenance management decisions. The problems described in his book are based on statistical approaches; this book also provides numerous illustrative examples. Extensive coverage of these methods is beyond the scope of *Uptime*, but be aware that these methods exist, they work and merit your consideration.

Many maintenance problems can be solved using data analysis tools—software programs that can manipulate the data and produce the answers. There are many of these software tools available; most are stand-alone programs that can be interfaced or integrated with corporate databases. Several collect condition-monitoring signals that are input from field sensors and use that data in real time with history data and economic inputs to produce recommendations about whether or not to run equipment or to shut it down for work. All of these tools depend on accurate data to produce the best results.

Suffice it to say that these methods produce statistically and economically sound decisions—provided that the data used as input is accurate. That raises a significant point. The data collected in many management systems today is often faulty and incomplete.

Many companies that have embraced these methods and trained engineers in their use have run into significant data roadblocks, and

---

8. Another excellent source of this information is "Maintenance Excellence, Optimizing Equipment Life-Cycle Decisions" by John D. Campbell and Andrew K. S. Jardine, (New York: Marcel Dekker, 2001).

missing data records about failures have led to misleading analysis—a failure rate may appear lower than it really is. Conversely, maintenance records that do not distinguish between repairs to failed equipment and repairs "just in case" can lead to the mistaken belief that failure rates are worse than they really are. Both problems—missing data and incorrect categorization of repairs—are widespread. One coal-mining operation in Canada had extensive maintenance records. Rather than relying on these records, the company resorted to data sampling and deployed its engineers to collect the data for analysis. The engineers compiled accurate data and this led to good results and significant improvements, but the data-gathering process took far longer than expected. In another example, a mobile equipment maintenance service provider hired a mechanical engineering student to visit the maintenance departments of four mines to determine actual life of some critical large components. The available data were so sketchy that the results of the study were estimated to be accurate within +50 percent at best! At present, the author is aware of only one company that is attempting to deal with the data problems using the solutions discussed in Chapter 7, and even this company has a long way to go.

Information Technology (IT) has come a long way since the first edition of *Uptime* was published in 1995. Unfortunately, the ability to use it has not kept pace. IT professionals often say, with some justification, that you can get a great deal of information from their systems. And you can, but those data are often in the form that the system designers thought you would use. Unfortunately, very few system designers know much about equipment reliability, and this sometimes defeats the objectives. For example, one simple piece of information that is often missing from corporate maintenance databases is whether or not the item that was repaired on any given work order was actually found in the failed state. It is nearly impossible to fill in those gaps in information collected in the past. That one piece of missing information renders many corporate maintenance databases almost useless from a reliability analysis perspective. It is not the fault of the IT people but a fault of poor integration and communication. The maintenance and reliability professionals have not told the IT people what they want. And often, that is because they themselves do not know what they want. Fortunately, as the maintenance profession becomes truly professional, this situation is likely to improve.

RELIABILITY AND SIMULATION MODELING

When determining the most important area of a plant to improve and deciding how to allocate scarce reliability engineering resources, some companies use elaborate ranking schemes. These schemes are often based on criteria that are important to the company because they impact safety, environment, and production output. Another technique is to build a computerized reliability model or a process simulation model of the plant systems. Reliability modeling involves complex mathematical models[9] that use computer software tools to model system reliability and availability. In simulation modeling, computers imitate, or simulate, the operations of various kinds of real-world systems, facilities, and processes using largely statistical models. Both of these modeling techniques are excellent tools for revealing just where the plant production processes are most bottlenecked or constrained. For example, if a certain machine tool's capacity or reliability is limiting production, it can be targeted for reliability improvements, capacity increases, or even for replacement with a higher capacity machine. Sometimes these constraints are obvious to those in the plant, but that is not always the case.

A simulation model was used in a facility that processed spent nuclear fuel bundles for long-term storage. The newly installed systems seemed to be incapable of performing even close to the desired production levels. The modeling revealed that the overall process could not reach desired throughput because of flaws in the combined reliability of all machines in the process. It also revealed that certain machines were not performing up to their expectations because of constraints on inputs from other machines. Overall, the processing line configuration was not well balanced. Various physical configuration and operating procedural changes were modeled and showed that performance could be substantially improved without substantial new investment. The changes were made and performance was improved (albeit not quite to the originally desired levels).

Simulation models can be used to simulate the anticipated benefits of various other improvement initiatives, such as RCM. If you

---

9. The mathematical tools use probability theory, stochastic processes, stochastic models, and Markov processes.

target an improvement in one critical area, you can often see the impact (positive or negative) on other areas. This can be a big help in planning improvement efforts that can achieve multiple desired results and avoid or ameliorate undesirable results in other areas.

INCREASING AWARENESS

Many professional development courses that focus on the methods and techniques discussed here are available to today's maintainers. Most of these courses are geared to promote a full appreciation of the value of support systems and data accuracy. Moreover, the mindset of maintainers is beginning to shift from "fix it when it breaks" to "be proactive in avoiding the problems in the first place." There are many things that you can do to enable this attitudinal shift within your company. Hopefully, one of those options will be sharing *Uptime* and its principles with your people. Explore the work of researchers in maintenance and reliability and investigate the numerous technological advancements being made in the field of condition monitoring. You will find that the more you learn, the more you need to know, and this, as it should, will lead to additional productive research because learning is a never-ending journey.

UPTIME SUMMARY

Equipment failures disrupt business. Once they have happened, you will want to avoid having them happen again. Future equipment failures can be eliminated through several reactive methods of asset reliability improvement, methods used after failures have occurred. Post-mortem analysis can teach us a great deal. Even if you have followed the proactive methods described in Chapter 8 of this book, there may be some failures you miss and these reactive methods are the answer. More reliable equipment means more uptime, and successful companies do all they can (proactively and reactively) to improve asset reliability.

Preventive Maintenance Optimization (PMO) arose from the need to improve maintenance programs that were failing to meet desired performance expectations. PMO uses RCM logic to analyze, eliminate, or modify maintenance activities of existing programs. It attempts to identify failure modes that may have been missed by the original maintenance program. Although its approach is not as thorough as RCM, it has achieved some very good results and merits consideration.

Root Cause Failure Analysis (RCFA) is entirely reactive to failures that have already occurred. RCFA is a method of performing a sort of post-mortem to determine what caused any particular failure. The intent is to eliminate the "root cause"—an identifiable cause that you can manage in some practical way.

Decision optimization techniques and tools help maintainers make fact-based decisions or improve on decisions already made. RCM can be used before an asset is put into service and, for this reason, decisions about task frequencies and failure modes are invariably subject to some degree of uncertainty. Once a program is put into place some unanticipated failures will surface or the frequency of failures may not match original estimates. Optimization techniques are used to analyze the in-service data to validate or modify the original decisions. It is a form of second-guessing that becomes more precise as failure data accumulated in service become available. These techniques can be very accurate provided the data they rely upon are accurate.

Reliability and simulation modeling are computer-based techniques that mathematically model the behavior of installed systems. They can reveal the location of process bottlenecks and predict whether (and where) another bottleneck is likely to surface once the first is handled. These models can also show the effect of various reliability improvements at different points in the systems and help focus engineering improvements efforts more effectively.

10

Team-Based Methods

How much should one maintain one's own motorcycle?
It seems natural and normal to me to make use of the small tool kits and
instruction booklets supplied with each machine, and keep it tuned
and adjusted myself . . . there is no manual that deals with the
real business of motorcycle maintenance, the most important
aspect of all. Caring about what you are doing is considered
either unimportant or taken for granted.
ROBERT M. PIRSIG, *Zen and the Art of Motorcycle Maintenance*

TEAMS IN GENERAL

The dominant methods used by companies that strive for superior results are team-based. There is a simple reason for this: These humanistic approaches work well. RCM, RCFA, and PM Optimization are all team-based methods that focus on assets. Developing an effective strategy and then following it also depends heavily on teamwork among maintainers, operators, finance, human resources, and supply chain. Multiskilling enables maintainers to work in smaller teams and sometimes even alone, but it also enables maintainers to work closely with operations, satisfying many of their immediate needs as important contributors to the production team. Work management also requires a form of teamwork because operations and supply chain both play critical roles in the process along with maintenance. Basic care utilizes a team approach—operators can do simple maintenance tasks and help maintainers while they do more complex work on systems that are shut down. Total Productive Maintenance, which is described in detail in this chapter, is also a team-based method. Teamwork is clearly important, but so are team size and structure.

In *The Tipping Point*, Malcolm Gladwell describes Robin Dunbar's 1992 anthropological work relating the brain size of primates to the number of group members in the primates' groups. Bigger brains are needed to handle larger groups with many more relationships. Humans are at the top of the list for brain size and for the size of the groups we interact with. And size matters. The number of people in a group that any one person can maintain genuine social relationships is approximately 150. Several organizations use this rule of 150 to determine maximum group size. Hutterite colonies are limited to 150 members before they split to form two colonies. Gore Associates (makers of Gore-Tex) limit their plant sizes to 50,000 square feet and their parking lots to 150 spaces. Once these are full, the company builds another small plant. In military organizations the world over, the basic fighting unit is the "company," which typically has between 120 and 150 soldiers. A company commander and all of his troops will know everyone else in the company, but a battalion command (a battalion contains several companies) will not. What these organizations have found is that small groups develop a form of group memory and the ability to transfer knowledge easily. They can work to common goals quite naturally. Within these small groups, informality works best. But larger groups, with more than 150 people, begin to need more formal structures simply because the relationships within those larger groups are less well developed. Smaller teams are quicker at decision making than larger ones and the quality of their decisions, as measured in results obtained from implementing them, is often better. They do not get bogged down in analysis paralysis, and they are less worried about company politics. These teams simply work!

In *Finding Our Way: Leadership for an Uncertain Time*, Margaret J. Wheatley describes living organizations in their own right and they are simultaneously made up of many other living organisms: people. If "command and control" are removed from these organizations, they (and the organization they inhabit) become self-organizing. Each self-organizing unit creates for itself the necessary aspects of organization used to achieve its goals, including communication networks, structures, values, and behavioral norms. Research shows that self-managed teams are far more productive than teams formed or organized in other ways. There is a clear link between participation and productivity, and productivity gains of up to 35 percent have been documented. Unfortunately, many organizations are designed to accommodate command and control by their leaders, often harming productivity. Teams and the benefits they can generate are stifled in such organizations.

Leaders of highly structured organizations argue that control is needed to manage the risks inherent to turbulent times. In military organizations, however, commanders learn that the greater the risk, the more they benefit from everyone's commitment and intelligence. By controlling too tightly, leaders stifle creativity and prevent intelligent work. In April 1992, Argentina occupied the Falkland Islands (Islas Malvinas) in the South Atlantic. British junior officers were given unprecedented authority to make decisions and simply get things done. The result was a rapid and very efficient mobilization of a large fleet sailing a long way from home on very short notice. As Wheatley noted, effective leaders are better at relying on their people and not controlling every detail themselves. Machinery needs structure; people do not. Machines cannot adapt to change; people can. Running an organization like a machine might maximize control but it suboptimizes performance.

Team-based methods for maintenance use small teams: groups of people who have a common mission, develop relationships, and create highly productive output. To confirm this point, just observe the results generated by teams of various sizes working on problems of any sort. Smaller teams will generally be far more productive. The cautionary note here is that quality suffers if a small team lacks diversity in experience and knowledge. Striking a balance between team size and composition also matters.

TOTAL PRODUCTIVE MAINTENANCE (TPM)

Total Productive Maintenance is an approach to managing physical assets that emphasizes the importance of teams of maintainers and operators working together to make equipment reliable. *Caring* about the job cannot be taught, but TPM creates an environment that encourages that kind of commitment. TPM is widely accepted by the automotive, light manufacturing, brewing, chemicals, and mining industries.

Management has always held an operator accountable for production output. This individual is now also responsible for product quality. Many factors affect how well product quality is achieved, including the way in which the workplace is organized as well as the equipment's effectiveness. When several people are involved, producing quality depends on teamwork. TPM makes it easier for individuals and groups to meet their primary goal: to produce quality products at the time and the rate required. In its broadest sense, TPM has three distinct features: 1) activities to maximize equipment effectiveness, 2) autonomous maintenance by operators, and 3) small group activities. Maximizing equipment effectiveness requires the elimination of failures, defects, and any other form of waste or loss incurred in equipment operation. This is entirely consistent with Zero-Defect and Six-Sigma approaches to quality management. TPM utilizes Overall Equipment Effectiveness[1] (OEE) as a common key measure for both maintenance and operations.

Autonomous maintenance by operators features them doing some maintenance activities and working with maintainers during repair periods. Cleaning activities can be viewed as a form of inspection. Training operators how to clean equipment without causing any damage (e.g., you don't want water from a hose to get into bearing housings) will help them understand how their actions can affect the equipment. Training them in what to look for while cleaning (e.g., leaks or looseness) is a way of making operators more aware of how the equipment works so they can recognize problems. Getting approval to conduct such training is sometimes challenging, especially in companies with formal labor organizations or strict rules about who does what work, but you can derive many benefits from this kind of training.

TPM is a formal way of becoming less formal in the way you manage equipment effectiveness. It moves you from hierarchical organizations with plenty of command and control, to small teams making and acting on their own autonomous decisions and creating value. In organizations where TPM has been applied, productivity gains of up to 60 percent have been documented.[2] TPM, as it is practiced now, began in Japan as a vital and necessary response to business imperatives to reduce waste, product variation, and production cycle times. It was a fresh approach to new challenges of the marketplace, not a logical progression of systematic maintenance management.

---

1. See Chapter 6.
2. Seiichi Nakajima, *TPM: Introduction to Total Productive Maintenance* (Tokyo: Japan Institute for Plant Maintenance, 1984; Portland, OR: Productivity Press, 1988).

Traditionally, maintenance was expected to keep a plant or an individual machine available for a targeted period of scheduled time, say 90 percent. Because of idle work-in-process inventories, most machines could be considered independent. If several machines in a series were maintained at 90 percent, the availability of the series was also 90 percent. If a machine varied much from the norm, the problem would eventually be noticed in final product quality inspection and traced back to the offending machine. Maintenance would then make corrections.

Just-in-time (JIT) techniques attacked all forms of waste: anything that did not add value to the manufacturing process. This meant the end of the idle work-in-process inventories. The machines in a sequential process became interdependent. Under these conditions, the success of the entire process relied on each machine working to a uniform plant load, or drumbeat. Thus, a six-machine process, with each machine maintained at 90 percent, no longer meant 90 percent availability overall but 90 percent times itself six times, or 53 percent. To complicate matters further, final quality control inspection was moving upstream in the process to eliminate defects and yield fluctuations at their source. As a result, machine performance problems were being identified much earlier. Demands for conformance and reliability were greatly increased, with more stringent variation checks. Maintenance management— or more correctly, the management of equipment effectiveness— had to adapt quickly to the new directives. The concept that evolved was TPM, sometimes known by its most prominent feature, autonomous (operator) maintenance.

OBJECTIVES AND THEMES OF TPM

TPM's three distinct features are reflected in its primary objectives:

- To maximize equipment effectiveness and productivity by eliminating all machine losses.
- To create a sense of ownership in equipment operators through a program of training and involvement so they can perform autonomous maintenance.
- To use small-group activities involving production, engineering, and maintenance to promote continuous improvement.

Each enterprise has its own unique approach and vision for TPM, but in most cases there are common elements and themes. There are seven broad elements in any TPM program. These have been summarized in the TPM wheel in Figure 10-1.

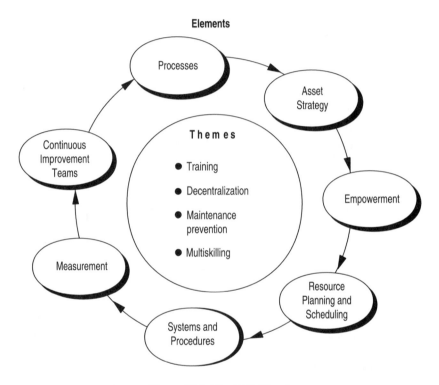

Figure 10-1. The TPM Wheel

Asset Strategy

TPM is commonly used to support and enable the principles of JIT and Total Quality Management (TQM). This usually involves moving some equipment into a cell arrangement and removing anything that is redundant. Setup modifications and upgrading machine requirements are also commonly part of the plan. Simplifying, streamlining, and automating the manufacturing process have an impact on the way maintenance is conducted. It is crucial, therefore, to dovetail the maintenance strategy with the new asset structure. Where JIT is introduced, maintenance management immediately gets involved in:

- *Layout evaluations,* including maintainability; operability; hydraulic, pneumatic, electrical, utility, steam, plumbing services; environmental concerns; and floor-loading considerations.
- *Equipment modifications,* such as solving chronic problems before a cell start-up. This can also mean providing enablers, color-coded service lines and machine air lifts, and reducing excess motion to reduce wear and noise.
- *Postmove services* to restore the equipment to satisfactory operating condition as a cell is formed. Of key importance is the initiation or revision of a specific *preventive maintenance program.* RCM is well respected as a method for achieving this aspect of TPM.

Empowerment

TPM puts the power to improve in the employees' hands. It grants workers autonomy, along with responsibility. At the same time, TPM recognizes that employees in one area have much to teach and learn from those in others. The entire organization gains strength and ideas from motivated continuous improvement teams.

A TPM environment encourages a skills exchange between operators and maintenance, and multiskill training in the various trades. It can provide increased job satisfaction for operations, tradespeople, engineers, and supervision alike. What is really exciting about TPM is that it can fundamentally change an organization's culture. Centralized, command-and-control maintenance structures cannot support a JIT–TQM–TPM initiative. Because TPM organizations become what Margaret Wheatley would consider truly living organisms, they are incompatible with overly rigid structures.

Operator ownership is not about boundaries or barriers around equipment or sections of the process. It is an expression of commitment and caring about conditions and causes and effects, an essence captured in Robert Pirsig's lament at the beginning of this chapter. Building operator ownership is mostly a matter of removing impediments and providing correct training and tools to encourage a supportive, technically informed relationship.

Resource Planning and Scheduling

During the introduction of TPM, there will be significantly increased demand on the maintenance department, especially as operators train to be more equipment conscious. As they discover the causes of chronic equipment losses or malfunctions, they will want to have them corrected quickly.

To encourage operators to be enthusiastic partners in equipment care, the maintenance department provides the infrastructure for managing their activities. It will have planning and scheduling procedures in place. The department has sufficient capacity and skills available to assign priorities and carry out the work quickly and professionally. As many organizations have found, it helps to dedicate specific tradespersons to particular areas. In this way, they become a permanent part of the team familiar with the equipment, forming closer ties with the operators and supervisors.

Systems and Procedures

As continuous improvement teams begin to focus on equipment performance, *best practice* operating and maintenance procedures will evolve. These practices in each area are documented and shared. It will quickly become daily routine to track information such as equipment histories, parts and materials, individual training progression, and costs. A well-chosen data management system can be an indispensable tool, provided it serves the purposes of the teams first!

Each team in each work cell seeks the most effective way to reduce or mitigate the risk of failure. First, the nature of failure in a specific case is understood. Then the remedy can be chosen, whether it is based on time, use or condition factors, or some other tactic.

Measurement

The current reality is compared against a future vision. In maintenance management, the prime objective is asset productivity: asset output divided by all inputs.

For TPM, it is useful to measure improvement success by teams. Monitor their individual and collective progress. From the beginning, spreading the good news about progress beyond the shopfloor will help to motivate everyone in the organization.

The future vision is best tempered with an understanding of what the competition, industry at large, or best-in-class have achieved. Benchmarking is useful in this regard, and some companies have gone to the extent of setting up entire benchmarking departments to facilitate this sort of industry-wide comparison. At GM's Saturn Division, extensive benchmarking is performed right down to the details of timing and methods of change-out of machine tools and dies.

A visible feature in TPM organizations is the extensive use of measures and their public graphic display. Performance statistics, trend, and Pareto charts are conspicuously posted, and the teams and individuals involved fully understand their contribution to those statistics. The single most important measure used in most TPM teams is OEE.[3]

Continuous Improvement Teams

Continuous improvement, based on *kaizen* principles in Japan, is central to TQM and JIT. Organizations that have begun implementing TQM, JIT, or Continuous Improvement (CI) processes have CI teams in place. CI teams can be formed to solve specific problems and disbanded when the solution is achieved, or they can be organization-based, usually centered on a work cell or manufacturing process. Most organizations use both.

TPM operators build strong relationships with their equipment. They drive an understanding within teams of failure causes, effects and impacts, and the resulting actions to eliminate these failures.

TPM teams base their agenda on management information, often stored in maintenance management systems (for example, equipment histories for failure analysis). Determination of what to do first often begins with a Pareto review of failure of the equipment or processes that govern bottlenecking, or those that add the most value to the product flow. One of the simplest yet most powerful tools to determine where to focus your efforts is the Pareto diagram. Vilfredo Pareto, an Italian economist (1842–1923), observed that 80 percent of the land in Italy was owned by 20 percent of the population. He thus came up with the legendary 80-20 rule that seems to apply in most fields of human endeavor. It is a

---

3. See Chapter 6.

"rule of thumb" and the percentages are not always exactly 80 and 20, but they will be close. For maintenance, the rule means that 80 percent (or so) of the problems are associated with 20 percent (or so) of the equipment. TPM teams can focus their efforts on the problematic 20 percent. Pareto diagrams are used to identify problems in planning and scheduling of work and to analyze Overall Equipment Effectiveness (OEE).

The Pareto diagram is a bar chart. The length of each of the bars corresponds to the number of occurrences of each failure type. It is used to help prioritize work and helps separate the vital few from the trivial many. In Figures 10-2, 10-3, and 10-4 the downtime of an Oriented Strand Board (OSB) plant manufacturing line is analyzed using monthly failure records. In Figure 10-2 you can see each step of the process in sequence, the number of failures, the downtime that each step incurred and the repair, downtime and total costs.

OSB Manufacturing Pareto Analysis

Step 8	Process Steps	8 of Failures	Total Downtime	Cost of Repair	Cost of Downtime	Total Downtime Cost
1	Log sorting	13	5	$5,000	—	$5,000
2	Jack ladder	12	7	$7,000	—	$7,000
3	Debarking	24	20	$20,000	—	$20,000
4	Stranding	18	35	$35,000	—	$35,000
5	Wet bins	2	1	$1,000	$5,000	$6,000
6	Drying	3	4	$8,000	$4,000	$12,000
7	Blending	5	7	$28,000	$7,000	$35,000
8	Forming line	7	9	$36,000	$45,000	$81,000
9	Pressing	3	8	$56,000	$40,000	$96,000
10	Finishing line	8	19	$19,000	$19,000	$38,000
11	Shipping	5	2	$2,000	—	$2,000
		100	117	$217,000	$120,000	$337,000

Figure 10-2. OSB Plant Downtime Data

The data can be sorted several ways to determine if equipment requires attention first. Figure 10-3 shows that problems can be sorted by number of failures, by downtime, by repair costs, and by downtime costs.

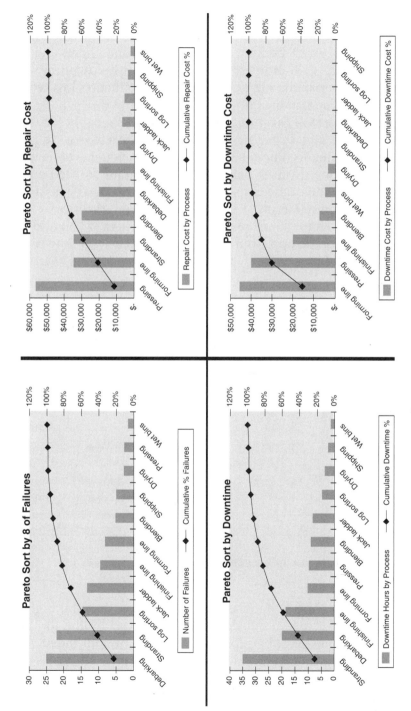

Figure 10-3. Various Possible Pareto Sorts

The process equipment that requires most attention is on the left-hand side of each plot. But notice that each sort provides a different initial focus. Debarking has the most failures, pressing the highest repair cost, stranding contributes the most downtime, and the forming line has the highest downtime (production loss) costs. Which is most important?

A maintainer will carry out repairs and will probably focus on numbers of failures or repair costs because these costs are paid from the maintenance budget. A production manager who is worried about getting product delivered will be more worried about downtime and downtime costs because they keep him or her from meeting production targets. These are competing priorities.

There is also a total business impact to consider. If you add the costs of repair to the opportunity costs associated with downtime, you get the total cost to the business overall. (See Figure 10-4.)

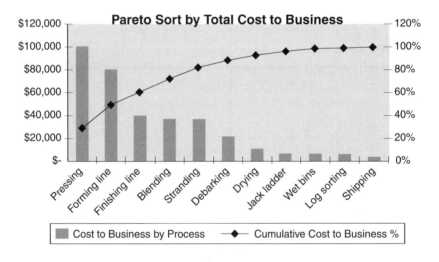

Figure 10-4. Pareto Sort by Overall Cost to Business

Figure 10-4 shows that the pressing process has the highest combined cost of repair and downtime, followed by the forming line and then finishing. By plotting the graph over different time periods (weekly, monthly, and annually), it is possible to discern which problems are chronic and which are acute.

Logarithmic scatterplots[4] can also be used to plot mean time to repair vs. frequency of failures and show lines of equal downtime. These are an excellent tool that reduces the effort required to compile the decision-making criteria from several Pareto charts into a single diagram as shown in Figure 10-5 (log scatterplot of mean repair times vs. number of failures). Lines of constant downtime are easily plotted showing, as in a Pareto diagram, which failures make the largest contributions to downtime. The plot can also be divided into quadrants showing acute and chronic failures. Acute failures are infrequent but significant contributors to overall downtime while chronic failures are those that occur frequently. The upper right quadrant includes top priority failures that have both high downtime and high frequency of occurrence. Efforts to improve the business overall will be focused on those areas that are most significant over the longer term.

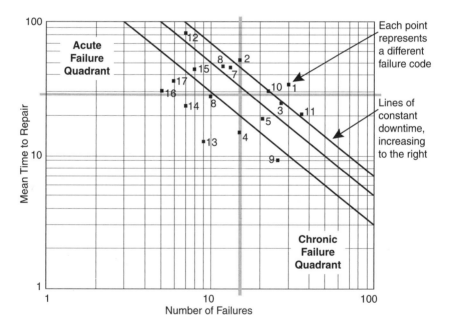

Figure 10-5. Log Scatterplot of Mean Repair Times vs. Number of Failures

4. Adopted from, "Downtime Priorities, Jack-knife Diagrams and the Business Cycle" by Dr. Peter F. Knights, Article first published in *Maintenance Journal*, Vol. 17, No. 2, pp. 14–21, Melbourne, Australia, May 2004.

Processes

TPM is often a radical change in the way asset maintenance is managed. Some of the traditional processes for managing programs of preventive, corrective, or breakdown maintenance, and for stores inventory control, are no longer appropriate. In the new climate of responsiveness, flexibility, and empowerment, the existing processes are often revisited. They are clearly understood, analyzed, and then redesigned to support TPM objectives. Each step along the way adds value and minimizes any waste in cost, time, service, quality, or other resources.

IMPLEMENTING TPM: THE ELEMENTS

What TPM means and what it will accomplish is different for each application. Even the implementation plan is specific to the situation and plant environment. A small woodworking firm with a tradition of production-maintenance integration will probably take a more informal approach than a large integrated steel mill. A basic methodology that has proved successful as a guide in many diverse applications is presented in Figure 10-6.

Following an implementation plan adapted from the Japan Institute of Plant Maintenance, the enterprise progresses through four phases in charting its new course. This route moves from stabilizing the mean time between failures and extending equipment life to predicting equipment life through condition monitoring. The four phases of activities are conducted by teams of production, maintenance, and engineering personnel working in concert. The entire implementation process is supported throughout by comprehensive education and training. (See Figure 10-7 on page 282.)

Awareness, Education, and Training

Learning underscores each element of TPM. At Nachi-Fujikoshi Corporation in Japan, "Cultivating equipment-conscious workers is the base upon which every other feature of [TPM] rests. Education and training is not only one of the fundamental improvement activities of TPM, it is a central pillar that supports the others."[5]

---

5. Nachi-Fujikoshi Corporation, eds., *Training for TPM: A Manufacturing Success Story* (New York: Productivity Press, 1990), p. 217.

	I. Stabilize Mean Time Between Failures	II. Lengthen Equipment Life	III. Periodically Restore Deterioration	IV. Predict Equipment Life
Autonomous (Operator) Maintenance	Restore accelerated deterioration by cleaning, lubricating, tightening, and correcting visible defects	Learn more about equipment mechanisms and functions; develop inspection skills	Conduct autonomous inspections and adjustments; organize and visually manage work areas	Manage operations, daily equipment care, and inspections autonomously; carry out simple repairs and replacements
Equipment Improvement	Prevent accelerated deterioration with improvements to: • Control contamination sources • Enhance accessibility for cleaning, lube, and inspection Address chronic equipment losses and prevent recurrence	• Correct design and fabrication weaknesses • Prevent operating and repair errors • Eliminate sporadic failures • Improve maintainability and operability		• Further extend life using new materials and technologies • Learn and apply advanced failure analysis techniques
Planned Maintenance	• Prepare equipment logs • Help operators establish daily inspection and lubrication standards • Introduce visual controls • Clarify operating conditions; comply with conditions of use	• Rank failures, prioritize PM work • Standardize routine maintenance activities • Create data management systems to monitor failures, equipment, spares, costs	• Estimate lifespans & learn early signs of internal deterioration • Set standards for periodic inspection and parts replacement • Improve efficiency of planned inspection and maintenance work; improve control of data and spares	• Apply condition-based monitoring techniques to predict life • Conduct periodic restoration based on predicted life
Quality Maintenance	Clarify relationship between quality and equipment, people, materials, methods		Establish and maintain equipment control conditions	• Build in QM controls at the design stage
Maintenance Prevention	Define data system requirements and begin documenting equipment improvements	Incorporate data from current equipment improvements in new equipment design specifications		

Figure 10-6. TPM Implementation

	General Management	Maintenance Engineering	Operations	Maintenance
TPM objectives, elements, themes	✓	✓	✓	✓
General equipment cleaning, inspection, monitoring			✓	✓
Problem identification, analysis tools		✓	✓	✓
Basic equipment functioning, adjustment, optimization of skills			✓	✓
Focused technical skills				✓
Maintenance prevention and equipment redesign		✓	✓	✓

Figure 10-7. TPM Education and Training

Managers, maintenance staff, team leaders, and equipment operators are all extensively involved in the learning process. Training supports:

- *Decentralization* of decision-making and empowerment of employees. This will help them act autonomously with knowledge and confidence and as team players who know where and when to ask for help.
- *Maintenance prevention*, or minimizing the amount of maintenance intervention without sacrificing reliability. This is accomplished with standard operating procedures and systematic analysis and treatment of equipment failures and other abnormalities.
- *Multiskilling* to maximize flexibility, efficiency, and job satisfaction for both maintenance and production workers.
- *Performance measures* to assess the cost-benefit ratio of TPM. Successes in the program are publicized and shortcuts to achieving resource productivity are abandoned.

The tools and techniques for problem identification, definition, solution, and team decision-making are shown in Figure 10-8. These aids are invaluable for the learning process.

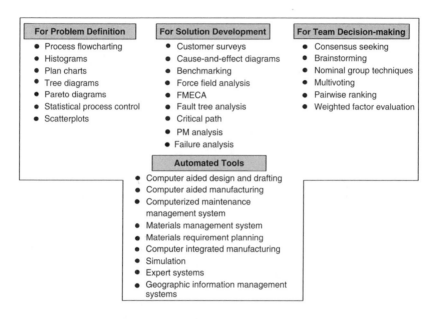

Figure 10-8. Tools and Techniques for TPM

Pilot Project

Beyond understanding the theory of TPM, you will probably want some practical knowledge of what it takes to implement before you set about making sweeping changes to the way you manage your operations and maintenance. A pilot project in one area of the plant can help to work out any kinks and build both experience and confidence in your implementation team and methods.

Of great help in a trial run is a detailed "before-and-after" study. One way to conduct this study is to have staff photograph or videotape the area, pointing out defects, disorder, and deterioration. Such varied industries as aluminum rolling, primary steel, and discrete manufacturing have found that a series of pictures is indeed worth a thousand words. Keeping a visual record is part of the following eight-step approach for piloting:

1. *Education (basics).* Hold a company-wide seminar on the elements, themes, and objectives of TPM, and how it relates to TQM, JIT, and CI programs that you may have in place already.

2. *Survey.* Determine which areas are likely to excel in a pilot program because of culture, attitude, preparation, or management style. You want to pick an area with a high probability of success.

3. *Selection.* Select the pilot area based on its probability of success and on the productivity improvement potential. The area chosen should also be representative of the organization at large so that what you learn can be applicable to other areas as well.

4. *Data collection.* Conduct Pareto or log-scatterplot analyses of the frequency and duration of losses caused by recorded failures, set-ups, idling, minor delays, quality, and yield losses.

5. *Education (specifics).* Present a detailed seminar for pilot area personnel, describing the selection process, data analysis for equipment losses, and TPM vision.

6. *Photographic tour.* Have pilot teams produce "as-is" photographs or videos of equipment deterioration, defects, disorders, housekeeping, and so on, in their area.

7. *Training.* Relate the Pareto analysis of losses to the results of the photographic tour. Also, provide training on how to minimize equipment deterioration and, therefore, equipment losses through the activities in Phase I: Stabilize Reliability.

8. *Kickoff.* Choose a formal kickoff date and location for Phase I. Assign responsibilities for improvements to production, materials, maintenance, and engineering and hold them accountable to support each other.

Measure the progress of the pilot program as a precursor to building the case for plantwide implementation. Monitor such "outputs" as:

- *Overall equipment effectiveness*—the product of availability, process rate, and quality rate.
- *Reliability*—mean time between failures.
- *Maintainability*—mean time to inspect, service, replace, or repair.
- *Set-up time*—the average and current best times for change out of dies or set-ups.

Also measure input such as:

- *Labor*, including degree of PM compliance, demonstrated proficiency in autonomous maintenance, crew size, and maintenance labor distribution.
- *Materials*, including engineering stores inventory turns, inventory service level, vendor partnering, and obsolescence.
- *Cost-effectiveness*, where costs are measured by function, area, equipment, job, and class of expense.

Key Success Factors

The single most important factor to implement TPM is true management commitment. Organizations with a high level of commitment are successful, even if they do not have the most comprehensive plan or a lavish budget. Management supports and nurtures the TPM teams, avoiding the temptation to control and direct them. Management attacks the problems, not the people.

Management's commitment is often shown by what it is willing to put on the line. The resources allocated are important, of course. But what counts even more is the time and visible involvement of senior management, for however long it takes (and this can be 3 to 5 years!), to put TPM into place. Other key success factors include:

- The team approach throughout the project cycle.
- The enthusiasm and team-building skills of TPM leaders or project managers.
- A clearly defined implementation methodology.
- The learning processes, particularly the communication between maintenance and operations in such vital areas as how the equipment does what it does and how to keep it operating effectively.
- The mechanisms in place to reinforce positive behavior and results.

TPM began in Japan and grew out of quality management initiatives that, oddly enough, originated in the United States. Today, many of North America's important manufacturers and processors are now fully immersed in TPM. DuPont Fibers attributes major gains in productive capacity to TPM: having skilled people getting equipment up to as-new condition and keeping it there, and eliminating failures through systematic long-term improvement. Others companies that have implemented TPM include Timkin, Pepsi,

Ford, Harley-Davidson, Wilson Sporting, MACI, Saturn Corp., Norton, John Deere, Miller Brewing, Unilever, Steelcase, and Toyota. But as Mark O'Brien of Yamaha observed, "As we looked around Japan and the U.S. for the perfect TPM recipe, we realized that no one has the cookbook." The ingredients, however, produce something quite good.

Successful implementation of TPM themes and elements certainly results in measurable benefits. Empowered, motivated employees contribute in significant ways to help improve asset productivity. The long-term benefit of caring about maintenance can be summed up in another quotation from Pirsig:

> Each machine has its own personality, that is the real object of motorcycle maintenance. The new [machines] start out as good-looking strangers and, depending on how they are treated, degenerate rapidly into bad-acting grouches or even cripples, or else turn into healthy, good-natured, long lasting friends. This one, despite the murderous treatment it got at the hands of those alleged mechanics, seems to have recovered and has been requiring fewer repairs as time goes on.

UPTIME SUMMARY

There's an old saying that "two heads are better than one." Teamwork has been proven time and again to produce superior results. It is the basis for many successful methods like RCM, PMO, RCFA, Total Productive Maintenance (TPM), and various quality improvement programs, such as Six Sigma. The importance of your people has already been stressed in Chapter 2. Choosing excellence goes beyond that: Self-organized teams bring out the best in people. They, in turn, deliver enhanced productivity and superior results.

Smaller teams tend to be more effective than larger teams, provided they have sufficient breadth and depth of knowledge to handle assigned tasks. When teams grow into large groups or departments, they begin to need more formal management structures and processes in order to remain effective. If you have a group with more than 150 people, you will find formalized approaches necessary. In a group with fewer than 150 people, a degree of informality works well. Some organizations strive to keep the number of people in an operational unit (a plant, for example) below 150. One of the reasons for the success of small teams and less formal organizations is that they do not rely so heavily on "command and control" to get things done. Command and control tends to stifle initiative and creativity and that can harm productivity.

Total Productive Maintenance (TPM) is a team-based approach to organizing and working that has proven highly successful in a variety of industrial environments. Similar to quality approaches, it emphasizes the importance of integrated teams of operators and maintainers who work together, care about their work, and are committed to team success. From that flows the overall success of the organization. The small team is one of the distinct features of TPM. Operators and maintainers work together toward the same goals with common performance measures and methods. The traditional work boundaries tend to blur between them and extensive training is used to help maximize flexibility and capability while retaining safety. The teams are allowed to operate autonomously, are responsible for their own decisions, and support overall plant or operational goals.

Teams optimize the value of employee input into your company, and TPM is an excellent approach that works well in the production environment. Blending maintenance and operations into autonomous self-directed teams achieving superior results, TPM provides a framework for exceptional team achievement.

11

Process Optimization

Drive thy business or it will drive thee.
BENJAMIN FRANKLIN (1706–1790)

Assets are used to produce products or deliver services. The "way" they are used can be called a "process." Businesses have financial, budgeting, hiring, payroll, supply chain, and other processes. In a production environment, it is a production process. In maintenance, it is a maintenance process. If a process leads to desired results at a low cost, it is a cost-effective process. If the results achieved are not the desired results or the cost of achieving the results is too high, a review of the process can present opportunities for improvement.

Companies that implement new computer systems and automate their processes often redesign their systems or their processes for greater cost-effectiveness. Companies that experience problems with their processes often modify them to handle or avoid similar problem in future. The people who use business processes often see ways to streamline them, remove or reduce the frequency of bottlenecks, or make them work better with other processes. They may change a process or find a work-around to make their own jobs simpler. It is in this manner that business processes evolve over time. Process evolution can be healthy, but the way it is approached can make a difference. With some approaches, processes can become overly complex and cumbersome.

In a natural gas pipeline company in the United States, for example, the capital acquisition process comprised over 240 steps. On average, it took more than two years to process any single request before the purchasing process could begin. Only 5 percent of the requests initiated actually got approved, and most of the rejections occurred about 18 months into the process. After a careful review and redesign, the company was able to reduce the process steps from 240 to 30. With fewer steps, most requests could be processed within 2 months (rather than 2 years), and most rejections occurred during the first week (rather than 18 months into the process).

Not every process is going to require radical redesign, but it makes sense to check your maintenance business processes periodically to ensure that they are achieving what you want to achieve without undue complexity. It also makes sense to ensure that your maintenance process integrates smoothly with other processes, like purchasing and production planning. Process redesign is often prompted by mergers or acquisitions. Integration of the processes of each previously autonomous company makes it possible for the new company to function seamlessly.

Regardless of the reason for process redesign, it is useful to have a logical approach that produces the desired results. This chapter provides guidelines for companies that are radically reengineering their entire maintenance and related processes as well as to companies that merely want to optimize existing processes, regardless of the reason.

Process reengineering was first discussed in Michael Hammer's *Harvard Business Review* article, "Reengineering Work: Don't Automate, Obliterate." It is a concept that represents a fundamental rethinking of process modification, one that posits that redesigning business processes should be revolutionary rather than evolutionary. The goal of radical redesign of business processes is to achieve dramatic performance advances in critical areas, such as cost, quality, service, and speed. Instead of fine-tuning the status quo with continuous incremental improvement, reengineering focuses on core business processes, such as new product development, order fulfillment, and maintenance management. It zeroes in on those processes that are crucial to success because they increase customer and shareholder value. (See Figure 11-1.) Since its introduction in the early 1990s, reengineering has been abused by companies seeking to make short-term cost reduction gains. Many of those short-sighted efforts met with eventual failure. Never-the-less, when used correctly, reengineering is a power-business tool when used as intended to achieve long-term sustainable improvement.

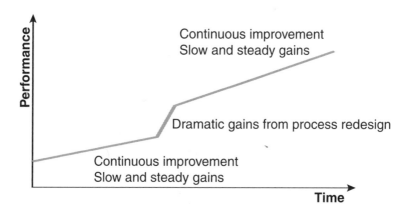

Figure 11-1. Quantum Leaps in Improvement

There are two ways to change processes. The first is to redesign or reengineer existing processes, and the second is to design entirely new ones. If you are starting up a new operation you will be designing your processes from scratch. The basic processes built into your software support systems are a good place to start, but part of the implementation of the software you have selected must include tailoring it to your specific requirements. If you are merging two companies, you may well have two sets of entirely different processes to manage. Some companies choose to leave things as they are, but most companies are now opting to institute a standardized approach across the board, regardless of the disruption this can cause during the transition. Often, this is driven by the desire to consolidate reporting at the executive level. Regardless of your reasons for doing redesign work, the approach is basically the same.

Implementing process changes across multiple sites, divisions, regions, and continents poses some interesting challenges. A good place to begin is to look at the underlying process optimization approach and then at some of the challenges you may encounter during large-scale transformations.

MAINTENANCE: IS IT A PROCESS OR A FUNCTION?

Traditionally, maintenance has been viewed as a function, a discipline, or a professional "silo." But this perception does not adequately (or accurately) define maintenance management, which is really a complex process that crosses many functional boundaries.

The problem with the traditional functional view is that it leads you to optimize the function and not the overall process. Maintenance, when viewed as a function, usually covers only the tradespersons and the management of work they do. When viewed as a process, however, maintenance is far more; it covers tradespeople, but it also covers purchasing, stores, production scheduling, operations, engineering, and several other management and administrative functions that all impact the ability to deliver uptime.

One example of the problems that can arise from viewing maintenance as a function is maintenance stores. When managed by maintenance, the critical measure for stores is service level, with finance and accounting viewing stores as an investment of the organization's working capital. When stores is managed by material handling (or others with little interest in the service level), the critical measure is minimizing inventory holding costs, which maintenance sees as an impediment to good performance. Depending on how you look at the function, you get different results. As illustrated below, each silo has its own agenda to optimize performance:

- *Maintenance.* Because it is responsible for equipment availability, maintenance does not want to be caught without any part on hand to respond to breakdowns. It minimizes these failures by scheduling time for PM work and component replacements. Maximizing inventory optimizes its performance as a function and open stores access across all shifts is preferable. Stores can become bloated with many "just-in-case" spares.
- *Production.* Its mandate is to produce during scheduled runs, so it does not want any equipment delays, not even for scheduled component replacements. Production is usually measured on income statement accounts and is not concerned with balance sheet accounts, such as stores inventory. Production people typically remain blissfully unaware of MRO inventory issues until maintenance people inform them that a job cannot be done because they are awaiting parts.
- *Materials.* Minimizing freight charges and personnel costs dictates slow logistics and single-shift coverage for stores. Maximizing space and orderliness makes the function run smoothly. Day-shift, controlled access ensures minimal discrepancies in inventory reconciliation. The prime driver for this function is control, not necessarily service.

- *Finance.* Concerned with controlling the balance sheet, finance likes to minimize stores investment and carrying costs, often to an arbitrary, fixed level.
- *Engineering.* As part of capital project planning, engineering sets rigorous specifications and follows a conservative route to maximize reliability when planning capital and replacement spares.
- *Purchasing.* Going out for numerous quotes and taking the lowest cost, while meeting the minimum specifications, ensures that cost savings targets are met but adds excessive variation in spare parts. The resultant acquisition of low-cost and often substandard parts can result in more downtime, more frequent parts' replacement, and poor equipment performance, leading to reduced product or service quality.
- *Plant management.* Often rooted in production or engineering, cost-cutting measures tend to be aimed at support functions like maintenance and stores.

Too often, the various departments involved negotiate an uneasy balance that favors one or two of them, and this suboptimizes the outcome. A better alternative is to view equipment effectiveness and cost efficiency as results of the entire maintenance process. That depends on developing rational principles that get the most from all functions, not any particular one. If you can do that, then the maintenance process can improve your results radically.

To redesign any process you need the participation and buy-in of all the various groups that are involved. Pull together a multi-discipline team from all the functions that make the process work. Depending on your organization's structure, this may include production, materials, engineering, maintenance, finance, human resources, and administration.

Many techniques and tools can be used to redesign a process. Consider process mapping, process analysis, value stream mapping, and customer interviews or surveys. You can also include automated tools to simulate how the redesigned process will work and benchmarking to help set goals and provide insights. The team develops a clear understanding of the overall vision of the business and what drives competitive advantage in your particular sector. Participants will learn what it is about maintenance that is critical to your business success, whether it is low cost relative to competitors, high reliability and uptime, rapid response to customer demands, or something else.

Next, map out the main working elements, such as how maintenance links or interfaces with other core processes like production and engineering. Delays and bottlenecks in processes often occur at these hand-off points where one group's priorities are different from another's. Broad, aggressive business goals (for example, achieving zero breakdowns in all scheduled runs within 36 months) are defined and agreed upon at this point. Beware that visionary goals can be unrealistic without carefully set and managed expectations. For example, if you anticipate a major process redesign (such as those that can occur when you implement new software systems), make sure that people are aware that:

- There will be a major restructuring in the way you are organized, the roles each person will play, the skills required, the way you are evaluated, the supporting technology, and maybe even the company culture.
- The top executive will commit an enormous amount of time at the site sponsoring and supporting the effort.
- There will be constant communication about the effort and progress that relate directly to profitability.

ANALYZING MAINTENANCE PROCESS FLOW

A process is a set of linked activities that takes an input and transforms it into an output. In maintenance, the inputs involve identifying equipment requirements and various materials, skills, and information. The linked activities include planning, scheduling, and the actual work. Outputs are available equipment, histories, and satisfied customers.

To redesign the maintenance process, begin with an understanding of how the current process is actually conducted. Your objective is to simplify it to reduce cycle times, work-in-process, waste, and duplication.

Process Mapping

A straightforward, activity-based mapping technique using block diagrams is usually quite sufficient, except for complex processes like the on-site rebuild of a major equipment system. Use a hierarchy and map at different levels, as shown in Figure 11-2. The first level may be the planned maintenance process. Level 2 delineates planned maintenance into the following steps: notify, prepare, fix, and review. Levels 3 and 4 are used to break down these steps to even further detail. At the finest level of detail, you can pinpoint where improvement has potential to provide the greatest benefit, because of high cost, long cycle time, frequency, quality problems or overall impact on the entire process.

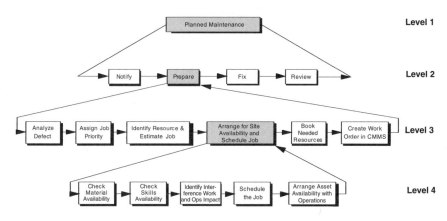

Figure 11-2. Process Flow Mapping

In mapping, you define the boundaries of the process, the beginning and end. For each activity, define "what it is." If that is not obvious, define where it starts and ends and who does it.

One successful technique for process mapping is known as the "brown paper process." This uses a large sheet of kraft wrapping paper, roughly 1.5 m × 2 m (4 ft. × 6 ft.) (Brown kraft wrapping paper is available in most industrial sites, hence the name "brown paper," but any large sheet of paper can be used.) Sketch the process flow, spreading it out over the entire paper. Indicate start and stop points and any decision points with the various "yes or no" process flows that result. Then attach copies of the various documents and reports used throughout the process at the appropriate points on the process diagram. Sample documents include copies of work orders at various stages in the processes, copies of purchase orders, drawings, plans, timesheets, etc. Include any "control documents," such as authorizations, approvals, and reports.

Process Analysis

Now that the process is mapped, you can analyze it for improvement potential. For each activity, determine what is being done, how it is done, why it is done, what the volume is, who is involved, how long it takes, and what it costs. Ask yourself, "Does this activity add value?" In other words, would customers pay for it if they knew you were doing it? If you are using a "brown paper" you can use Post-it™ notes to identify any areas of uncertainty or confusion. (The team resolves any confusion before moving on to redesign.)

List activities that do not add value: move, inspect, file, store, retrieve, count, travel, or wait. They cannot all be eliminated, but they are good places to start streamlining. Figure 11-3 shows how to begin the value test, using a work request process as an example. Look for:

- *Overall process effectiveness.* Does it achieve what it is supposed to achieve? The example shows that scheduling for nonemergency work is missing, and you may want to add that to the process.
- *Management and control effectiveness.* Is the process really being controlled by the elements that are in place now? Are the various control elements working? The example shows little of the control elements used to control the process. Samples of work requests, work orders, etc., would help to answer these questions.
- *Risk management.* Are risks being managed? In the case of emergency requests cited in the example, do they get handled early enough in the process and rapidly enough to meet the demands of the situation? There appears to be no place where information is gathered for overall process and risk management.
- Who is involved? How much effort is required of each participant? Average times for each step would be helpful.
- Is the organization structured to support the process or does it cross departmental boundaries? In the example, you might consider whether or not planners should be involved in emergency request evaluation or whether the initial investigation should go directly to the crew supervisor.
- Do all interested parts of the business receive adequate communication and information about the process? In the exam-

ple, the initiator is notified, what happens if this person is off-shift at the time?

• Are the measures being used monitoring efficiency and effectiveness of process execution? The measures indicated in the figure give some indication of work request flow, but there is no indication of the backlog that might be building or of average compliance to schedule.

• Does the process involve the customer or outsiders? In the example, the initiator is advised of progress along the way but no on seems to be reporting to management.

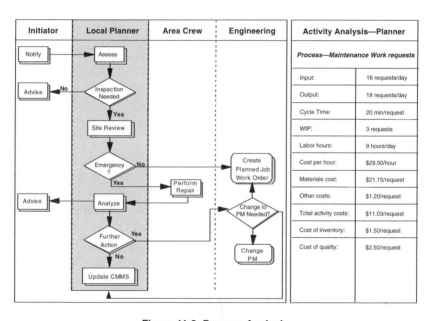

Figure 11-3. Process Analysis

You will probably come up with specific ideas for changes to the process or its documentation or controls. In some cases, you may even see how potential changes to the process flow can improve it.

Now you are ready to critique the process. There are tests that can be applied to each process and activity to determine its value. Can bureaucracy be reduced to eliminate unnecessary communications? Are there excess moves, waiting, filing, or rework? Is there an easier, simpler, or more streamlined approach, perhaps by changing the order, balancing tasks, or combining them? You can often eliminate duplication by looking at redundancies or multiple versions. If you conduct activities in sequence, consider whether they can be done in parallel or along a critical path. When you look at the root cause of errors or quality problems, consider error proofing through standardization or using a specialist. Finally, consider automating the simple, repetitive tasks.

Value Stream Mapping

Value stream mapping is similar to process analysis and sometimes the two names are used interchangeably. However, value stream mapping goes a bit further. In addition to mapping the main process flows, it also includes the flows of information and the management systems that support the basic process. This is particularly helpful when examining process flows as part of a computer system implementation project where information flows are critical. It can provide insights into the process and how it is managed, which process mapping alone can fail to provide.

Visioning

Once the current process is understood in detail, you can question the purpose for it all and decide on what you want the end result to be. Ask basic, hard questions, such as, "Why do we maintain our own equipment?" or "Does time-based PM work actually reduce our failure rates?" Also ask yourself whether you need to be doing the process (or parts of it) at all.

For parts of the process that are not working as well as you would like, brainstorm, use cause-effect diagrams, and ask the "Five Whys" to get to the bottom of what is not working.

After you have asked the basic questions, you may want more ideas about what the ideal process may look once implemented. Benchmarking, particularly in businesses not related to your own but facing similar challenges, is a valuable tool. It shows what the best are doing, and it can provide excellent targets to set as part of your vision.

Redesign

The vision you build is the foundation of the redesign process. The detailed plan, costs, and cycle times are the mechanics. Figure 11-4

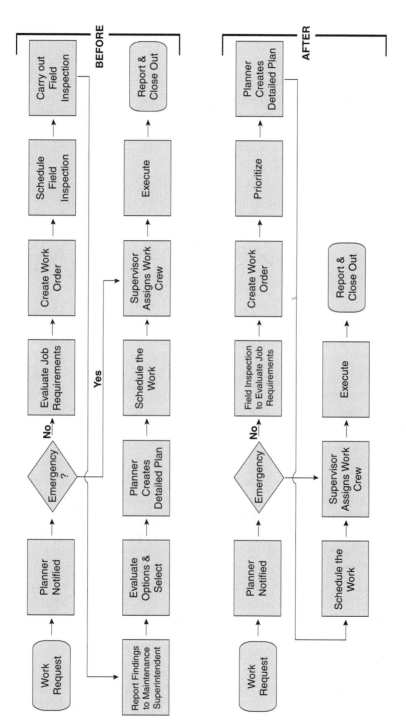

Figure 11-4. Simplifying the Corrective Maintenance Process

shows an example of how a common process, managing corrective (demand) maintenance, can be simplified. Specifically, the example shows that by utilizing the planner skills more effectively, it is possible to remove three steps and the participation of the superintendent without compromising work quality.

As you go through the redesign stage, barriers to potential change and adjustments will soon become evident. The real issues will take shape as the organization struggles to restructure. Supporting it all is senior executive leadership.

Management commitment to change cannot be stressed enough. There is no point beginning the exercise if you are not prepared to follow through. One utility company recently reorganized into business units, consolidating many of its maintenance specialists into a services unit. The makeover progressed rather smoothly. As people were becoming comfortable with the change, one of the managers introduced a maintenance process reengineering exercise for civil works. The team took up this initiative and produced results that were clearly superior to the status quo. Executive management cheered the reengineering exercise as a new approach to cost-effectiveness; however, it was not prepared to implement the result, which basically contradicted the earlier maintenance centralization effort. Everyone went back to the old, familiar ways. By allowing this to happen, management failed to empower its workforce.

Process redesign can produce radical and dramatic results, gigantic leaps in contemporary measures of performance. On occasion, it can also be a little nerve-wracking. One large brewery in the United States has implemented what many would consider an ideal TPM program. Within this organization, operators and maintainers work together without separate operations and maintenance budgets. Compared with other breweries' costs, the company's overall operations costs are low, but it is impossible to tell if this comes from operating or maintenance practices because its TPM program precludes comparisons at that level. While the overall result is gratifying, the company cannot use benchmarking to determine if there is further room for improvement because no other company is organized the same way. The brewery has taken a path that deviates sharply from that traveled by others, both in methods and performance. That sort of dramatic change can shake an operation to its roots, and it is not for the faint-hearted. Yet it is precisely such bold and innovative moves that forward-looking companies embrace to forge ahead in today's borderless and fast-paced business world.

LARGE-SCALE TRANSFORMATIONS

As Chapter 2 of this work explained, it is sometimes difficult to implement dramatic and even subtle changes in the way people work in small organizations and single-site operations. The challenges are amplified if the process optimization is being carried out for multiple-site operations, for several divisions of a company, or for a company that is the product of a merger.

Invariably, different sites, different divisions, and different companies do things differently. Over time they have all adapted to their respective business circumstances: their unique client demands, ways of handling suppliers, equipment environments, or manufacturing process idiosyncrasies. Add to that the complexities of different regulatory environments, different cultural norms, different languages, different work ethics, different social values, and different levels of skill, and you have a complicated transformation challenge.

The approaches that work with a unionized workforce in a large urban environment may not work in a remote, nonunion rural environment or in a developing nation. Even in the relatively homogeneous environment of North America, computer-generated report scripts that are written for English-speaking operations get rewritten for French and Spanish readers. Expand that company into Europe or Asia and the complexity grows substantially.

Underlying business processes that the corporation insists must be consistent throughout an entire company (e.g., finance, budgeting, and accounting) will need to be taught to parts of the organization that are adapting. Many other business processes, notably maintenance and its related supporting processes, rarely need to be consistent from site to site. For maintenance, only financial reporting truly needs to be consistent with corporate standards and requirements; other maintenance processes can be different without impacting on corporate reporting.

As discussed earlier in the book, small organizations can successfully rely on less formal approaches and less structure than larger organizations. People work best in an environment that does not have an overwhelming number of superimposed interrelationships to grasp and keep track of. Formalizing processes can stifle human creative energy. The more formal and more bureaucratic the processes, the greater the potential for stifling. If the processes do not support the individuals in executing their roles successfully, they will find work-arounds. This becomes highly evident every time someone leaves the organization. A task or job that seemed easy suddenly becomes difficult. The individual who once did the job was very likely working outside established processes and systems that he or she found constricting or impractical and was getting things done. The individual who has taken over must either work within the procedures and systems or, in time, develop his or her work-around. And the latter will probably happen. Recognize that this is human nature. Imposing a standard solution or process on anyone is likely to meet with resistance, either passive or overt.

The key to success in a large transformation is to provide core processes at the corporate level and allow for local solutions and process variants. Do not attempt to overcontrol or manage each site from the head office. It just won't work. The local variants on business processes will account for local conditions and factors that help to make things move smoothly—in that location or area. These versions must of course feed the process requirements (usually information) at the corporate level. What matters is that they work together consistently, not how they do it. Complex corporate transformations can be successful if they accommodate local preferences and differences. It is far easier to accommodate the seemingly chaotic mix of local approaches that work to meet a common standard than it is to impose common approaches and hope that the standard will be met. The following example illustrates how well this can work. A global mining company based in North America was expanding through acquisition and new start-ups. Already conducting operations on five continents and with a labor pool speaking seven languages, the company had recently acquired another mining enterprise with several mines in Asia. Aware of the challenges associated with such corporate diversity, company leadership invested in an external review of its practices. The scathing report that was issued after the review pointed out that the company was not taking advantage of numerous opportunities to improve overall cost performance. In addition, the report recommended that the company take steps to extend the lives of several of its mines by finding a more economical way to mine lower grades of ore. The company began to act on these recommendations and, among other initiatives, set its sights on becoming a leader in maintenance.

The strategy was simple and effective: a set of corporate standards that would be introduced and implemented throughout the organization, but not by traditional command-and-control means. The company would allow individual sites all the latitude they needed to meet those standards while it supported the site efforts on an as-requested basis.

A team of maintenance leaders from each region met and, with the help of an outside facilitator, developed the standards to be used at all sites. Inputs from the newly acquired company were welcomed. As it happened, this company had already begun a similar initiative and had done some of the groundwork. The standards the maintenance leaders created set minimum requirements that each site had to meet but stopped short of telling the sites how this was to be done. Each regional operation and each site had to come up with its own plan. The corporate team visited each site to facilitate the start-up process. The team performed site reviews comparing site practices with the new standard. Team members worked with site leadership to develop improvement plans that would eventually bring each site into compliance with the standard and then left the sites. Corporate support was available to provide advice, assistance, and training, and sites were required to report on progress and show results. An enterprise asset management system was implemented, again allowing leeway for local variations and languages. As a result of the review effort, local maintainers were exposed to people and ideas from other sites and from the head office. Communication between and among the sites and between sites and the head office increased, and practices, processes, methods, and tricks were shared. After two years, the corporate team revisited each site and performed another review. The report issued after this review showed that much had improved.

By accommodating local differences and by sharing information and ideas rather than imposing them, the company was able to improve maintenance practices at all of the sites. Maintenance costs per ton of ore produced were reduced by nearly 20 percent and safety and environmental performance improved. Life-of-mine forecasts were extended at two of the company's operations.

UPTIME SUMMARY

Whenever you are following a set of steps to achieve some goal you are following a process. Your people do their jobs through day-to-day implementation of those processes in order to deliver results. If the processes are ill conceived or inefficient things move slowly and results are more expensive to obtain than they need to be. Well-designed, efficient processes that integrate with other related business processes keep things running smoothly, keep costs down, and keep people motivated.

Over time, a natural tendency to want to do things "better" prompts companies to redesign their business processes. They streamline here and add something there, all in an effort to deal with changing circumstances. Unfortunately, this approach tends to add complexity rather than take it away. In fact, this is how bureaucracy grows and becomes bloated.

Maintenance is a business process that works best when it is tightly integrated with materials management, supply chain, human resources, and engineering. If these "departments" operate independently of each other, they will tend to optimize their own results, sometimes at the expense of others'. If they work together, the result is optimization of the entire business.

From time to time, it makes sense to take a hard look at your maintenance processes and how they integrate with other business processes and then evaluate whether or not you really need all of the existing processes and all the steps they entail. Sometimes dramatic changes can arise from what is learned during these reviews. If the changes are dramatic, they are often called "reengineering." More often, the changes are fairly minor, a continuous improvement process.

There are a variety of tools for analyzing process flows: process mapping, process analysis, value stream mapping, visioning, and redesign. All of these can help wring more value from business processes.

In organizations with corporate-wide management systems, there is a tendency to impose consistent business processes on all parts of the company. This is better in theory than in practice because it fails to take account of the unique circumstances that exist at each location and business unit. Local thinking and methods are often more effective than ideas imposed from on high or elsewhere. For large-scale corporate transformations across multiple sites, it is best to lay out standards and expectations but leave the decisions about execution at the local levels.

PART IV

Epilogue

Uptime provides an overall strategy for excellence in maintenance management based on practices observed in high-performing companies in capital-intensive industries. The three parts of the *Uptime* Pyramid of Excellence deal with specific activities, methods, tools, and approaches that can be applied. Excellence is not a destination: When you think you have arrived, you will discover there is more that can be done. If you do not find opportunities for improvement at every stage of the journey, your competitors will. The more you and your company learn about managing maintenance, the more you will discover. Choosing excellence as a journey entails a great deal of commitment and resolve. Maintenance as a topic for management discussion is not considered very "sexy," but it is an important part of any capital-intensive business that consumes resources, time, and money. It also affects every aspect of a company's performance. Maintenance impacts uptime and revenues, downtime and losses, safety and environmental performance, energy efficiency, and regulatory compliance. Getting it right can bring substantial benefits; getting it wrong can be disastrous.

12

Excellence

If you are going to achieve excellence in big things,
you develop the habit in little matters.
Excellence is not an exception,
it is a prevailing attitude.

COLIN POWELL

Excellence is a journey. You will never achieve perfection, but you can always do better. If you do not improve, your competitors will, and this is a compelling reason to achieve more all the time. In maintenance, it is your people using your process to get the most out of your assets that make improvements happen. Within this framework, as Colin Powell observed, are a host of big things that are dependent on "habit in little matters." Excellence is an accumulation of those habits—all of them important in their own ways as parts of the greater whole.

Companies that are high performers[1] in maintenance are invariably high performers in virtually every other aspect of their business as well. There is an atmosphere of achievement and a positive attitude that never quits; they expect top performance. Like professional athletes, they make it look easy because they are so good at what they do, and they constantly strive to do better. For these companies, change is normal, and they are good at managing change. Moreover, they stay focused on the changes and complete them before moving on to the next thing. They finish what they start and realize that every journey is made up of many small steps. They embrace new technology, new methods, new ideas, and

---

1. A "high performer" has a low cost per unit of output, an excellent safety record, an excellent environmental record, and focuses only on success—consistently and efficiently achieving what it sets out to achieve.

inputs from their people. They invest in the future and in their own success, and know that investments in maintenance improvement contribute to the bottom line. Their people are active and fully engaged participants. They take part in the choices that affect what they do, how they do it, and when. They are highly motivated, and they genuinely enjoy what they are doing. They share in the company's success through job satisfaction, compensation, job security, and a safe, clean, and pleasant working environment.

In many companies, however, the business environment seems to drive mostly short-term thinking. Executives at these companies are challenged to create long-term value while under pressure to perform today. Many companies start change initiatives but never finish them. They are too busy reacting to finish what they start. Even those things that are finished are not executed effectively. These companies evolve very slowly; they are rarely, if ever, leaders.

Regulatory requirements legislated in the wake of the big financial scandals of the early 2000s have driven increasingly tighter and more stringent controls. Many of these laws were passed by the U.S. Congress, but their effect is felt by businesses worldwide, and other countries' lawmakers are following suit. The actions of a few unscrupulous business leaders have led to a legislative backlash.

Nevertheless, some of the regulations that overcontrol and overregulate the current business environment do have some very positive by-products. Everyone is compelled to be more careful and most people think twice before making decisions that will have an adverse impact on others or on the environment. Although fear of being held accountable, not altruism, often motivates this caution, the results are positive just the same. Care and caution have become constants in most organizations and in their various departments and functional units.

Maintenance, which has an impact on virtually all aspects of business in a capital (asset) intensive company, is also affected by this careful and cautionary mode. There is less and less tolerance for errors that injure or kill people, harm the environment, cause loss of public services and utilities, or put shareholders at significant and avoidable financial risk. When maintenance decisions are made correctly, physical and financial injury can almost always be prevented.

Increasingly complex equipment and systems are handling materials at higher speeds, levels of precision, and throughputs, and this increases levels of randomness, induces failures, and leads to serious consequences. Many industrial accidents occur during maintenance activities or as a result of equipment failures. The physical assets of most companies contain and process raw materials and products, hazardous and nonhazardous alike. Equipment that does what it is supposed to do handles hazardous materials safely. Equipment failure can release hazardous substances into the atmosphere or water or elsewhere, increasing risks to safety and violating environmental regulatory compliance. If the failures are bad enough, they can put operating permits and licenses in jeopardy. If they are deemed to be the result of negligence, they can embroil an organization in unpleasant legal confrontations and irreparably damage a company's reputation. Doing the right maintenance the right way keeps people, systems, and equipment working properly so these risks are reduced.

Equipment and systems that are working properly are also more fuel efficient, keeping some of our variable operating costs down. Equipment that is working properly is more precise and produces on-spec product, reducing product rework, recycle, and scrap, and also keeping our variable costs down. Equipment and systems that are well maintained through programs that consider failure consequences and directed by people who make good decisions about failure management will experience fewer significant consequences. The reduced risks spill over into reducing the need for and cost of warranties and insurance. The pattern is cumulative: The better assets are maintained, the more benefits will accrue. There is a lot involved in achieving these cumulative benefits, and *Uptime* only scratches the surface.

In the distant past and in recent decades, companies or whole industries have been targeted by specific campaigns to wipe out practices like child labor, excessive forest harvesting in sensitive environmental or wildlife areas, excessive effluent flows, and chemical bleaching in paper-making processes. Changes occurred when society's consciousness of injustice to people or harm to the environment made it bad business to continue such practices and many took hold and became solidly entrenched in corporate cultures and values. Financial markets are now responding to investor demands for greater "corporate social responsibility."

When "irresponsible" practices of companies are observed and made public, those companies tend to change. Investors are willing to pay more, but not much more, for enhanced performance. At the same time, they expect to get higher rates of return from these more sustainable businesses and they are starting to see that result. Maintenance contributes to this movement by keeping the assets performing well and meeting the increasingly demanding requirements we place on them.

An interesting pattern has emerged from this sequence of events. Many companies are now becoming responsible without being pushed into responsibility by government regulations, social outrage, or investor prodding. Often, the results are most evident in maintenance management and the tangible benefits that it can produce.

Those who invest in maintenance are investing in a long-term process with long-term payback. Companies that have chosen this path and stuck to it have seen significant results. They have not wavered from conviction that the payback is worth the investment in people, tools, and strategies and they have not succumbed to short-term pressures to cut staff or cut budgets when things are going well. They understand that maintenance performance is a journey and that continued good performance relies on continuously improving the people, tools, and strategies involved.

Excellence is a choice that entails ongoing effort. Starting the journey can be a daunting initiative but once momentum is gained, it is relatively easy to continue. Much of the direct effort is required from your employees, and from those who provide support to them in your storerooms, purchasing, engineering, information technology, and human resource departments. Your role as a manager or executive is to provide support for their efforts and to nurture them. This support entails more than just words. You must walk the walk and lead by example.

The manager of the future embraces change and guides people through the transformations change brings. Your people may keep things off balance and will make mistakes along the way, but mistakes are part of the learning curve. There is little value in looking over their shoulders and micromanaging. Provide guidelines and standards and then let them do their jobs. Help them to get it right, but don't ride herd on them.

Many skilled workers have reached or are quickly approaching retirement age and skilled workers to replace them are increasingly hard to find. Demographics are not on your side, and you will be faced with some tough choices.

- You can hunt for increasingly rare talent and expect to pay a great deal for it. Skilled trades know that they are in demand and the price is going up.
- You can import talent from overseas if you can find it.
- You can set up and run your own training and apprentice programs. Waiting for governments to do this is bound to fail. Government follows trends; it does not set them.
- You can cut down on the work that needs to be done through outsourcing, although that may be limited by the same demographic problem.
- You can cut down on maintenance work by building less maintenance-intensive designs when you acquire new assets.
- You can cut down on maintenance work through methods like RCM that will produce the most cost-effective maintenance program and respect safety and environmental concerns.
- You can reduce the nonvalue-added work that maintainers do. Get rid of bureaucracy and meetings that are not essential. Plan well and redesign your maintenance processes so that no one is standing around doing nothing.
- You can unleash the latent creativity and enthusiasm of your workforce by allowing it the autonomy it needs to self-organize.
- Above all, keep the workforce you already have motivated and happy. You want them to stay.

You will probably need a combination of these solutions, and some will undoubtedly increase your cost of doing business. But doing nothing will cost more. Whatever you choose, get started soon. Time is against you on this one. Maintenance staffing and capability concerns are already on the agenda of executive meetings in many industries. It is to your advantage to stay ahead of the game.

The industrial age has ended in the Western world. Even the information age is drawing to an end and giving way to wisdom. Old management habits are no longer sufficient to meet today's business demands and new habits take their place. Awareness of new processes, new ways of doing things, and new solutions are the stepping-stones to success. One of the first steps is unleashing the latent talent in your workforce, and that means choosing to educate your people. If this book helps you to make that choice and start that process, it has succeeded in starting something truly extraordinary.

Whole books (in some cases, many books) have been written on each of the topics covered in these pages. One of the objectives of *Uptime* is to raise your awareness of the scope and depth of what is out there. Hopefully, this has occurred.

Appendix A

The Maintenance Management Diagnostic Review

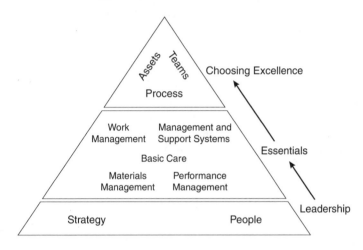

A diagnostic review is used to observe what is being done in each of the key areas of maintenance management depicted in the Pyramid of Excellence. By gathering objective data, carrying out a thorough visual tour and "inspection," and asking questions of various individuals who work in these areas and their "customers," we get a very clear picture of what is happening and how it is being viewed internally.

It is possible to judge how well things are being done, but a great deal of caution is required in doing so. There is no single "right way." What may appear to be less than ideal practice may actually work extremely well in a particular situation; conversely, what seems to be ideal is not viable in another. It is always the results that matter; as long as they are legal, methods do not.

It is best to avoid making judgments about what is good or bad practice. After collecting the review information and evidence of results, compare what you have been doing with what other high performers are doing. Remember to focus on results rather than on practices observed.

An example that illustrates the reason for this distinction between observing practices and results concerns a newsprint paper mill using a homegrown CMMS to manage work. The company had high compliance with its work schedules, a low incidence of rework, a high ratio of planned to unplanned work, smooth shutdowns, and relatively few emergencies. Despite the homegrown CMMS, which is often considered a "worst practice," things were going very well and the company was achieving desired results. The homegrown system had been perfectly designed to match their business processes, it was fully utilized to support those processes, and the company was making very good use of it and getting excellent performance from its maintenance group. Of course, the homegrown system did not work as well in all respects. For instance, it was not particularly suitable for financial reporting because it did not track maintenance cost details. Overall costs were tracked separately in an accounting system. At budget time, to support their forecasts for the following year, the maintainers manually correlated their work reports with financial reports. A fully integrated CMMS, EAM, or ERP system may have been more useful than their homegrown stand-alone systems for that purpose. The question here is which result was more important to the business: managing the maintenance process or managing maintenance financial reporting? The implications of this kind of trade-off are important. If a commercial, fully integrated system is not used by the maintenance tradespersons because it is "user-hostile," then it is better to use a homegrown system. If the cost of management's budgeting processes outweighs the benefits of excellent work management, using a homegrown system is ill advised.

A diagnostic review can point out the cost-benefit ratio between practices and even suggest other options. Choices can then be made with a full awareness of the trade-offs, and these choices are the product of "conscious management."

Whenever a company makes choices consciously, it has a much greater chance of achieving its goals. Leaving these choices to others is a way of abdicating the responsibility of managing your business. Moreover, relinquishing your control means giving that control to others even though the ultimate results will be your responsibility. Later, if something is not working, blaming those others for your choices is not going to solve your problems.

Conscious management is characterized by being aware of your options and making choices based on that awareness. Although you do not need an outsider for this, you do need to maintain objectivity, and this is sometimes difficult for anyone who has a stake in the outcome.

Often, the best solution to this objectivity issue is a diagnostic review performed by an independent third party. The following outline shows key areas examined during a maintenance diagnostic review. A partial list of specific items reviewed in each rubric is provided below.

1. Overall business context
2. Leadership
   - Maintenance strategy and its fit with the business context
   - Organization and people management
3. Essential practices
   - Work management
   - Materials management
   - Basic care
   - Performance management
   - Management and support systems
4. Methods
   - Asset-centric methods
   - Team-based methods
   - Process optimization
5. Results

KEY AREAS FOR ASSESSMENT

Overall Business Context

Business plan and competitive dimensions; nature of the business cycle
Products and customer profile
Role of the plant/facility or fleet in meeting the overall business plan
Special regulatory, environmental, safety, or material-handling considerations
Plant layout, facilities, fleet sizes and makeup, age
Process flow and technology; equipment criticality
Capital expenditure history; plant upgrades

Leadership

Maintenance Strategy and Its Fit with the Business Context
Documented, communicated, and understood vision, mission or
   mandate, principles, objectives, and improvement plans
Degree of fit with business characteristics
Organization level of maintenance management
Overall maintenance budget over past several years
Use of contractors, outsourcing, cosourcing, partnering
The annual budgeting process and involvement

Organization and People Management
Organization structure and labor levels
Existence of maintenance planning, maintenance engineering
Number of personnel, by trade and function
Key accountabilities of each key position; overlaps and gaps
Communication styles and effectiveness
Training processes: technical, general, supervisory, problem solv-
   ing, teamwork
Compensation system, incentives, recognition, rewards
Performance evaluation, employee development, career progres-
   sion; selection of new employees
Succession planning

Essential Maintenance Practices

Work Management
Responsibilities for fault identification, general work identification
Priority setting, collaboration; scoping the work
Planning activities, sequencing, coordinating skills, estimating
Scoping for parts, components, materials; cost allocation
Availability of special tools, mobile equipment, rigging
Reference drawings, safety reminders
External contractor arrangements, special orders
Use of standard procedures for repetitive work
Backlog of special work, preventive maintenance, shutdowns
Coordination with production, stores; daily, weekly meetings
Net capacity review for special skills
Scheduling horizons for production planning, labor balancing
Use of decision support tools, large job scheduling techniques

Use of work-order types: PM, lubrication, corrective, urgent, standing
Authorization levels and procedures, costing technique
Use of work-order records: costs, productivity, failure analysis, job
plans, backlogs, scheduling
Feedback provided on actual vs. planned
Quality control and management on maintenance activities and
schedules

Materials Management
Clear purchasing policies, procedures, accountabilities
Vendor qualification; performance monitoring on cost, accuracy,
quality, service, stability
Vendor partnering, systems contracts, cooperative negotiations
Approval process, levels for purchase requisitioning
Coordination with maintenance on specifications, quality, service
Level of urgent, emergency requisitions from maintenance
Purchasing performance monitoring recost, customer satisfaction
Expediting procedure
Administrative processes for procurement, accounts payable
Warranty management procedures, discrepancies
Use of purchasing for obsolescence, engineering changes, new item
testing
Stores layout, locations, access, space, racking, security
Availability and use of mobile equipment and stores management
tools
Degree of automation, bar coding
Use of substores, shopfloor stores, free-access items
Receiving, issuing, stocking schedules, labor, procedures
Direct charge item storage
Parts and materials quality assurance, accuracy
Management of telephone orders, delivery, kitting/pick lists
Consignment stock locations, vendor access
Requisitioning procedures
Catalogs, referencing, online information
Inventory reconciliation and absolute value of deviation
Use of statistical analysis by inventory category, stock history
Measures of investment efficiency, turnover, value, number of SKUs
Obsolescence review, no usage analysis
Stock control techniques, max-min, EOQ, EOP
Control of repairable items/rotables

Service level/stockout measures, back orders
Stock counting policies, schedules

Basic Care
Compliance tracking for applicable regulations (safety, environment, etc.)
General housekeeping and equipment condition
Coverage of equipment, areas for planned maintenance
Level of detail on preventive, predictive maintenance routines
Work generated as a result of inspections
Use of condition-based and nondestructive techniques
Drawings for layout, equipment configuration, updating, control

Performance Management
Cost reporting, availability of information, cost control
Key performance indicators that are in use and how they are estimated or measured
Data collection, data entry, integration
Records management for personnel, equipment, costing
Use of dashboard or score cards
Visibility of performance reporting
Acceptance of performance management within workforce

Management and Support Systems
Completeness of equipment records
Identification of critical equipment, configuration management, asset lists
Availability of nameplate and procurement information with bill of materials
Assets clearly marked, nameplated
Records management for manuals, drawings
Is there a CMMS either in place or planned?
Degree of CMMS use and coverage
Capability of modules, functions (do the capabilities match business processes?)
Integration with other systems
Degree of user friendliness (is it used by shopfloor personnel?)
Use of analytical and decision support software tools
Use of automation in stores, shops, etc.
Are work-around solutions in place?

Methods

Asset-centric Methods

Has RCM been used or is it being used?
Are past RCM program results reviewed for relevance over time?
Are reliability results used to upgrade or change RCM decisions?
Is the PM program clearly linked to RCM outputs?
Use of RCFA
Availability of histories of faults, failures, causes, repairs, actions, costs, times
Access to records, use of records for prediction, problem solving, capital replacement, life-cycle management
Use of equipment histories and mathematical models for fault/failure analysis
Decision support methods and tools in use

Team-based Methods

Degree of autonomy, self-direction, teamwork
Are RCM and other task force teams truly empowered?
Is a TPM program in place?
Are TPM principles being followed?
Suggestion plans, continuous improvement teams
Documentation of downtime, causes, corrective action, inspection schedules

Processes Optimization

Processes documented and followed?
Operating policies, plans, and schedules
Are there clear links between maintenance, materials management, supply chain, administrative processes?
Do processes share common goals, objectives, customer orientation, process orientation?
Are work-around processes in place and why?
Review cycle for business process optimization

Results

Safety record, loss prevention, analysis and correction, discipline, participation
Overview of plant, facility, fleet condition, and housekeeping

Overall working conditions, degree of satisfaction, labor relations
Morale, absenteeism, turnover, grievance level
Level of unplanned, urgent, emergency, standing work orders
Level of planned, preventive, predictive scheduled maintenance
Degree of compliance with planned work schedules
Accuracy of costs, estimates, and budget control
Equipment performance for frequency and duration of failure,
  speed, precision, availability, utilization, reliability
Process performance, such as work orders by status, PM compliance, time on planned work, backlog, new tactics applied
Employee performance, specialty training, application of skills,
  teamwork, progression
Response time to urgent calls, flexibility, coverage
Housekeeping after repairs
Level of confidence in maintenance by production

Appendix B
Glossary of Maintenance Terminology

Term or Acronym	Definition
Acceptable condition	That condition agreed for a particular use, not less than that demanded by statutory requirements; meeting a functional standard for equipment operation.
Activity board	An information-sharing display prepared by a team or group to facilitate communication between operators and maintainers in a TPM environment.
Acute loss	Infrequent or one-time performance shortfall, the gap between actual and optimal performance; usually associated with a major defect.
Adjustments	Minor tune-up actions requiring only hand tools, no parts, and usually lasting less than a half hour.
Apprentice	A tradesperson in training.
Area maintenance	A type of maintenance organization in which the first-line maintenance foreperson is responsible for all maintenance trades within a certain area.
Asset(s)	The physical resources of a business, such as plant, facilities, fleets, or their parts and components.
Asset list	A register of items usually with information on manufacturer, vendor, specifications, classification, costs, warranty, and tax status.
Asset management	The systematic planning and control of a physical resource throughout its economic life.

Term or Acronym	Definition
Asset number	A unique alphanumerical identification of an asset on a list, often in a database, which is used in its management.
Autonomous maintenance	Routine maintenance, PM and predictive maintenance (PdM) carried out by operators, with or without help from maintenance tradespersons who are often a part of the same team as the operators.
Available	The state of being ready for use, includes operating time and downtime for reasons other than maintenance.
Availability	The period of scheduled time for which an asset is capable of performing its specified function, expressed as a percentage.
Backlog	Work that is waiting to be done; it is estimated and awaiting planning, prioritization, scheduling, and execution.
Bar code	Symbols for encoding data using lines of varying thickness, designating alphanumeric characters.
Benchmark	A measurable standard for high performance based on a survey or study of comparable businesses or business processes having similar key performance drivers.
Benchmarking study	A formal study aimed at determining benchmarks and practices used to attain those high levels of performance.
Best practice	see Successful practice
Bill of materials (BOM)	List of components, from complete assemblies to individual components and parts for an asset, usually structured in hierarchical layers from gross assemblies to minor items.
Breakdown	Failure of an asset to perform to a functional standard.

Term or Acronym	Definition
Breakdown maintenance	A policy where no maintenance is done unless and until an item no longer meets its functional standard, often when the asset is no longer able to operate at all.
Call back	A job that is redone because the original repair did not correct the failure.
Call out	The practice of calling maintenance workers in to work at times outside of their normal workday.
Capital spares	Spares, usually large, expensive, difficult to obtain, or having long lead-times, that are acquired as part of the capital purchase of the asset for which they are intended to be used or later, after the risk of not having them is realized; accounting often treats these spares as capital items with their value depreciated over time.
Catalogue	Description of a part or other stock or non-stock item that is used in the maintenance of equipment.
CBM	see Condition-based maintenance and Condition-based monitoring
Change-out	Remove a component or part and replace it with a new or rebuilt one.
Charge-back	Maintenance costs charged to the user department that requested the work.
Chronic loss	Frequently occurring performance short-falls, the gap between actual and optimal performance.
Cleaning	Removing all sources of dirt, debris, and con-tamination for the purpose of inspection and to avoid chronic losses.
CMMS	Computerized maintenance management system.
Code	Symbolic designation, used for identification.

Term or Acronym	Definition
Component	A constituent part of an asset, usually modular and replaceable, that is sometimes serialized depending on the criticality of its application and interchangeability.
Component number	Designation, usually structured by system, group, or serial number.
Computer, mainframe	A digital processor with the highest capacity, speed, and capability, normally used at the corporate level of a company.
Computer, micro	A digital processor having moderate capability relative to a mini- or mainframe computer, usually desktop, operated by individual user.
Computer, mini	A digital processor having significant capacity but less than a mainframe, often used at the corporate or site level.
Computer, workstation	Equipment, usually a keyboard and display, used to access a mainframe or mini-computer; sometimes used to describe an office work area for one person; sometimes used to describe a desktop microcomputer for individual use.
Conditional probability of failure	The probability that a failure will occur in a specified period given the condition that the item has survived to the beginning of that period.
Condition-based maintenance	Repair or restoration of an asset based on its condition at the time; also known as on-condition maintenance.
Condition-based monitoring	The monitoring of equipment performance or other condition parameters to determine the condition or "health" of the equipment or system. Condition-based monitoring is used as a part of a predictive maintenance program to determine the need for condition-based maintenance.

Term or Acronym	Definition
Contract maintenance	Maintenance work performed by contractors.
Contractor	An individual or company providing specific services to another under contract for those services, tasks, or specific results.
Coordination	Daily adjustment of maintenance activities to achieve the best short-term use of resources or to accommodate changes in needs for service.
Corrective maintenance	Maintenance done to bring an asset back to its standard functional performance.
Costs, life-cycle	The total cost of an item throughout its life, including design, manufacture, operation, maintenance, and disposal.
Critical spares	Spare parts that have high value, long lead-times or are of particularly high value to the important and unspared equipment on which they are used. They are carried to avoid excessive downtime in the event of a breakdown.
Criticality	A measure of the importance of an asset relative to other assets.
Defect	A condition that causes deviation from design or expected performance, leading to failure; a fault.
Deferred maintenance	Maintenance that can be or has been postponed from a schedule.
Detective maintenance	Testing an asset to make sure it is still functional; used primarily to check dormant devices that can fail in such a way as to be undetectable until it is needed to function.
Deterioration rate	The rate at which an item approaches a departure from its functional standard.
DM	see Detective maintenance
Down	Out of service, usually due to breakdown, unsatisfactory condition, or production scheduling.

Term or Acronym	Definition
Downtime	The period of time during which an item is not in a condition to perform its intended function whether scheduled or not. The distinction between "scheduled" and "unscheduled" downtime is stated where it is relevant to the discussion.
EAM	Enterprise asset management system.
Emergency	A condition requiring immediate corrective action for safety, environmental, or economic risk, caused by equipment breakdown.
Engineering work order (EWO)	A control document from engineering authorizing changes or modifications to a previous design or configuration.
Equipment configuration	List of assets usually arranged to simulate the process, functional, or sequential flow.
Equipment repair history	A chronological list of defaults, repairs, and costs on key assets so that chronic problems can be identified and corrected, and economic decisions made.
Equipment use	A measure of the accumulated hours, cycles, distance, throughput, etc., that an asset has performed its function.
ERP	Enterprise resource management system.
Evident failure	A failure mode that, on its own, becomes apparent to the users of the asset under normal operating circumstances.
Examination	A comprehensive inspection with measurement and physical testing to determine the condition of an item.
Expert system	Decision support software with some ability to make or evaluate decisions based on rules or experience parameters incorporated in the database.

Term or Acronym	Definition
Failure	Termination of the ability of an item to perform its required function to a desired standard.
Failure analysis	A study of failures; to analyze the root causes, develop improvements, eliminate or reduce the occurrence of failures.
Failure coding	Indexing the causes of equipment failure on which corrective action can be based, for example, lack of lubrication, operator abuse, material fatigue, etc.
Failure effect	A statement of what chain of events follows occurrence of a failure.
Failure-finding task	A scheduled task used to detect whether or not an asset is in a failed state, generally used on assets that are normally dormant (e.g., safety devices, backups).
Failure mode	The event that leads to failure.
Fault	see Defect
Fault tree analysis	A review of failures, faults, defects, and shortcomings based on a hierarchy or relationship and beginning with statement of an undesirable event, such as "failed;" used to find the root cause or multiple causes of the event; used primarily where reliability is of utmost importance (e.g., airlines, nuclear power, pharmaceuticals).
Five S	Derived from the Japanese words *seiri* (organization), *seiton* (tidiness), *seiso* (purity), *seiketsu* (cleanliness), *shitsuke* (discipline); focused on the workplace and successful habits that contribute to equipment condition.
FMECA	Failure mode, effect, and criticality analysis; a logical, progressive method used to understand the root causes of failures and their subsequent effect on production, safety, cost, quality, etc. Used as part of RCM.

Term or Acronym	Definition
Forced outage	Downtime caused by a failure.
Forecasting	The projection of the most probable: as in forecasting failures and maintenance activities.
Functional maintenance structure	A type of maintenance organization where the first-line maintenance foreperson is responsible for conducting a specific kind of maintenance, for example, pump maintenance, HVAC maintenance, etc.
Hard time maintenance	Periodic preventive maintenance based rigidly on calendar time.
Infant mortality	Failures that occur prematurely; often these occur because of design, material, workmanship, installation, or quality problems in any work that was done prior to starting the asset up for service.
Inspection	A review to determine maintenance needs, condition and priority of equipment.
Inventory	Stock items that are actually on-hand in a storeroom or elsewhere ready for use.
Inventory control	Managing the acquisition, receipt, storing, and issuance of materials and spare parts; managing the investment efficiency of the stores inventory.
Inventory turnover	Ratio of the value of materials and parts issues annually to the value of materials and parts on-hand.
Issues	Stock consumed through stores.
Labor availability	Percentage of time that the maintenance crew is free to perform productive work during a scheduled working period.
Labor utilization	Percentage of time that the maintenance crew is engaged in productive work during a scheduled working period.

Term or Acronym	Definition
Lean manufacturing	A manufacturing system that focuses on minimizing the resources required to produce the product or service.
Level of service (stores)	Usually measured as the ratio of stock-outs to total stores issues.
Life cycle	The sequence of stages in the existence of an asset: conceptualization, plan, evaluate, design, build/procure, operate and maintain, modify, dispose.
Life-cycle cost (LCC)	The total of all costs of the asset throughout its entire life cycle, including all work done on or to the asset, depreciation, and other costs of ownership; normally LCC takes account of the time value of money.
Logistics engineering	A systems engineering concept developed for military weapons systems; it advocates maintenance considerations in all phases of an equipment program to achieve specified reliability, maintainability, and availability requirements.
Maintainability	The rapidity and ease with which maintenance operations can be performed to help prevent malfunctions or correct them if they occur, usually measured as mean time to repair (MTTR).
Maintenance	Any activity carried out to retain an item in, or restore it to, an acceptable condition for use or to meet its functional standard.
Maintenance audit/review	A formal review of maintenance management practices and results carried out by an independent third party for the purposes of evaluating performance, identifying areas of strength, weaknesses, and opportunities for improvement.

Term or Acronym	Definition
Maintenance engineering	A staff function intended to ensure that maintenance techniques are effective, equipment is designed for optimum maintainability, persistent and chronic problems are analyzed, and corrective actions or modifications are made.
Maintenance history	A record of maintenance activities and results.
Maintenance policy	A principle guiding decisions for maintenance of an asset (e.g., this asset will be run-to-failure and then repaired vs. this asset will be monitored for vibrations to avoid having it fail unexpectedly).
Maintenance prevention	Design of assets to avoid the need for maintenance.
Maintenance route	An established route through a facility along which a maintainer carries out proactive maintenance, detective maintenance, and minor repairs on a routine basis.
Maintenance schedule	A comprehensive list of planned maintenance and its sequence of occurrence based on priority in a designated period of time.
Maintenance shutdown	A period of time during which a plant, department, process, or asset is removed from service specifically for maintenance.
Maintenance strategy	A high-level statement of vision, mission, and objectives with a description of a general plan for achieving them; also used to describe the specific approach to be used for maintaining a specific asset.
Maintenance window	The time frame in which maintenance work can be performed without incurring any unplanned production losses.
Major defect	A single defect that can cause equipment breakdown and operational losses.

Term or Acronym	Definition
Material safety data sheet (MSDS)	Information sheets that come with chemical products giving the formal name of the chemical/compound, a description of its toxicity, handling instructions, warnings about its use, and first-aid treatment for exposure.
Menu	A selection of functional options in a software display.
Meter reading	A numerical reading of the accumulated usage of an asset using an hour meter, odometer, or other device.
Minor defect	A single defect that cannot cause losses on its own but may contribute to losses in combination with other minor defects.
MRO	Maintenance, repair, and overhaul; used in describing the material resource requirements to support maintenance activities.
MTBF (mean time between failures)	see Reliability
MTTR (mean time to repair)	see Maintainability
Natural deterioration	The inherent deterioration that occurs in an asset as a natural result of its usage or age.
NDT	Nondestructive testing of equipment to detect abnormalities in physical, chemical, or electrical characteristics, using such technologies as ultrasonics (thickness), liquid dye penetrants (cracks), x-ray (weld discontinuities), and meggers (voltage generators to measure resistance). Some forms of NDT carry a risk of damaging an item or increasing the probability of failure for the item being tested (e.g., meggers and dye penetrants that require equipment disassembly) and some are completely nonintrusive (e.g., x-rays).

Term or Acronym	Definition
Nonroutine maintenance	Maintenance (usually repairs) performed at irregular intervals, with each job unique, and based on inspection, failure, or condition.
OEE	see Overall equipment effectiveness
Online	The state of being available and accessible while the CMMS is operating.
Opportunity maintenance	Maintenance work that is performed in an unanticipated maintenance window or to take advantage of a planned maintenance window to get more work accomplished than scheduled.
Outage	A term used in some industries, for example, electrical power distribution, to denote when an item or system is not in use.
Outsourcing	Contracting of all or a major part of the maintenance work required by an organization.
Overall equipment effectiveness	OEE is a measure combining availability, production rate (i.e., utilization of the available time), and quality rate of an asset.
Overhaul	A comprehensive examination and restoration of an asset to an acceptable condition.
Pareto	Analysis to determine the minority of equipment that is causing the majority of the problems.
PCR	Planned component replacement. See scheduled discharge.
PdM	see Predictive maintenance
Pending work	Work that has been issued for execution but is not yet completed; maintenance work in process.
Performance indicators	Measures that indicate the degree to which a specific function is being performed.

Term or Acronym	Definition
Performance management	The act of using performance measurement as a means of identifying shortfalls and correcting them with an aim to improve overall performance results.
Performance measurement	The act of measuring performance using performance indicators.
Periodic maintenance	Cyclic maintenance actions carried out at regular intervals, based on repair history data, use, or elapsed time.
Pick list	A selection of required stores items for a work order or task normally used by stores to prepackage the needed materials for use.
Plan	The comprehensive description of maintenance work to be done, including task list, parts and materials required, tools required, safety precautions to be observed, permits and other documentation requirements, and estimate of the duration of the work, effort, and costs.
Planned component replacement (PCR)	see Scheduled discard
Planned maintenance	Maintenance carried out according to a documented plan of tasks, skills, and resources.
Planner	An individual who plans work (see plan); often planners also schedule work.
PM	see Preventive maintenance
PM frequency	The frequency for performing PM work, also used for inspections, PdM and DM frequencies.
PMO	see Preventive maintenance optimization
Potential failure	A detectable operating or equipment condition that can be used to indicate that a failure is about to occur or in the process of occurring.

Term or Acronym	Definition
Predictive maintenance (PdM)	Use of measured physical parameters against known acceptable limits for detecting, analyzing, and identifying equipment problems before a failure occurs; examples include vibration analysis, sonic testing, dye testing, infrared testing, thermal testing, coolant analysis, tribology, and equipment history analysis; used to identify the need for CBM.
Preventive maintenance (PM)	Maintenance carried out at predetermined intervals, or to other prescribed criteria, and intended to reduce the likelihood of a functional failure.
Preventive maintenance optimization (PMO)	A process of analyzing an existing PM program with the intent of optimizing its performance, sometimes used as an alternative to RCM.
Priority	The relative importance of a single job in relationship to other jobs, operational needs, safety, etc., and the time within which the job should be done; used for scheduling work orders.
Proactive	A style of initiative that is anticipatory and planned for; includes PM and PdM.
Process safety management (PSM)	Regulatory requirements designed to increase safety and environmental performance in manufacturing processes.
RCFA	see Root cause failure analysis
RCM	see Reliability-centered maintenance
Reactive maintenance	Maintenance repair work done as an immediate response to failure events normally without planning, always unscheduled.
Rebuild	Restore an item to an acceptable condition in accordance with the original design specifications.

Term or Acronym	Definition
Refurbishment	Extensive work intended to restore a plant or facility to acceptable operating condition.
Reliability	The ability of an item to perform a required function under stated conditions for a stated period of time; usually expressed as the mean time between failures.
Reliability analysis	The process of identifying maintenance of significant items and classifying them with respect to malfunction on safety, environmental, operational, and economic consequences. Possible failure mode of an item is identified and an appropriate maintenance policy is assigned to counter it. Subsets are failure mode, effect, and criticality analysis (FMECA); fault tree analysis (FTA); risk analysis; and hazardous operations (HAZOP) analysis.
Reliability-centered maintenance (RCM)	A method used to determine the appropriate failure management policies for any asset in its present operating context.
Repair	To restore an item to an acceptable condition by the renewal, replacement, or mending of worn or damaged parts.
Restoration	Actions taken to restore an asset to its desired functional state.
Return on investment (ROI)	Financial performance of an investment.
Return on net assets (RONA)	Profits generated expressed as a percentage of the net value of physical assets that produced that profit.
Rework	Work that has to be done over.
Root cause failure analysis (RCFA)	Analysis used to determine the underlying cause or causes of a failure so that steps can be taken to manage those causes and avoid future occurrences of the failure; sometimes called root cause analysis (RCA).

Term or Acronym	Definition
Rotable	Components that are rebuilt after their useful life and rotated through maintenance stores back to use; a repairable item.
Routine maintenance	see Scheduled maintenance
Running maintenance	Maintenance that can be done while the asset is in service.
Run-to-failure	A failure management policy that allows the asset to be run to the failed state without any effort to predict or prevent it before it occurs.
Schedule	A time-phased list of work to be done.
Schedule compliance	The number of scheduled jobs actually accomplished during the period covered by an approved schedule; also the number of scheduled labor hours actually worked against a planned number of scheduled labor hours, expressed as a percentage.
Scheduled discard	Replacement of an item at a fixed, predetermined interval, regardless of its current condition; a type of PM, a planned component replacement (PCR).
Scheduled maintenance	Any maintenance that is prioritized to be done at a predetermined time; scheduled work may be planned or unplanned.
Scheduled outage	Downtime that was intended for maintenance, servicing, operational, or other purposes.
Scheduled restoration	Repair or restoration of an asset at a predetermined interval, regardless of its current condition; a type of PM.
Scheduler	An individual who schedules work; see Planner.
Scheduling cycle	The length of time for which scheduling is normally done for work backlog, often weekly or biweekly.

Term or Acronym	Definition
Scoping	Outlining the extent and detail of work to be done and the resources needed.
Seasonal maintenance	Maintenance work carried out at a specific time of year, e.g., repair of potholed roads in northern climates, repairs to school buildings during vacation periods.
Service level	An expression of the percentage of spares that are issued on demand; also a specification of the desired service standards to be met by a contractor.
Servicing	The replenishment of consumables needed to keep an item in operating condition (e.g., lube oil, ink, wearing surfaces, cleaning of working surfaces).
Set-up and adjustment	A process of changing from one manufacturing configuration to another to accommodate a change in product being produced on the same asset.
Shelf life	That period of time during which materials in storage remain in an acceptable condition.
Shutdown	That period of time when equipment is out of service; also refers to major maintenance work where primary producing assets are down while the maintenance is being performed.
Shutdown maintenance	Maintenance done while the asset is out of service, as in the annual plant shutdown.
Six losses	In TPM these are the major losses that occur due to inadequate equipment operation or condition; i.e., breakdown, setup, and adjustment; minor stoppages; speed reductions; quality defects and rework; yield reductions.
Specifications	Physical, chemical, or performance characteristics of equipment, parts, or work required to meet minimum acceptable standards.

Term or Acronym	Definition
Sporadic loss	see Acute loss
Standard job	A preplanned maintenance job with all details required for work execution delineated and stored (usually in the CMMS, EAM, or ERP) for repeated use.
Standby	Assets that are used as backups to others, that are installed or available but not in use.
Standing work order (SWO)	A work order that remains open, usually for the annual budget cycle, to accommodate information on small jobs or for specific tasks.
Stock	A term used to describe parts that are normally kept onhand in storeroom
Strategy	The overall approach for managing the life cycle of a specific physical asset (e.g., its maintenance strategy); an overall direction and flexible high-level plan for business.
Successful practice	A practice that leads to superior performance or results in a specific process; sometimes called "best practice," but this implies that it is the only way to execute the practice.
Superintendent	A second-line manager who is responsible for a maintenance group or department.
Supervisor	A first-line manager who is responsible for a group of tradespersons.
Survey	A formal inspection of a plant, facility, civil infrastructure, or vehicle to look for condition and defects.
Tactics	The choices made to implement a strategy and manage the people, processes, and physical asset infrastructure that make up your business.
Task	A single item on a task list that informs an inspector or maintainer what to do, an instruction.

Term or Acronym	Definition
Task list	Directions to an inspector or maintainer telling him or her what to do and in what sequence, e.g., check oil level, clean, adjust, lubricate, replace, etc.
Terotechnology	An integration of management, financial, engineering, operating maintenance, and other practices applied to physical assets in pursuit of an economical life cycle.
Total productive maintenance (TPM)	Company-wide equipment management program emphasizing operator involvement in equipment maintenance and continuous improvement in equipment effectiveness.
Trade	A specific skill or set of related skills in a particular area (e.g., millwright, electrician, machinist, boilermaker, carpenter, rigger, etc.).
Tradesperson	Skilled worker who normally has completed an apprenticeship program; in some jurisdictions certain tradespersons must be tested and licensed in their respective trades
Unplanned maintenance	Maintenance done without planning; could be related to a breakdown, running repair, or corrective work; unplanned maintenance may be scheduled during the normal schedule cycle.
Up	Used in reference to an asset that is available and being used.
Uptime	The period of time during which an item is in a condition to perform its intended function, whether it is in use or not.
Utilization factor	Usage of an asset expressed as a percentage of schedule time.
Variance analysis	Interpretation of the causes for a difference between actual and some norm, budget, or estimate.

Term or Acronym	Definition
Visual control	The use of easy-to-read indicators to show equipment status and performance (e.g., red, yellow, or green gauge markings; normal reading zone indicators; color-coded oil cans and filler caps).
Warranty	Coverage for repair costs incurred in the event of a defect caused by a supplier of equipment, materials, or services.
Work-in-process (WIP)	Partially completed production "product" at some interim stage in the production process; product that is still being worked on prior to being considered ready to deliver.
Work order (WO)	A unique control document that comprehensively describes the job to be done; may include formal requisition for maintenance, authorization, and charge codes, as well as a record of what work was actually done, time, and materials used.
Work request (WR)	A simple request for maintenance service or work requiring no planning or scheduling but usually a statement of the problem; usually precedes the issuance of a work order.
Workload	The number of labor hours needed to carry out a maintenance program, including all scheduled and unscheduled work and maintenance support of project work.

Bibliography

Bossidy, Larry, and Ram Charan. *Execution: The Discipline of Getting Things Done*. New York: Crown Business, 2002.

Campbell, John D., and Andrew K. S. Jardine. *Maintenance Excellence: Optimizing Equipment Life-Cycle Decisions*. New York: Marcel Dekker, 2001.

Campbell, John Dixon. *Uptime: Strategies for Excellence in Maintenance Management*. Portland, OR: Productivity Press, 1995.

Cher Min Tan and Shin Yeh Lim, *Application of Wiger-Ville Distribution in Electromigration Noise Analysis*, IEEE Transactions on Device and Materials Reliability, Vol. 2, No. 2, June 2002.

Coetzee, Jasper L. *Maintenance*. Hatfield, South Africa: Maintenance Publishers (Pty) Ltd., 1997.

Collins, James C., and Jerry I. Porrass. *Built to Last: Successful Habits of Visionary Companies*. New York: HarperCollins, 1997.

Cotts, David G., and Michael Lee. *The Facility Management Handbook*, AMACOM, a division of American Management Association, New York, 1992.

Covey, Stephen R. *The 7 Habits of Highly Effective People*. New York: Simon & Schuster, 1989.

Covey, Stephen R. *The 8th Habit, From Effectiveness to Greatness*. New York: Simon & Schuster, 2004.

Foot, David K., with Daniel Stoffman. *Boom, Bust, & Echo*. Toronto, Ontario, Canada: Stoddart Publishing, 1998.

Gladwell, Malcolm. *The Tipping Point*. London: Abacus, 2000.

Gleick, James. *Chaos: Making a New Science*. New York: Penguin Books, 1987.

Goldratt, Eliyahu M. *The Goal*. 2nd revised edition. Great Barrington, MA: North River Press, 1992.

Hammer, Michael. "Reengineering Work: Don't Automate, Obliterate," *Harvard Business Review*, 1990.

Hammer, Michael. *The Agenda: What Every Business Must Do to Dominate the Decade*. New York: Crown Business, 2001.

Hammer, Michael, and James Champy. *Reengineering the Corporation*. New York: HarperCollins, 1993.

Handy, Charles B., *The Age of Unreason*. Boston: Harvard Business School Press, 1991.

Higgins, Lindley R. *Maintenance Engineering Handbook*. 5th ed. New York: McGraw Hill, 1995.

Humphries, James B. "Best-in-Class Maintenance Benchmarks," *Iron and Steel Engineer*, October 1998.

Jardine, A.K.S. and Albert H.C. Tsang *Maintenance, Replacement, and Reliability Theory and Applications*. Boca Raton, FL: CRC Press, Taylor and Frances Group, 2006

Jones, James V. *Integrated Logistics Support Handbook*. New York: McGraw Hill, 1987.

Kaplan, Robert S., and David P. Norton. *The Strategy-Focused Organization*. Boston: Harvard Business School Press, 2001.

Kaplan, Robert S., and David P. Norton. "The Balanced Score Card: Measures That Drive Performance," *Harvard Business Review*, 1992.

Kelly, Anthony. *Maintenance and Its Management*. Monks Hill, UK: Conference Communication, 1989.

Kelly, Anthony. *Maintenance Strategy: Business-Centred Maintenance*. Oxford, UK: Butterworth-Heinemann, 1997.

Kepner, Charles, and Benjamin Tregoe. *The Rational Manager: A Systematic Approach to Problem Solving and Decision Making*. New York: McGraw Hill, 1965.

Kotter, John P. *Leading Change*. Boston: Harvard Business School Press, 1996.

Latino, Robert J., and Kenneth C. Latino. *Root Cause Analysis: Improving Performance for Bottom Line Results*. Boca Raton, FL: CRC Press, 2002.

Levitt, Joel. *Managing Factory Maintenance*. New York: Industrial Press, 1996.

Levitt, Joel. *The Handbook of Maintenance Management*. New York: Industrial Press, 1997.

McNeilly, Mark. *Sun Tsu and the Art of Business*. Oxford, UK: Oxford University Press, 1996.

Moore, Geoffrey A. *Crossing the Chasm*. New York: Harper Business, 1999.

Moore, Ron. *Making Common Sense Common Practice: Models for Manufacturing Excellence*. Woburn, MA: Butterworth-Heinemann, 2002.

Moss, Marvin A. *Designing for Minimal Maintenance Expense*. New York: Marcel Dekker, 1985.

Moubray, John. *RCM II Reliability-Centred Maintenance*. Oxford, UK: Butterworth-Heinemann, 1991.

Nachi-Fujikoshi Corporation, eds. *Training for TPM: A Manufacturing Success Story.* Cambridge, MA: Productivity Press, 1990.

Nakajima, Seiichi. *TPM: Introduction to TPM, Total Productive Maintenance.* Cambridge, MA: Productivity Press, 1988.

Nakajima, Seiichi. *TPM Development Program, Implementing Total Productive Maintenance.* Cambridge, MA: Productivity Press, 1989.

Nowlan, F. S., and H. Heap. *Reliability-centered Maintenance.* Springfield, VA: National Technical Information Service, US Department of Commerce, 1978.

Peters, Thomas J., and Robert H. Waterman, Jr. *In Search of Excellence: Lessons from America's Best-Run Companies.* New York: Harper & Row, 1982.

Peters, Tom, and Nancy Austin. *A Passion for Excellence.* New York: Warner Books, 1985.

SAE, JA1011, "Evaluation Criteria for Reliability-Centered Maintenance (RCM) Processes," August 1999, Warrendale, PA.

Shirose, Kunio. *TPM for Workshop Leaders.* Cambridge, MA: Productivity Press, 1992.

Smith, Anthony M. *Reliability-Centered Maintenance.* New York: McGraw Hill, 1993.

Stack, Jack, with Bo Burlingham. *The Great Game of Business.* New York: Doubleday, 1992.

Suzuki, Tokutaro. *New Directions for TPM.* Cambridge, MA: Productivity Press, 1992.

Tajiri, Masaji, and Fumio Gotoh. *TPM Implementation: A Japanese Approach.* New York: McGraw Hill, 1992.

Tomlingson, Paul D. *Effective Maintenance: The Key to Profitability, A Manager's Guide to Effective Industrial Maintenance Management.* New York: John Wiley and Sons, 1998.

Tsang, Albert H. C., Andrew K. S. Jardine, John Dixon Campbell, and James V. Picknell. *Reliability Centred Maintenance: A Key to Maintenance Excellence.* Hong Kong: City University of Hong Kong, 2000.

Turner, Steve. "PM Optimization—Maintenance Analysis of the Future." www.pmoptimisation.com.

Ulrich, Dave, Jack Zenger, and Norm Smallwood. *Results-Based Leadership.* Boston: Harvard Business School Press, 1999.

Wheatley, Margaret J. *Finding Our Way: Leadership for an Uncertain Time.* San Francisco, CA: Berrett-Koehler, 2005.

Wireman, Terry. *Developing Performance Indicators for Managing Maintenance*. New York: Industrial Press, 1998.

Wireman, Terry. *Benchmarking Best Practices in Maintenance Management*. New York: Industrial Press, 2004.

Index

Accidents, 10, 113, 115
Accounting, 135, 214
Aerospace industry, 226
Age-related failure, 122–23, 124
Airline industry, 125, 225–26, 249
Airport facility, 187
Alcan, 83–84
Annual plan, 92–94
Antitrust laws, 170
Apprentice programs, 64
Art of War (Tzu), 4
"As built" drawings, 17
Asset-centric methods, 38
Asset functions, 232–33
Asset life cycle
  costs, 16, 184
  long-range plans, 92
  multi-step management process, 14
  overlapping steps in, 17
  strategy examples, 4
Asset management. *See* Physical asset
  management
Asset optimization tools, 260
Automated fault diagnostic tools, 184–85
Automobile industry, 108, 121
Autonomous crews. *See* Self-organized
  teams
Autonomous maintenance, 270, 271
Availability, 223

Baby boom generation, 18, 42
Backlogs, 59, 98
Backlog time standards, 106–7
Balanced scorecard, 158, 173–76, 177
Banks, 12
Basic equipment care
  beyond the minimum, 115–18
  condition-based maintenance, 127–32
  cost of tactics, 132–33
  minimum, 113–15, 134
  preventive maintenance, 132
  tactical options, 118–27
Batch process, 101
"Bathtub curve," 122, 123, 124
Bell-Mason type spider diagram, 28, 29
Benchmarking
  activity examples, 169–70, 275

basic approach, 168
best practices database, 26
in change management, 51–52
customers' input, 169
determining successful strategies, 25–26
findings, uses for, 30
maintenance, 167–77
study results, 171–72
"Best practice," 25, 26, 30, 39, 108, 274
Bhopal, India, 113
Blank, Warren, 70
Boeing aircraft, 226
Bottlenecked production process, 8–9, 263,
  265, 294
Brainstorming, 26, 257, 259, 298
Break-in work, 82
Brewery, 101–2, 129, 131, 210–14, 300
"Brown paper process," 295, 296
Budget, 92–94, 111
Built-in redundancy, 228
Business case, 24, 25
Business strategy, 5–6
"Buy-in," 5

Canada, 11, 59, 65, 172, 210–14, 262
Capability, 218
Capacity
  constraint, 8–9
  fixed asset, 8
  idle excess, 8
  lost, 87
  net, 86, 87, 98, 109, 110
Capital-intensive industries, 8, 249
Capital planning, 260
Capital projects, 95–96
Carling O'Keefe, 211
Case study, multiskilling, 64–66
Catalogue items, 141
Cause-and-effect analysis, 257, 298
CBM. *See* Condition-based maintenance;
  Condition-based monitoring
Centralized maintenance organizations, 54
CFO (Chief financial officer), 189
"Champion," 33, 211
Change management
  assessments and plans, 46
  benchmarking, 51–52

communication, 51
driven from within, 43–44
factors changing simultaneously, 44–45
fear of change, 47–51
leadership in, 53
reason for change, 46–47
steps in process, 45–46
Chief financial officer (CFO), 189
Churchill, Sir Winston, 251
CI. *See* Continuous improvement
Client-server technology, 216, 217
CMMS. *See* Computerized Maintenance
  Management Systems
Command and control, 268, 303
Commercial airline industry, 225
Communications
  change management, 51
  CMMS and, 209
  modern technology, 110
  remote site, 109–10
Companywide strategic direction, 34
Compensation and rewards
  base pay, 72
  benefits, 73–74
  employee retention, 71–72
  gain sharing, 73
  for multiple skills, 75
  nonmonetary rewards, 74
  overtime, 72
  perquisites, 74
  profit-based incentive pay, 72–73
Competition avoidance laws, 170
Competitive advantage, 36
Complete overhaul, 118, 126
Computerized Maintenance Management
  Systems (CMMS), 186–217
  age of system, 188, 200
  basic functionality, good system, 190,
    192–93
  capability categories, 193
  case study, implementation, 210–14
  delivery methodology steps, 200–207
  future, 214–17
  "going live," 206
  homegrown, 316
  implementation, 198–207
  Internet access, 195–96
  justifying cost of, 207–10
  key modules, 196
  methodology, major steps in, 202–6
  objectives, 199–200
  overview, 193–98

for smaller companies, 190
  tailoring, multiple sites, 207
  two most important features, 190
  See also MARS system; Software
Computer software. *See* Software
Conditional probability of failure, 122–27
  "bathtub curve" pattern, 124
  best new pattern, 125
  constant pattern, 125
  operating age and, 123
  slow aging pattern, 124
  worst new pattern, 125
  worst old pattern, 124
Condition-based maintenance (CBM), 120,
    127–32
  components suited for, 127–28
  criteria for, 237
  favored by RCM, 228
  lubricants, 129–30
  method selection factors, 128
  in RCM process, 241–42
  system performance, 130–32
  temperature, 130
  vibration analysis, 129
Condition-based monitoring (CBM), 120,
    239
Condition monitoring, 126, 131, 181–83
Constrained production process, 263
Continuous improvement (CI), 105, 251–65
  with CMMS, 194
  Decision Optimization, 259–62
  increasing awareness of, 264
  PM optimization, 252–54
  reliability and simulation modeling,
    263–64
  root cause failure analysis, 255–59
  time standards and, 105
Continuous process, 101
Contract maintenance, 37
Contractors, 95, 99
Contract penalties, 90–91
Control, 191
Coopers and Lybrand, 172
"Core" vs. "noncore" activities, 35
"Corporate memory," 42
Corporate responsibility, 56, 311. *See also*
  Social responsibility
Corporate-wide management systems,
    304–5
Corrective maintenance process, 82, 299
Cost-benefit ratio, 316
Cost-effective maintenance tactics, 236, 237

Cost performance, 162–63
Costs
  fixed, 7, 8
  hidden, 135, 136
  life-cyle, 260
  RCM and, 244–45
  variable, 7, 8, 9
Covey, Stephen R., 18
Creativity, 191, 269
Critical path
  job, 97–98
  method, 103–4
Cullen, Lord William Douglas, 113, 115
Culture
  of change, 47
  focusing on execution, 53
Cumulative probability of failure, 123, 124
Customer feedback, 166–67, 169
Customer satisfaction, 157
"Cycle of loss," 48–49

Data
  exchange standard, 216
  management, 155, 185–86, 218, 261–62
  mining, 188
  warehouse, 182, 216–17
Decision optimization, 259–62, 265
Decision support tools, 183–85, 186
Defect elimination, 108
Delivery problems, 90–91
Demographics, 18, 42–43, 313
Deregulation, 15
Design flaws, 17
Design, Measure, Analyze, Improve,
    Control (DMAIC), 255
Design-out maintenance
  equipment upgrade, 121
  redesign, 120–21
  redundancy, 120
Detective maintenance, 82
Diagnostic review, 315–22
  barriers and, 33
  basic care, 320
  benchmarking and, 30
  essential maintenance practices, 318–19
  leadership, 318
  management and support systems, 320
  materials management, 319–20
  methods, 321
  overall business context, 317
  performance management, 320
  results, 321–22

rubric, items in each, 317
Direct maintenance labor and parts costs, 9
"Direct purchase," 142
Disasters, 10, 113, 115
Discrete smoothed pseudo-Wiger Ville
    distribution (DSPWVD) technology,
    131
Dispatch office, 109
DMAIC (Design, Measure, Analyze,
    Improve, Control), 255
Downtime, 99, 106. *See also* Emergency
    maintenance; Shutdown management;
    Unplanned downtime
Draconian management techniques, 105
DSPWVD (Discrete smoothed pseudo-
    Wiger Ville distribution) technology,
    131
Dunbar, Robin, 267
DuPont, 171, 285

EAM. *See* Enterprise Asset Management
    systems
E-business, 148–50
Efficiency gains, 38
80-20 rule, 275–76
E. I. du Pont de Nemours & Co., 171
Eisenhower, Dwight D., 53, 105
Electric utilities
  deregulation of, 110–11
  mobile workforce, 15
  privatization, 17
  scheduled switching operations, 127
Electronics industry, 131
Emergency maintenance, 82, 98, 111, 132
Emotional intelligence, 70
Employee
  associations, 95
  motivation, 105
  trade skills, 217
  turnover, 42, 61
  See also People
Engineered Performance Standards, 105
Engineering approach. *See* Design-out
    maintenance
Enron, 10
Enterprise Asset Management (EAM)
  systems, 186–217
  future, 214–17
  growing popularity of, 189
  transaction control, 191
Enterprise management systems, 140, 141,
    146

Enterprise Resource Planning (ERP)
  systems, 186–217
  array of functionality, 189
  future, 214–17
  integrated tools for, 191
  percent of usable functionality, 190
  transaction control, 191
Environmental regulatory compliance, 311
Equipment
  effectiveness, 293
  history, 90, 106, 185
  maintenance tips, 126
  meriting most attention, 106
  modifications, 273
  performance, 159–62, 233
  upgrade, 121
  See also Basic equipment care; Failure;
    Failure patterns
ERP. See Enterprise Resource Planning
  systems
Europe, 171, 259
Excellence, 309–14
  choosing, 286
  as journey, 39, 75
  See also Quality; Pyramid of Excellence
Executive management, 56–57, 300, 312
Expert systems, 179, 184–85
Exxon, 10

Failure
  -finding tactics, 240
  frequency, 106
  mechanisms, 126, 134
  modes, 234–36
  random events and, 92
  risk and, 311
Failure patterns, 122–27
  age-related, 123, 127
  conditional probability of, 123–25, 226
  failure modes and effects, 234
  standards of performance, 248
  statistical sampling studies, 126
  "tribal knowledge" and, 126
Fault Tree Analysis, 242
Fault trees, 254, 257
Fear of change, 47–51
  "cycle of loss," 48–49
  force field analysis example, 50
  unknown, facing the, 51
Feedstock, 100
Firefighting, 90, 213
Fishbone diagram, 257, 258

Five Whys, 255–57, 259, 298
Fixed asset capacity, 8
Fixed costs, 7, 8
Fixed interval maintenance, 119, 124, 228
Fixed maintenance costs, 9
Fleet assets, 4, 115–16
Fluor Daniel, 173
Focused factories, 56
Forest products company, 172
Fuel efficiency, 311
Functional boundaries, 33
Functional capability deterioration, 239
Functional silos, 15, 291–93
Function failure, 235, 248
Future vision, 274–75
"Fuzzy logic," 179

Gain sharing, 38, 73
Gantt, Henry T., 102
Gantt chart, 102–3
General Motors (GM), 83–84, 171, 275
Genesis Solutions, 173
Geographic Information System (GIS), 110,
  112
GIS (Geographic Information System), 110,
  112
Gladwell, Malcolm, 267
Globally integrated software platform, 205
Global Positioning Systems (GPS), 110, 112
GM (General Motors), 83–84, 171, 275
GPS (Global Positioning Systems), 110, 112
Graphic user interface (GUI), 212
Greenfield scenario, 231, 247
GUI (Graphic user interface), 212

Hammer, Michael, 290
Hand-held devices, 183
Hands-free invoice payment, 214
Hands-on-tools time, 106
Handy, Charles B., 67
Hardware and software tools, 180–86
  condition monitoring, 181–83
  data, importance of, 185–86
  decision support tools, 183–85
  hand-held devices, 183
  portable computers, 183
  See also Computerized Maintenance
    Management Systems
Hastings, Dr. Nick, 183
Hazardous materials, 311
Heating, ventilation, and air conditioning
  (HVAC), 35, 56

Herzberg, Frederick, 105
Hidden failures, 240
High-performance companies, 309–10
Histogram, 28, 29
Human resources. *See* People
Hutchison Whampoa, 179
HVAC (Heating, ventilation, and air
    conditioning), 35, 56
Hydroelectric generating industry, 172

IBM minicomputers, 211
IDD ("If-Down-Do") jobs, 97
Idle excess capacity, 8
"If-Down-Do" (IDD) jobs, 97
IISI (International Iron and Steel Institute),
    171–72
Industrial accidents, 10, 113, 311
"Information age," 18
Information management, 208–9
Information sharing, 155
Information technology, 188, 262. *See also*
    Hardware and software tools;
    Software
Infrared monitoring equipment, 130
Inspection, 99, 142–43
Insurance, 11–12, 311. *See also* Warranties
Intelligent reasoning engines, 184
International airport facility, 187
International Iron and Steel Institute (IISI),
    171–72
Internet
    architectures, 218
    e-business, 148–50, 155
    virtually everywhere, 188
    See also Software
Internet-based standard, 216
Inventory
    "free issue," 145
    holding account, 141
    "insurance spares," 144
    management system, 149
    repairable items, 145
    shrinkage, 144, 145
    spoilage, hazardous consequences, 145
    stale, 139
    stockouts, 147
    stockpiles, 136
ISO 9001-2000, 11

Japan, 55, 171, 270, 275, 285
Japan Institute of Plant Maintenance, 280
Jardine, Andrew K. S., 261

Jardine, Dr., 183
JIT (Just-in-time) manufacturing
    philosophy, 56, 246, 271, 272
Just-in-time (JIT) manufacturing
    philosophy, 56, 246, 271, 272

Kaizen, 275
Kaplan, Robert S., 158, 173
Kepner Tregoe Problem-Solving and
    Decision-Making Method, 259
"Kitting" of parts, 146

Labor pool. *See* People
Ladbroke Grove train tragedy, 113, 115
Large-scale transformations, 301–4
Latent talent, 58, 313
Latino, Robert J. and Kenneth C., 259
Laws, 170. *See also* Regulatory compliance
Lay-down area, 143
Layout evaluations, 273
Leadership
    in change management, 53
    emotional intelligence, 70
    strategy and, 38
Lead-time, 98
Learning, training, and development
    plant variation and, 67
    scope of requirements, 69
    strategy, 68
Lever, 64–66, 71
LHD (Load-haul-dump) trucks, 229
Liability, 56–57
Life-cycle asset strategy. *See* Asset life cycle
Li Ka-shing, 179
Line support resource pool, 213
Load-haul-dump (LHD) trucks, 229
Local business preferences, 302, 303, 305
"Lock down" date, 98, 99
Log-scatterplots, 106, 255, 279
Long-range planning, 92
Lord William Douglas Cullen, 113, 115
Lost capacity, 87

Machine learning, 186
Maintenance
    budget, 92–94
    definitions, 82–83
    maturity grid, 31–32
    outsource service provider, 173
    process, 195
    productivity, 208
    scorecard, 176

stores, 292
See also Measurement of maintenance
Maintenance and Repair Contract (MARC)
  agreements, 37–38
Maintenance management
  crossing functional boundaries, 291
  diagnostic review, 315–22
  downtime, 7
  "language," 82–83
  long-term payback, 311
  six core steps, 84–90
Maintenance, repair, and overhaul (MRO),
  136-137, 150-54, 155, 229
Maintenance strategy, 18, 39
  background documentation, 6
  banks, 12
  basic program examples, 117
  components of, 22–23
  contract maintenance, 34–38
  development of, 23–25
  elements of, 5–6
  fixed and variable costs and, 9
  framework for, 18–22
  implementation plan, 33–34
  insurance, 11–12
  quality programs, 11
  regulatory compliance, 10–11
  review, 27–33
  timing tactics, 119, 122
  vision, development of, 25–27
  warranties, 12–13
Maintenance Task Analysis, 245–46
Management commitment, 300
Management information systems, 217–18.
  See also Computerized Maintenance
  Management Systems; Enterprise
  Asset Management systems;
  Enterprise Resource Planning systems
Mandatory jobs, 87
Manufacturers' recommendations, 116,
  117–88, 252
MARCAM (ShawWare), 211
MARC (Maintenance and Repair Contract)
  agreements, 37–38
Margin, 7
Market conditions, 7–8
MARS system, 212–14
Materials management, 135–55
  e-business, 148–50
  "just-in-case" materials, 143
  MRO improvements, 150–54
  process integration, 155

seven process steps, 136–48
stores upgrade activities, 151–54
See also Inventory
Materials management process steps,
  151–54
  analyze the data, 147–48
  control, 144–46
  order, 141–42
  source, 13–141
  specify, 137–39
  store, 142–44
  use, 146–47
Materials process, 194
Mathematical models, 184, 263
MDT (Mean Down Time), 224
Mean Down Time (MDT), 224
Mean Time Between Failures (MTBF),
  168–69, 223, 224
Mean Time to Repair (MTTR), 106, 224
Measurement of maintenance
  cost performance, 162–63
  equipment performance, 159–62
  process performance, 163–67
  productivity, 159
Metal extrusion plant, 30, 33
Methods-Time-Measurement, 105
Mexico, 65, 140
Microelectronics company, 168–69
Micromanaging, 53
Military organizations, 268, 269
MIMOSA, 216
Mining industry, 8–9, 37, 167–68, 225, 247,
  262, 302–4
Mission, 6, 22, 34
Mobile workforce management, 108–11,
  112
Molson Breweries, 101–2, 210–14
Monitoring devices, 181–82
Moore, Geoffrey A., 50
Moore, Gordon, 188
Moore, Ron, 7
"Moore's Law," 188
Motivated workforce, 105
Motivation Hygiene Theory, 105
Moubray, John, 221, 222
MRO (Maintenance, repair, and overhaul),
  136-137, 150-54, 155, 229
MSG-3, 226
MTBF (Mean Time Between Failures),
  168–69, 223, 224
MTTR (Mean Time to Repair), 106, 224
Multidiscipline team, 293

Multiskilling, 58–67
case study, 64–66
flexibility and, 59, 76
introduction of, challenges, 60
long-term benefits, 64
planning and training for, 61–64
skilled trades availability and, 59
in TPM environment, 273
union resistance to, 60–61
Multiticketed tradesmen, 60

Nachi-Fujikoshi Corporation, 280
NAFTA (North American Free Trade
Agreement), 65, 66
Natural gas pipeline company, 289–90
Naval ship design, 225
Net capacity, 86, 87, 98, 109, 110
Neural networks, 186
Nominal group technique, 26
Noncompliance, 10. See also Regulatory
compliance
Noncritical equipment, 246
Noncritical jobs, 98
Nondestructive testing techniques, 131
Nonproductive working time, 87
Non-value-adding activities, 296
North America, 9, 140, 285, 301, 302
North American Free Trade Agreement
(NAFTA), 65, 66
Norton, David P., 158, 173
Nowlan and Heap report, 123
Nuclear power generation, 249

O&M (Operating and maintenance) costs,
16
OEE (Overall Equipment Effectiveness),
270, 276
Off-site strategic planning session, 26
Oil-loading facility, 256–57
Oil refining, 98
On-condition maintenance. See Condition-
based maintenance
"Open stores," 87–88
Operating age, 123
Operating and maintenance (O&M) costs,
16
Operations research, 260
Operator ownership, 273
Organization of maintenance structure,
53–58
decentralization, 55
hybrid model, 55–56

self-organizing structures, 53–54, 76
traditional centralized system, 54
Organized labor. See Unions
Oriented Strand Board (OSB), 276
OSB (Oriented Strand Board), 276
Outsourcing
determining cost effectiveness of, 36
maintenance, 35–36, 39
service provider, 173
Outstanding work, 98
Overall Equipment Effectiveness (OEE),
270, 276
Overhaul, 118, 126

Paper mill, 88, 172
Pareto, Vilfredo, 275
Pareto analysis, 255, 276
Pareto diagram, 106, 275–76, 276–78, 279
Pareto sorts, 277, 278
Parts
availability, 87–88, 139
costs, 9
"kitting" by work order, 146
Pay-for-knowledge systems, 63
P-cards (purchashing cards), 142, 147
People
aging workforce, 58
change management, 43–53
CMMS investment and, 207
compensation and rewards, 71–75
control and, 191
learning, training and development,
67–71
as most important asset, 41–43
multiskilling, 58–67
organization of maintenance structure,
53–58
skilled tradespeople, 42, 146–47, 213
"skills," 43, 76
See also Employee
Performance benchmarks, 163–66, 174
Performance management, 157–77
balanced scorecards, 173–76
benchmarking maintenance, 167–76
measuring maintenance, 159–67
Performance standards and function
failure, 235
Permits and licenses, 311
Personnel. See People
Peters, Tom, 157, 175
Petrochemical industry, 120, 171
P-F interval, 239

Physical asset management, 3–4
  beyond traditional boundaries, 14–15
  for delivering uptime, 134
  functions of assets, 232–33
  as new paradigm, 57
  older equipment, 116
  organization chart, 57, 58
  repair vs. replace, 122
"Piper Alpha" offshore rig, 113, 115
Pirsig, Robert M., 267, 273, 286
Plan-Do-Check-Act sequence, 229–43
  apply RCM process, 232–41
  diagram, 23–24
  implement selected tasks, 241–42
  optimize tactics and program, 242–43
  prepare for RCM project, 230–32
  select plant areas, 229–30
Planned job, 82
Planned maintenance, 82, 85, 93
Planned shutdown. See Shutdown
  management
Planners, 70–71
Planning and scheduling tools, 102–4
Planning horizons, 91–96
  annual plan and budget, 92–94, 111
  life-cyle plans, 92
  long-range plans, 92
  projects and shutdowns, 95–96
  work orders and specific jobs, 94–95
Planning standards, 105–8
  backlog time standards, 106–7
  Pareto diagram, 106
  quality standards, 108
PMO (Preventive Maintenance
  Optimization), 121, 126, 252–54, 264
PM (Preventive maintenance), 132
Portable computers, 183
Postmove services, 273
Powell, Colin, 309
Predictive maintenance, 82, 228
Preventive Maintenance Optimization
  (PMO), 121, 126, 252–54, 264
Preventive maintenance (PM), 83, 132
Prioritization matrices, 26
Privatization, 17
Proactive maintenance, 83
  predictive maintenance, 82, 120, 228
  preventive maintenance, 83, 119–20, 132
  tasks, failure management, 236–41
  See also Reliability-centered maintenance
Process
  analysis, 296–98

  flow mapping, 295
  mapping, 294–95
  performance, 163–67
  performance measurements, 163–66
  redesign, 290–91
  safety management regulations, 113–15
Process optimization, 289–305
  large-scale transformations, 301–4
  maintenance, process or function,
    291–94
  maintenance process flow, 294–301
  quantum leaps in improvement, 291
Productive working time, 87
Productivity, 159
Progressive shutdowns, 100–102
Pulp and paper company, 172
Purchasing cards (P-cards), 142, 147
Pyramid of Excellence, 1
  histogram representation, 28, 29
  Innocence to Excellence score, 30, 31–32
  ten elements of, 28, 29, 30, 31–32

Quality, 11, 108, 244
Questionnaire, 28, 29

Random failures, 118
RCFA (Root Cause Failure Analysis), 242,
    254, 255–59, 265
RCM. See Reliability-Centered
    Maintenance
RCM II, 227
Reactive maintenance, 83, 85, 119. See also
    Emergency maintenance; Firefighting
Receiving areas, 143
Redesign engineering approach, 120–21
Redesign of business processes, 290–91,
    298–301
Redesign tactics, 241
Redundancy, 15, 120, 228
Reengineering, 290–91, 304
Regulations
  beyond the minimum, 115–18
  minimum, 113–15
  violations of, 114
Regulatory compliance, 10–11, 310, 311
Reliability
  analysis, 183
  -centered processing, 212
  defined, 224
  engineer, 90
  improvement, 168–69
  management, 223

uninterrupted service, 15
Reliability and simulation modeling, 265
Reliability-Centered Maintenance (RCM),
    224–49, 227–43
    actions to implement, 242
    analysis, 68, 92
    background on, 225–27
    benefits of, 244–45, 249
    in capital-intensive industries, 226, 249
    decision logic diagram, 238, 239
    pilot project, 231
    Plan-Do-Check-Act sequence in, 229–43
    for proactive failure analysis, 126
    seven-step approach, 227–28
    simplified methods, 245–46
    successful implementation, 246–48
    three complementary activities, 243
    trades-tasks relationship, 62
Reliabilityweb.com, 173
Repairs, 262
Replacement asset value, 163
Replacement of asset, 122
Reputation, 10, 311
Response time, 166–67
Return on investment, 13
RFP response, 205
Risk-effective default actions, 236
Risk reduction, 11, 114, 229, 245, 311. See
    also Regulatory compliance
Root Cause Analysis, 259
Root Cause Failure Analysis (RCFA), 242,
    254, 255–59, 265
Rule of 150, 268, 286–87
Rules, 23
Run-to-failure, 114, 119, 228, 240–41

SAE, 226–27
Safety regulations, 113–15
Scheduled component replacement, 119–20
Scheduled maintenance, 83
Scheduled overhaul, 120
Schedule overruns, 104
Scheduling and planning tools, 102–4
Self-administered questionnaire, 28, 29
Self-managed work environments, 53–54,
    58, 76
Self-organized teams, 76, 88–89, 191, 268,
    286, 287. See also Mobile workforce
    management
Senior management, 56–57, 300
Service, 244
"Service level agreements," 37

Service providers, 37–38
ShawWare (MARCAM), 211
Shrinking labor pool, 43
Shutdown management, 96–102
    master schedule, 99
    meetings, 100
    planned vs. unplanned, 96–97
    progressive shutdown, 100–102
    projects and, 95–96
Silos, 15, 291–93
Simulation and reliability modeling,
    263–64, 265
Sir Winston Churchill, 251
Six maintenance management steps, 84–91
    assign, 88–89
    close, 89–91
    execute, 89
    identify, 85
    plan, 85–86
    schedule, 86–88
Six Sigma method, 11, 108, 121, 255, 270
Six-step work management process, 80–81
Skilled tradespeople, 42, 146–47, 213
SKUs (Stockkeeping units), 187
Small companies, 190, 191, 301–2
Social responsibility, 42, 114–15, 311
"Soft maintenance," 102
"Soft" skills, 43
Software
    data-analysis tools, 261
    front-end complexity, 193
    homegrown, 188
    for maintenance management, 94–95,
        107
    user-friendly navigation, 188, 190
    "user-hostile," 190, 192
    See also Computerized Maintenance
        Management Systems; Hardware and
        software tools; Internet
Spares, 17
Specific maintenance jobs, 94–95
Spider diagram, 28, 29
Standards. See Planning standards; Time
    standards
Statistical techniques, 187, 261
Steel industry, 136, 143, 171–72
Stock items, 141
Stockkeeping units (SKUs), 187
Stockouts, 147
Stores inventory, 214, 292
Stores upgrade activities, 151–54
Strategic direction, companywide, 34

Strategic planning session, 26
"Strategic Sourcing," 140
Strategy development, 4, 23–25, 39
"Stuck" switches, 127
Suboptimizing performance, 158
Supervisors, 99
Supplier partnership, 140
Supply chain, 139, 146
Support systems. *See* Hardware and
    software tools
Support vector machine methods, 186

Tactics, 3, 22
Talent, 58, 313
Target timing, 22–23
Team-based maintenance methods, 267–87
    small teams, 268, 269, 286
    teams in general, 267–69
    total productive maintenance, 269–71
    TPM implementation, 38, 280–86
    TPM objectives and themes, 271–80
Teamsters union, 65. *See also* Unions
Technically feasible tactics, 236, 237
Technical skills, 70
Thermography, 130
Time, 245
Time-based discard tactics, 240–41
Time-based maintenance, 122, 228, 237
Time-based repair/restoration tactics, 240
Timeslotting, 106–7, 108
Time standards, 105, 106–7
Timing maintenance tactics, 119
Total-cost-of-maintenance curve, 133
Total productive maintenance (TPM),
    269–87
    asset strategy, 272–73
    awareness, education, and training, 280,
        282–83
    companies utilizing system, 285–86
    continuous improvement teams, 275–79
    decentralization and, 55
    elements of, seven broad, 272
    empowerment, 273
    implementation, 280–86
    key success factors, 285–86
    measurement, 274–75
    pilot project, 283–85
    RCM and, 225, 246, 251
    resource planning and scheduling, 274
    systems and procedures, 274
    three distinct features, 271
    tools and techniques for, 282–83

wheel, 272
Total quality management (TQM), 246, 272
Toyota Production System, 55, 255
TPM. *See* Total productive maintenance
TQM (Total quality management), 246, 272
Trade certification, 59
Tradespeople, skilled, 42, 146–47, 213
Trades-tasks relationship, 62
Trade unions. *See* Unions
Training. *See* Learning, training, and
    development
Turner, Steve, 252
Turnover, 42, 61
Typical asset life cycle, 14
Tzu, Sun, 4

Unilever, 64–66, 71
Unions, 60–61, 65, 95, 301
United Kingdom, 9, 10, 17
United States, 10, 55, 65, 140, 171, 285
Universal Maintenance Standards, 105
Unplanned downtime, 12, 83, 97
Unplanned shutdown. *See* Shutdown
    management
Unplanned work, 132
Unscheduled maintenance, 7
Unscheduled shutdowns, 97
Up-front analysis, 17
Uptime Pyramid of Excellence. *See*
    Pyramid of Excellence
Urgent maintenance, 83
Usage-based maintenance, 122
"Useful running life," 85

Value, 244–45
Value stream mapping, 298
Variable costs, 7, 8, 9
Vendor management, 139–40, 145
Vendor solution, CMMS, 203–205
Vendor-supported software, 188
Visible assets, 135
Vision, 5, 22, 24, 25–27, 33, 39, 45
Visioning, 24, 298
Visual tool. *See* Gantt chart

W3 (Win-Win-Win) proposition, 1
Warranties, 12–13, 117, 311
Web-architected technology, 216, 217
Weibull analysis, 126
Wheatley, Margaret J., 58, 268, 269
Win-Win-Win (W3) proposition, 1
WIP (Work-in-process), 101, 271

Wireman, Terry, 173
Wood products plant, 209–10, 276–78
Workforce. *See* People
Work-in-process (WIP), 101, 271
Work management, 79–112
  avoidance of downtime, 80
  cycle, 79–84
  linked materials and, 138
  mobile workforce, 108–11
  planning and scheduling tools, 102–4
  planning horizons, 91–96
  planning standards, 105–8
  shutdown management, 96–102

six key steps, 79, 84–91, 111
unplanned vs. planned, 84
Work-order management systems, 146
Work orders, 94–95, 98
Work priority schemes, 87
WorldCom, 10

Zen and the Art of Motorcycle Maintenance
  (Pirsig), 267
Zero-based budgeting and planning, 93
Zero-based functional approach, 253
Zero-defect quality management
  approach, 270

About the Author

James V. Reyes-Picknell is founder and president of Conscious Asset Management in Toronto, Canada, and provides management consulting services in the area of physical asset and maintenance management. A licensed professional engineer, he is a certified RCM II practitioner and graduated with honors from University of Toronto with a degree in mechanical engineering. He has done postgraduate studies at the Royal Navy Engineering College, the Technical University of Nova Scotia and Dalhousie University.

Before founding Conscious Asset Management, Mr. Reyes-Picknell was already recognized as a leading authority on the Enterprise Asset Management practice of IBM Business Consulting Services (formerly PwC Consulting, PricewaterhouseCoopers, and Coopers & Lybrand). He worked as a marine engineer afloat in the Canadian Navy, as a specialist machinery engineer with Exxon Chemicals in Canada, as the maintenance and support planning manager for a large warship design and construction project, and as logistics support manager for helicopter and microwave landing systems projects.

In his capacity as maintenance management consultant, the author has assisted numerous clients worldwide to achieve significant improvements in maintenance and overall business objectives. His extensive experience includes plant, fleet and facility maintenance, strategy development and implementation, reliability management and engineering, spares and operating supplies, life-cycle management and analysis, diagnostic assessments, benchmarking for best practices, business process design, and enterprise asset management systems. James Reyes-Picknell has coauthored or contributed materials to several books; his articles on maintenance management have been published in numerous trade journals and periodicals. He has also taught Physical Asset Management at the University of Toronto's Professional Development Centre.